Combing the Coast

HIGHWAY ONE FROM SAN FRANCISCO TO SAN LUIS OBISPO

Combing the Coast

HIGHWAY ONE FROM SAN FRANCISCO TO SAN LUIS OBISPO

RUTH A. JACKSON

CHRONICLE BOOKS · SAN FRANCISCO

Printed in the United States of America.

Library of Congress Cataloging in Publication Data

Jackson, Ruth A.
    Combing the coast.

    Includes index.
    1. California—Description and travel—1981–
—Guide-books.   2. Coasts—California—Guide-books.
I. Title.
F859.3.J3   1985   917.940453   85-7687
ISBN 0-87701-285-7 (pbk.)

Editing: Deborah Stone
Book and cover design: Naomi Schiff
Composition: Accent & Alphabet, Seattle

Chronicle Books
One Hallidie Plaza
San Francisco, CA 94102

Photo credits:

Edna Bullock: pp. 41, 42, 44, 95, 98, 106, 120, 124, 126, 143, 145, 149, 152, 156, 158, 163, 164, 167, 168, 172, 182
Jim Fee: p. 24
Richard Frear: pp. viii, 5, 54
Alexander Lowry: p. 62
Ruth Jackson: pp. 2, 6, 13, 18, 20, 22, 24, 26, 33, 34, 45, 48, 56, 57, 58, 61, 67, 68, 75, 87, 89, 90, 92, 108, 113, 123, 130, 133, 135, 136, 139, 150, 160, 166, 171, 173, 190, 193
Donna Starr: pp. 8, 15, 16, 30
Morli Wilson: p. 36
Baron Wolman: front cover
Big Basin Redwood State Park: p. 65
California Department of Parks & Recreation: p. 155
The Cambrian: p. 186
Monterey Bay Aquarium: p. 118, back cover
Monterey Peninsula Visitors Convention Bureau: pp. 100, 116
Pacific Grove Chamber of Commerce: p. 66
Courtesy of Roaring Camp Railroad: p. 63
San Luis Obispo Chamber of Commerce: pp. 171, 178, 180, 194, 196, 200
San Mateo County Historical Association: p. 39
Santa Cruz Chamber of Commerce: pp. 73, 77, 80
Courtesy of Seattle Aquarium, Seattle, WA: p. 146
Wells Fargo History Room, San Francisco: p. 28
Courtesy of The Wine Institute: p. 203

Preface

*C*ombing the Coast is for those who like to explore
for a day, a weekend, or a lifetime.

Whatever your special interests, you'll probably
find them listed here. Beachcombing, antiques and
crafts, fishing, hiking, horseback riding, dining,
wildlife and bird watching, swimming, sunbathing
every round inch at nude beaches, golfing, surfing,
and biking: These are just a few of the activities
waiting for you. Use the index of this book as your
gold mine to dig out the pastimes and places that
appeal to you.

A range of restaurants, places to stay, and, whenever possible, phone numbers are mentioned. For
information on state park campsites and the popular
Hearst Castle tour reservations, you can now call,
toll-free (800) 952-5580, Monday through Friday
from 8 A.M. to 5 P.M. Actual reservations, however,
must still be made through Ticketron outlets. Call
(415) 393-6914 to find the one closest to you. Also,
when possible, ways to cut costs are mentioned.

But times change. Although listings were checked
right up to press time, you may discover that the
"find" of a restaurant or art gallery has changed
hands or that the Victorian house you were counting
on has been demolished. I hope such incidents will be
rare and suffered with understanding.

If you've reserved a place to stay, or even if you
haven't, take this book in hand, load up your camera,
pack your bag, and start combing this beautiful
length of sea, sand, mountains, and forests—the
Central Coast of California.

Contents

It's not far from the city to the edge of the sea, where San Francisco's Cliff House is a good place to start south, combing the coast.

1

San Francisco to Pacifica

It's only minutes away, ready to be enjoyed for an hour or a day—that great stretch of the Pacific Ocean, rimmed by sand, surf, high bluffs, and coastal hills overlooking miles of view. Most of this precious edge of the continent is now part of the world's largest urban park, the **Golden Gate National Recreation Area,** thanks to the persistence of the late congressman, Philip Burton, and others who realized the importance of this healing sea-washed oasis so close to the concrete city.

One of the many bonuses of combing the beautiful stretch of coastline south from San Francisco is that you can enjoy it all year, even when fog mutes its harsh edges. The best months for this area are usually in early spring and late fall, when the days are clear and the temperature ranges from crisp to surprisingly warm. From Memorial Day until Labor Day, expect some fog. It usually clears in the afternoon; and if you plan your route carefully you might avoid the fog entirely.

Along Skyline Boulevard, that winding Highway 35 on the spine of the coastal hills, you'll get more fog. One resident who kept track discovered that in addition to rain, five inches of moisture dripped off trees each year. South of Daly City, inland areas—including the big redwood parks—are often sunny when a cotton batting of fog may be clinging to the shoreline and skyline. Beaches vary in this regard. In Pacifica you may be discouraged by impenetrable fog just south of Mussel Rock and then find Pedro Point, a few miles farther south, bathed in sunshine.

As for winter rains, which usually occur from late November through February, unless you melt in rain, why not don rubber boots, rain gear, and go? This is the time the prized driftwood, fishing floats, and other booty wash in, and you may have miles of beach all to yourself. Besides, the rain washes the air to give you those glorious clear days in between.

Please don't wait only for calm days, or you will miss the drama of a storm at sea. As you stand,

The Sea — A Warning

Before you comb the California coast, remember—the **Pacific Ocean** is not always pacific. The sea has sometimes been called a siren, and sirens can lure you to destruction. That surf can be misleading. This is why those wise to the ways of the sea always keep an eye on incoming waves even while merely strolling on the beach.

It's not true, as rumor has it, that every seventh wave is dangerous, but the power of moving waves is awesome. Killer waves, perhaps even tidal—or seismic—waves caused by earthquakes or volcanic eruptions (far away, we hope) are rare occurrences. Standing with your back to the ocean, you might be surprised by a killer wave or Big Roller, twice as moun-

The sea is to be enjoyed, but always be alert to its awesome power, especially off rocky promontories along this coast.

tainous as other waves, rising up out of a heavy sea. These waves have been known to reach ninety-seven feet high. Farther north, near the Columbia River's mouth, a 135-pound rock was hurled higher than the Tillamook Rock lighthouse, which is 139 feet above the water.

Be cautious; stay on established trails even if you are high above the surf. Cliffs can and do crumble; it happens too often and can be fatal. As for swimming (only if you enjoy turning blue with cold!), brave the water at the few protected beaches at Santa Cruz, on the Monterey Peninsula, and at Avila Beach near San Luis Obispo. Besides the too brisk water temperature, there are rip tides to contend with, especially on incoming tides.

Rip tides are a legacy of the winter storms that batter against and chew up sandy shores. (In just a few hours during the January 1983 storms, 150 miles of central California beaches were pounded and scoured away into the raging sea.) Until July or August, when the waves again build up the gentle, sandy slopes, much of the sand is deposited in offshore sandbars. Waves that break over these bars are trapped; when they find an opening they surge through in a powerful funnel. Beware if you notice dirty, sandy, foamy, choppy water or a body of water traveling seaward through an area of little or no wave activity. All this indicates dangerous current conditions. If you find yourself caught in the vicinity of this surge, you could be swept out to sea in waters that range in temperature from the high forties to low fifties. If you do get caught in a rip tide, don't fight the current; experts advise swimming at right angles to the tide and parallel to the shore until the rip tide feathers out and you can make it in.

As important is the warning to stay out of sea caves, where you can become trapped if the ocean turns treacherous. Too many people living along the Pacific have encountered dead bodies washed up on shore. They know that even at low tide the ocean can turn on the careless. So check your tide tables, keep your eye on the surf, and use commonsense caution.

bundled up against the rain and howling wind, or sit protected in your car, you will feel the immense presence of the ocean, as wave after wave thunders in, perhaps hurling surf across Highway 1. Afterwards, walking on the wet, shining sand among driftwood and shredded seaweed can be as peaceful as a benediction.

Of course, all along this coastline you have the magic chance to see and compare sunsets. Perhaps on a crystal-clear dusk you may glimpse the rare but vivid emerald, or liquid jade, color for one split second before the sunset disappears. Even after dark, the ocean can be mesmerizing, especially when the waves are edged with microorganisms that make them fluorescent. (Microorganisms, incidentally, may also be responsible for the foam that sometimes billows along the surf line. Unfortunately, though, pollution from detergents can cause this same phenomenon.)

Before you start down the coast south of San Francisco, treat yourself to the four-plus miles of the exhilarating—that is, breezy—**Ocean Beach,** presided over by **Cliff House,** just south of where ships head in toward the Golden Gate. To reach the Cliff House area from downtown San Francisco, drive straight west on Geary Boulevard and park in the sizable parking areas to the north; one is called "Merrie Way." If you're busing, take the #38 Geary to the end or call (415) 673-MUNI for alternative transportation. This is great country for biking, too. Part of the **Pacific Coast Bikecentennial Route,** popular with cyclists, runs from San Francisco to Santa Cruz. Call or write the Division of Highways (916/323-2544), 1120 N Street, Sacramento, CA 95814 for information.

Since 1863, millions of tourists have visited the many Cliff Houses that have been built here and burned down: The first went up in smoke in 1887 when a schooner loaded with dynamite foundered on the rocks below. On the outside, the present Cliff House is squat and forgettable; unfortunately it's not the 1905 version, a many-storied gingerbread palace. Yet the Cliff House is worth visiting for the views from its oceanside windows and concrete terraces. On a clear day you can see west eighteen miles to the Farallon Islands, north along the entire Marin coast to Point Reyes, and south to Pacifica's Pedro Point. If you want a higher vantage point and quieter atmosphere, walk up past two huge stone lions to Sutro Heights, to the east of Cliff House.

Arrange your schedule so you'll have a meal or at least a cocktail at Cliff House. The Sea Food and Beverage Company (415/386-3330), specializes in

Within camera range of San Francisco's famous Cliff House, seals and barking sea lions share Seal Rock.

fresh netted seafood and sunset watching. They open as early as 11 A.M., and Sunday brunch starts at 9 A.M. Upstairs at the Cliff House (415/387-5847), you'll find more modest prices. They open for breakfast at 9 A.M. and they also serve dinner. Cliff House offers you two choices of lounges in which to quaff beer or cocktails, both with ocean views. A series of smaller restaurants is strung up the curve above Cliff House, so there's no danger of starvation. However, if you can, squeeze into Cliff House.

You'll probably want to check out the ruins of the **Old Sutro Baths,** built in 1896. At the height of its glory, as many as 30,000 people could bathe in its five elaborate saltwater pools and one freshwater pool, with temperatures varying from cold to hot. A steep trail leads down to the mammoth ruins, but it's only for the sure of foot. Whether you descend on the trail or just marvel from above, don't get too close to the edge. Too often unwary people have been swept into the ocean by high waves. The mostly deserted baths burned in the 1960s, but some of its antique musical and other coin-operated machines are on view in a Cliff House museum. In this same complex is a visitors center for the Golden Gate National Recreation Area.

Another relic—this from the days when Playland-at-the-Beach (now filled with condos and a big Safeway) flourished across the highway with its Loop-the-Loop and Laughing Sal—is the thirty-year-old giant camera mounted on a concrete terrace below Cliff House. This rare attraction, housed in a garish building shaped like a box camera, is a camera obscura, built after a design by Leonardo da Vinci. Its revolving eye takes pictures of the whole sweep of

view and reflects it all inside on a huge parabolic disc. This view—in some ways more encompassing than the one outside—is worth the small admission fee.

Another irresistible attraction for you and for the tourists who pile in and out of the chartered buses that snort up to the curb near the Cliff House are the gulls, pelicans, and other sea birds that rest on nearby Seal Rocks. Don't confuse the rocks' larger tenants, the California sea lions, with seals, as many do (see page 54).

For the next dozen miles south of the Cliff House, especially in San Francisco and Daly City, the ocean beach is definitely no-frills. So before you leave, take advantage of the last touches of civilization at Cliff House: restrooms, telephones, bars, a souvenir shop that sells film, and restaurants. You'll find some of these facilities further south, but not all together.

Wide, sandy Ocean Beach is usually crowded all year long with picnickers, strollers, joggers, and their frisking dogs, for this is one of San Francisco's favorite escapes to serenity. You'll see few people in swimming. Though the surf along here is treacherous and the water cold, you will spot intrepid, and wetsuited, surfers.

As you drive south along the Great Highway you'll pass the tip of San Francisco's **Golden Gate Park** with its miles of greenery, small lakes, a waterfall, and recreational facilities. The Dutch windmill at the north edge of the park has been rehabilitated through private donations. The Murphy windmill to the south still stands, naked, without its blades.

All along the coast, the shoreline is eroding, receding from an inch to several inches a year. Until

Gossamer hang-gliders ride the winds off Fort Funston, a beautiful but breezy beach.

the improved San Francisco sewer to the ocean is finally finished (they call it pollution control), sand excavated in the project is supposed to be dumped west of the Great Highway in the hopes of keeping Ocean Beach more secure. Until 1986 or later, the highway near the project funnels into two lanes of frequent bumper-to-bumper traffic.

Storms and general erosion aid in historical research. In 1984, at the foot of Noriega Street, the skeleton of the old clipper ship, the *King Phillip,* which went aground on Ocean Beach in 1878, was uncovered. At very low tide you might see the stern of this 182-foot-long ship, although the sands may have covered it again before you arrive.

A popular spot with all ages, 3 to 103, is the **San Francisco Zoo,** just off Sloat Boulevard inland. Besides the usual lions, tigers, elephants, and such, a children's zoo has domesticated animals that children can pet. A small train equipped with a guide meanders throughout the zoo grounds, a boon for the footsore.

Just past the zoo turnoff, where the Great Highway meets Skyline Boulevard at the northern edge of **Fort Funston,** you'll see a small parking lot toward the ocean. It's an easy incline to the beach from here, and the cliff to the south is pockmarked with sandy caves and indentations where you can relax, out of the wind, when the sun is shining. (Remember, the sun usually shows up in the afternoon.)

Fort Funston is an exciting park to visit, especially when the wind is blowing ten miles an hour or more, enabling the colorful hang-gliders to take off from the cliffside to soar and swoop above you; you can watch from an observation platform. Near the primi-

tive restrooms you'll see the wheelchair-accessible Sunset Loop Trail that covers a gentle one and a half miles of coastal scenery. Look the other way from the ocean and you'll see Lake Merced and the backside of San Francisco: an arresting sight.

It's thrilling to watch these gossamer craft ride the wind. But if it's one of those rare windless nonfoggy days, enjoy. Find one of the picnic tables near the Sunset Trail or a niche in the sand where you can sunbathe, or clamber down the steep path to **Burton Beach.** Among other Fort Funston features, besides those old concrete batteries, are phones, benches, and a truck that sells snacks and hotdogs on weekends.

Whether you stay on Highway 1 through San Francisco, start south along the sweep of Ocean Beach, or go west on Highway 35, you'll get tantalizing glimpses of ocean, but rows of "ticky-tacky" houses creeping over those foothills also assault your eyes. These are the houses that inspired the late Malvina Reynold's hit tune, "Little Boxes." The subsequent publicity upset the Daly City fathers, but it was too late to stem the pastel tide.

For a change of pace, why not climb on a horse to investigate the trails that overlook the ocean? You can rent horses just north of the junction of Alemany Boulevard with Highway 35, at the Palo Mar Stables (415/991-9682).

Much of the old Highway 1 along the coast here crumbled away in the 1957 landslide and because of damage in the 1906 and 1957 earthquakes. You can see pieces of old Highway 1 asphalt from above. At last report the turnoff to **Thornton Beach State Park** was closed off because of crippling storm damage. You can still reach the beach part of

Tips on
Mussel Gathering
and Cooking

Vitamin-rich **mussels** are common all along the Central Coast. They're tasty but neglected shellfish, treasured by many Europeans, including Portola and his explorers who journeyed up the coast in 1769. But first a reminder: You need a valid California fishing license for mussel prying, as well as clamming.

Then a warning! Mussels can contain poison during summer months, when they get a deadly toxin from the organism called *Gonyaulax,* which gives the ocean a reddish color when it's about in great numbers. Mussels filter it in for food; consequently, they are quarantined from May through October and sometimes much longer. Check with the nearest state park rangers. Don't take chances; the toxin can cause lethal nerve paralysis. Since California abalone, crab, and shrimp don't feed on the poison-producing *Gonyaulax,* there's no danger from eating them any time.

Plan to gather mussels when the tide is really low so the maximum number of rocks will be exposed. Mussels attach themselves with strong whiskers to rocks at the midtide zone. Pry them loose with a tire iron or similar tool, knock off the barnacles, scrape off other encrusted sea creatures with a knife or stiff brush, and wash them several times to get rid of any sand. Then drain the mussels for at least half an hour and steam them in a pot with garlic, green onions, parsley, butter, and a dash of white wine. Dish them out the minute they open or

The author valiantly tries to pry mussels off rocks in anticipation of a delicious feed.

they may turn as tough as tire rubber. Then just savor each pink morsel along with fresh French bread and an adequate white wine.

Thornton Park from Burton Beach or from Mussel Rock City Park (415/726-6238) to the south. Gone, however, at least for a while, is the chance to picnic at tables right on top of the San Andreas earthquake fault.

Mussel Rock is a breezy two-mile hike from Thornton Beach. Provided the cliffsides are dry and you are part mountain goat, you can try the trail that drops to the ocean near the San Francisco Community Center (in Daly City) at tiny Northridge Park on Northridge Drive, which loops around from Skyline Drive. Coming south, take Westmoor Avenue to Skyline Drive, which parallels Highway 35. From Pacifica, the next town south, take the Paloma turnoff and continue north until you intersect with Skyline Drive. Or call SamTrans (San Mateo County Transit Information) at (415) 871-2200 to find out how to get there by bus.

Walk to the edge of the bluff overlooking the ocean near a fence by the Nichiren Shoshu Buddhist Center Academy (on private property). Notice how tiny the figures appear on the beach below. Watch gulls who have caught the updraft soar by, noiselessly, without moving their wings. Notice, too, that though the sun may be shining on the sea below, the updraft is bringing up moist sea air and turning it into fog. If you're still insistent on living dangerously and trying the trail, which was badly damaged by erosion, start out and hope you won't slide, especially where the gravel acts like ball bearings.

A much easier way to reach Mussel Rock is to park in the big lot near the Daly City transfer station—in plain terms, the dump. From the north, continue on Skyline Drive, which curves down, until you see the entrance sign. Coming from Pacifica, take the Paloma turnoff and continue north. Don't let the word *dump* bother you. This is not an old smelly dump with gulls hovering; the building is discreetly tucked away, almost out of sight. This beach access is now called **Mussel Rock City Park,** and the view is great from the top and all the way down the steps or trail to the water's edge.

The beach is a lovely sandy stretch, a good place for gazing at and listening to the roaring sea. It is also fine for strolling unless you arrive at the same time— usually late in May—as hundreds of *Velella lata,* commonly called jellyfish. These purplish-blue hydroids grow to four inches long and have a graceful, diagonal saillike fin on top making them look like tiny sailboats. Jellyfish resemble the Portuguese man-of-war, but are not poisonous.

However, velella are sticky underfoot, and they smell. Eventually they dry up, and all is forgotten until winds blow them ashore to litter the beach again the following year.

Fishing is popular along here (see page 12 for ocean fishing tips). The calmest and warmest periods along the shore occur during early spring and late fall before the northwesterly winds start blowing. However, from May through October, even in fog or wind, fishermen catch the most striped bass when they cast into and beyond the breakers. Stripers usually weigh from five to eight pounds, although some caught here have reached fifty pounds.

If you prefer clamming, you won't dig this shoreline. Vitamin-rich **mussels,** however, are common here and all along the coastside. They're a tasty but neglected shellfish, treasured by many Europeans, including Portola and his explorers, who passed this way in 1769. Tips on gathering and cooking mussels are on page 6.

Where to stay? Those ornate Cliff House rooms overlooking the crashing surf are no more. A small motel, Seal Rock Inn (415/752-8000), located a few blocks east of Cliff House at Point Lobos and Forty-Eighth Avenue, does have a sea view. A fraction of that view is also visible from their restaurant, which serves breakfast and lunch, with an emphasis on omelets. For more information on motels, hotels, and RV parks, contact the San Francisco Convention and Visitors Bureau (415/974-6900), P.O. Box 6977, San Francisco, CA 94101 or drop by the center at Hallidie Plaza at Powell and Market streets, on the lower level, to obtain maps, a lodging guide, and other information.

If you're on a strict budget and adventurous, the **San Francisco International Hostel** (415/ 771-7277), part of American Youth Hostels, Inc., has accommodations for ninety-six in a historic Civil War barracks at Fort Mason. Enter the fort at Franklin and Bay. The view is inspiring, and the hostel encourages you not to be put off by the word *youth*—all ages are welcome. Still, since the accommodations are in dormitories for four or eight and there is a curfew plus other restrictions—like no alcohol—few oldsters pay the modest fee.

The campgrounds and accommodations farther south are described in each chapter. It's wiser to reserve ahead, but even if you haven't, there are a few spots where you can try your luck at the last minute. So bon voyage along the coast.

Pacifica's castle, known by locals as McCloskey's Castle, has had a checkered past.

2

Pacifica to Devil's Slide

WHERE THE HELL IS PACIFICA?

Yes, Virginia, there is a **Pacifica.** No, it is not lost in the fog somewhere southwest of Daly City; Pacifica even has sunshine, often just inland and frequently near Pedro Point. Yes, there are interesting sights and sidelights in this town, so close to San Francisco and the Peninsula. Perhaps some defensive inhabitants have those bumper stickers because the town sprawls along Highway 1 for twelve or so miles, and like Oakland (with apologies to Gertrude Stein), there's "no there, there." Originally Pacifica consisted of several small towns that joined together and suffered many growing pains to achieve the present population of over 37,000.

Worth a glimpse to your left across the highway, just before the Paloma Avenue turnoff, is Anderson's nostalgic red two-story general store, built in 1907 and a friendly place to buy groceries.

The forbidding looking castle on the hill, also to your left, was modeled after a Scottish royal dwelling and was built of concrete and steel to withstand earthquakes. Finished in 1908, according to legend, instead of housing royalty, it served as an abortion mill in the 1920s, as a speakeasy during Prohibition, and later as a Coast Guard headquarters. It's now a private residence owned by Sam Mazza, who has filled the rooms with funky and exquisite collectibles. Mazza will occasionally let organized charitable groups sample the castle's ambience and enjoy the view. He can be contacted through the Pacifica Chamber of Commerce (415/355-4122).

Visit or write the Chamber of Commerce, 80 Eureka Square, Pacifica, CA 94044 for maps and brochures extolling Pacifica's virtues. Take the Paloma turnoff and cross over Highway 1 or the Sharp Park turnoff and double back to get to Eureka Square. Among the establishments catering to Pacifica citizens' daily needs is the Periwinkle Art Supplies and Framing Shop (415/359-5230). Enid Emde, the ebullient manager, has her finger on the pulse of local cultural activities, especially art and artists, and it's a pleasant place to browse. If you're hungry, join locals at the nearby modestly priced Muffin Mine.

Next? Even if you don't wish to catch a big salmon or several large crabs for dinner, the L-shaped **Pacifica Municipal Pier,** which juts 1,020 feet out over crashing surf, is worth a visit for its panoramic views of the coast and close-up glimpses of sea birds and, perhaps, whales.

To reach the pier from Highway 1, take the Paloma turnoff, turn left on Palmetto Avenue, right on San Jose, and park. If you've passed the Sea Horse Saloon (offering country music Friday and Saturday night) or the Amused Carrot Co-op, you've gone too far. Or, after taking the Paloma turnoff, continue to Beach Boulevard before turning left. Don't worry; 1,020 feet of pier is hard to lose.

Ignore the signs about closing hours; there are none, and some great catches have been made at night. The pier has fish-cleaning sinks and benches; two too-well-ventilated restrooms; and a bait shop that sells cold sandwiches, snacks, and beer. The pier clientele is varied; you'll hear many languages and dialects. Clothing is informal, with windbreakers de rigueur for breezes that usually have a bite.

Views? On a clear day the blue horizon is framed on your right by San Francisco's Golden Gate and sometimes even farther north to Point Reyes. To the south is nearby Gray Whale Point, named for the gentle giants that migrate south from the Bering Sea to Baja California from the last of November into February, returning with their calves in March or April. During the crucial weeks, a few of these mammoth creatures swim right under the pier. Some whales have been seen rubbing their bellies on the sand nearby to rid themselves of barnacles. Unless you take an excursion to Lower California during the whale's winter mating season, this is probably as close as you'll ever get to these exciting fellow warm-blooded creatures.

Many sea birds, including gulls, cormorants, and pelicans, keep a sharp eye on the fishing. As always, it is a thrill to see the ungainly brown pelicans plunge, like graceful dive bombers, into the surf. They are often closely followed by gulls or terns who try to snatch the catch. And you can see this whole show from the pier.

Fishing, of course, is the main reason why up to 600 people at one time will line the Pacifica Pier, and it's all free. You don't have to buy a fishing license to try your luck off public piers. Catches here have varied from small kingfish, flounder, and perch to a thirty-seven-pound salmon, a forty-three-pound bass, and a sixty-pound halibut.

The paradox of fishing, especially noticeable on a pier, is that a luckless fisherperson can be standing without a bite within a few feet of another bringing in two or three fish at a time. The small crescent-shaped area at the end of the pier before it turns into its *L* often seems a lucky spot for buckets full of kingfish.

Incidentally, the large Spanish-style building with arched windows across Beach Boulevard to the south is not a discreet hotel or convent. It is Pacifica's Sewage Treatment Plant; the Pacifica City Council holds its meetings upstairs here.

A short distance to the south is the 18-hole public **Sharp Park Golf Course** (415/751-2997), often referred to as the "poor man's Pebble Beach." This championship-length course was designed by the same Scotsman who did Pebble Beach. The putting greens are free, and you should reserve by Monday to play the course on weekends. A well-kept secret is the Sharp Park Restaurant (415/355-9200), which serves breakfast, lunch, and dinner (no dinner on Monday). You don't have to be a golfer to enjoy the many specials or what devotees say are the best steaks in the area. Notice the small murals here, done by the W.P.A. during the Depression years.

Ecologists and birders enjoy the migratory water-fowl who use the few acres of swampy land in the golf course for nesting and wintering, but the birds may get in your way if you're a golfer. Also frequently on the course are endangered San Francisco garter snakes: red with some blue and white on their backs and turquoise undersides. They're live bearing; they don't lay eggs but have baby snakes. Besides being endangered and beautiful, they are harmless. Drive or walk on past the golf course for an easy-to-reach beach. The ocean's edge here is often lined with surf fishermen during the striped-bass season.

In early 1984, after years of suspense, 1,100-acre, two-mile long **Sweeney Ridge** was finally purchased by Uncle Sam and incorporated into the Golden Gate National Recreation Area. This historic ridge is one of the highlights of the entire coast. A stone marker honors Gaspar de Portola (close to a big green water tank); here, on October 31, 1769, Portola and some of his scouting party became the first whites to glimpse San Francisco Bay. Near the Portola marker is a memorial dedicated to the late Carl McCarthy, who never gave up hope that this inspiring acreage would one day belong to the public. His memorial points out highlights of the view: The

The public 18-hole Sharp Park Golf Course in Pacifica has a pleasant ocean view and is close to San Francisco.

Farallon Islands, Point Reyes, Mount Tamalpais, San Bruno Mountain, Mount Diablo, Mount Hamilton, the Montara Mountains, and Point San Pedro.

You also see, of course, the southern portion of the great San Francisco Bay, which Portola's group found by mistake. The views on a clear day, plus the thrill of standing on the discovery spot, make the two-plus mile hike in well worth the effort. But one question has never been answered. Who was Sweeney? Did he run cattle on the hill or was he one of the Irish who came to this area to farm potatoes and cabbage? No one knows for sure.

Until more access routes are worked out, the easiest way to reach this spot is the steep, private one-lane road to the Shelldance Nursery (415/ 355-4845), 2000 Cabrillo Highway. You can probably park here for your walk up the trail to the spine of the mountain. If it's a weekend, take a peek at the exotic tropical plants in this nursery, which special-

izes in bromeliads. The road up to Shelldance Nursery comes soon after Highway 1 loses its center divider. However, the road is dangerous to turn left onto in heavy traffic. Continue on to the stoplight at Reina del Mar, make your turn, and come back for your jaunt up to the "Plymouth Rock of California."

Back to Highway 1, continue south for a mile. On your left, by a car wash, are the remains of a depot, the first visible remnant of the ill-fated **Ocean Shore Railroad,** easily visible from the Reina del Mar turnoff. Following the collapse of the railroad, this depot spent many distinguished years as the High Iron Restaurant. Eventually, the establishment was gutted by fire, then rebuilt as the present Vallemar Station. It may have opened as a restaurant once again when you visit.

The Ocean Shore Railroad was started in 1905. Ambitious plans called for a double-track line from San Francisco to Santa Cruz, clinging to the edges of

Ocean Fishing Tips

If you like **fishing,** the Central Coast is your country, for you'll find almost every variety—pier, surf, spear, party boat, or you name it. But before you load up your gear, be sure you have three items to make your fishing legal and more profitable. First, you need a California fishing license, available at most big sporting goods stores. Then pick up a tide table; they're available early in the year at sporting goods stores, bait shops, and many coastal service stations. Tide tables are calculated for a definite location, like San Francisco's Golden Gate, so follow the compensation direction provided.

Order the next items by mail: ocean fishing maps number 53—for San Francisco, San Mateo, and Santa Cruz counties—and number 54—for Monterey County and points south—from the Office of Procurement, Publications Section, P. O. Box 1015, North Highlands, CA 95660. For $1 each, you get easy-to-follow maps as well as advice on where, how, and with what to fish. Even experienced anglers might pick up pointers.

Rock fishing, either from shore or from small boats, can be great, especially after winter storms when fish seem to move in from the deeper waters. you'll find prime spots from Mussel Rock at the edge of Pacifica to Montaña de Oro State Park, south of San Luis Obispo. Besides steady legs and sturdy equipment, you need patience. Keep small pieces of fresh bait on your rig and try to keep that rig down on the rocks. You must time your casting to the surf action. Since your hooks and sinkers are likely to get tangled in the rocks, kelp, or seaweed, have a good supply of hooks. If the bottom is rough, you might use cheap sinkers; even old bolts, sparkplugs, or sand-filled tobacco sacks will do. The catch here will be cabezon, lingcod, and other rockfish, all of which can be whoppers.

Surf fishing? Surf-washed beaches are waiting for you all the way south. Odds are better if you try where the sand is coarse and the beach drops off steeply. The calmest and warmest periods along the shore occur during early spring and late fall before the northwesterly winds start blowing. However, from May through October, even in fog or wind, you can catch bass if you cast into and beyond the breakers; some bass weigh in at fifty pounds.

Other fish you can catch from the shore are surf perch, jacksmelt, white croaker, flounder, sand sole, shark, and ray. For surf perch, cast out into the breakers, let the bait sink almost to the bottom, and reel in the slack. You'll have no problem knowing when you get a bite. Surf perch are fighters, and you may have to work to drag them and your sinker through heavy surf. Keep your line taut when you're reeling one in. They travel in schools and are voracious eaters; if you manage to catch one by hit-and-miss casting, you'll probably get others in the vicinity. Some authorities insist that an incoming tide is best; other say it makes little difference. You can catch jacksmelt and surf perch

Fishermen line the shore below Santa Cruz, but there are still fish left for future anglers.

with small hooks or even on hand lines. Throwing bread into the water may make these schooling fish congregate.

Another tip for catching the big ones: Look for flocks of birds diving for and feeding on anchovies. You can be quite sure that bass or salmon are feeding below and forcing those anchovies up to the surface. This is why many fishermen swear by live anchovies as bait. But many also rig their lines so they can quickly change to lure fishing at the first indication that stripers are about. For these fish, they use metal spoons, leadhead, or squid, and cast out a good distance.

What's the most productive way to bring back a catch? Trying your luck on a **party boat** is number one, according to fish and game experts. They estimate that each California party boat angler brings back an average of better than eight and one half fish per capita per trip. But to get in on that largess, you have to reserve ahead and pay for a fishing license, the boat trip, and often extras.

If you prefer **pier fishing,** all you need is a rod, reel, a bucket or container for your catch, your favorite fish knife, and luck. You don't need a license, and you can come and go as you please. No wonder you see eternal optimists holding rods lined up at piers down the coast, including Pacifica, Princeton, Santa Cruz, Seacliff State Park, Cayucos, and Port San Luis.

There are a few ways you can increase your odds. One is to get going early. Most fishermen are early risers, believing in early mornings on an incoming tide. If you hit this combination on a windless day, the odds are even better. As for bait, most pier fishermen use pile worms that they buy, but a few prefer anchovies or mussels. Although a number 2 hook seems to work well for most fish, some experts swear by hooks as small as a number 6. Their theory is that you're sure to catch small fish and there's always the chance a big one will grab one of those small fish. A few catch small ones at the shallow end of the pier and then move to the deep end with the live wiggling bait they've just caught.

Without a net, hoisting record-size catches the considerable distance from the waterline onto the pier can be heartbreaking if the hook rips out of the fish's mouth. So why not bring along a crab net to use for those crucial moments when you're landing your prize? Besides, you might snare some crabs if the big fish aren't biting.

The most optimistic of all who hope to bring home a seafood dinner are skin divers. Authorities insist the skin diver's average is only half of a less prestigious fish per day. To a skindiving addict, perhaps it doesn't matter.

coastside cliffs most of the way. The 1906 quake destroyed most of the track and equipment. The railroad never recovered from this and numerous other misfortunes: landslides, rebuilding costs, and strikes, to name a few. Eventually, with passengers often seated on top of flat cars, a few trains rattled off from San Francisco on this "cool scenic route." At Tunitas Creek, where a few crumbling concrete blocks from the trestle remain, passengers were transferred to a Stanley Steamer. They climbed aboard the train again at Swanton to chug into Santa Cruz. The trip was advertised as taking five and a half hours, but it's doubtful if this schedule was ever kept. Although there is still an Ocean Shore Railroad office in San Francisco, the last trains under its banner ran in 1920. With the collapse of the railroad, coastside hopes of hauling produce and of importing tourists also collapsed.

Several other Ocean Shore Railroad depots remain. Those at Pedro Point, Montara, and Half Moon Bay are now private homes; the one at El Granada is a real estate office.

Rockaway Beach, just south of the depot, is a pleasant crescent of sand, often lined with fishermen during the run of stripers sometime after July Fourth. The beach is flanked by a small motel and the area contains a plethora of restaurants: Italian, Chinese, Mexican, and American steak and seafood. The most publicized restaurant is Nick's (415/359-3900), which lights the ocean at night for the romantically inclined. Most of these eateries discourage bare feet. On Highway 1 immediately before the Rockaway Beach turnoff, there's a deli and a fried chicken outlet.

On the landward side of Highway 1 at Crespi Drive, about three-fourths of a mile south of Rockaway Beach, is a state historical marker honoring Portola's expedition. Here's what it says, so you won't have to stop:

> Captain Gaspar de Portola camped October 31, 1769 by the Creek at the South of this valley. To that camp scouting parties brought news of a body of water to the East. On Nov. 4 the expedition advanced, turning inland. Here they climbed to the summit of Sweeney's Ridge and beheld, for the first time, the Bay of San Francisco.

On the ocean side, just past Crespi Drive, is the city-run **Pedro Beach,** a pleasant mix of sand and surf. There's also plenty of parking space, restrooms, and the Pacifica police often allow self-contained RVs to stay overnight. Call them at (415) 875-7314. Pedro Beach is a quick drive from San Francisco and also easy to reach by public transportation. SamTrans (415/573-2200) runs frequent buses that connect with BART (Bay Area Rapid Transit) in Daly City. Incidentally, those black shiny mammals bobbing in the water are probably not seals but human surfers. Just south of the park must be the most scenic hamburger stand along the coast, the A & W, where you can sit outside within a few feet of the surf and watch dogs running happily along the beach.

The **Sanchez Adobe** is less than a mile inland along the Linda Mar Boulevard. Francisco Sanchez, proprietor of the almost 9,000-acre Rancho San Pedro, finished this historic adobe in 1846. Several huge Monterey pines and cypresses near the adobe have survived from this period. Sanchez was the son of a commander of San Francisco's presidio, a militia captain, and repeatedly an *alcalde*—magistrate—of San Francisco. The building, constructed of adobe bricks from an earlier mission outpost (you can see the outline), was the scene of many brilliant social events. After Sanchez died in 1862, the structure had a checkered career as a roadhouse, a speakeasy (and possibly worse), and then a shed for artichoke packing.

The building itself has been artfully restored and contains tools, clothes, household items, and other artifacts from early days. Few of the original furnishings from the rancho period are here; most of the items were donated from other sources. Yet you can still get the feeling of how life must have been during its rancho period. Since the original mission outpost was started to produce food for San Francisco's Mission Dolores, a garden has been planted on the grounds. Plans are also in the works to reproduce the willow huts and perhaps the sweat houses used by the earlier inhabitants, the Ohlone Indians.

A bonus to your visit is **San Pedro Creek,** which runs along one edge of the grounds. This is a green, peaceful area, where you might see the steelhead spawning or meet the kingfisher hunting up and down the creek.

When Proposition 13 was passed, cutting back California state expenditures, the Sanchez Adobe had to be closed. History buffs came to the rescue, however, and the adobe is now open Tuesday and Sunday from 1 P.M. to 4 P.M., with a coordinator on hand. Groups wishing to see the historical building on other days can call (415) 359-1462.

Farther along on Linda Mar Boulevard is the entrance to Pacifica's **San Pedro Valley County Park,** open 8 A.M. to dark. In its 1,150 acres you can enjoy family picnic sites with barbecue pits, a self-guiding nature trail, and loop hiking trails. Two

The Sanchez Adobe in Pacifica has been artfully restored and is open to the public Tuesday and Sunday.

freshwater creeks run through the park, and when natures cooperates during the rainy season, Brooks Falls, with a drop of 175 feet in three tiers, puts on a water show.

One big advantage of San Pedro Valley County Park is that it is often sunny when the coastal area only two miles away is shivering in fog. So if fog and wind have driven you away from the oceanside, come in to warm up. Friday, Saturday, and Sunday from 1 P.M. to 4 P.M. you can also peek into the brand new Visitors Center (415/355-8289)with its environmental museum and restrooms. Eventually there may be trails connecting with those to Sweeney Ridge and to the newly acquired McNee Ranch section of Montara State Park on the coastside. If your children want structured activities, there is a playground at the small **Frontier Park** nearby; you can also barbecue here.

The **Linda Mar Shopping Center,** where Linda Mar meets Highway 1, is not photogenic, but its supermarket, drugstore, hardware store, wine shop, service station, and other establishments are appealing if you need gas, beer, sunburn lotion, or whatever to ease your travel.

Even if you're not a surfer, **Pedro Point,** directly across from the shopping center, might be worth a visit, and perhaps the Vagabond Restaurant will have reopened. Take San Pedro Road toward the point, turn right on Danmann Avenue, and park. At the end, you'll see one of the few remaining stations of the ill-fated Ocean Shore Railroad, this one now a private dwelling. The edifice on your right with a tower is the Arts and Heritage Building: Activities held there include frequent jazz concerts on Sunday. Call (415) 359-5230. Point Surf, across the road, caters to the many enthusiasts who flock here.

Shelter Cove, a private beach and now more private than originally intended, is at the end of a narrow path to the north at the end of Danmann Avenue. About fifty people, including artists and a botanist, live here facing the raw Pacific. Waves often crash over the seawall; one once picked up a van and threw it onto a porch. The climax came when a recent storm destroyed the only road, one lane wide. This means the inhabitants must pack everything in along that precarious path, which may go in the next big storm. Yet the Shelter Cove people consider themselves lucky to have a front-row seat to the drama of the sea and to watch, close up, great gray whales scraping against the Pedro Point rocks to rid themselves of barnacles. Residents can also enjoy the year round wildflower display; the fog helps keep plants blooming throughout summer.

Off Pedro Point you can indulge in crabbing and almost any variety of fishing, and this is excellent rockfishing and skindiving country. If you can, wangle yourself into a skiff or small boat or bring an inflatable rubber boat with an outboard motor (the small docking facility here does not rent boats). You'll probably fish just beyond the breakers. Try for king salmon, when they're running, though you'll probably have more luck bringing in blue rockfish, black rockfish, white croaker, lingcod, cabezon, jacksmelt, and kelp greening.

If you decide to stay over in Pacifica, choices are limited. There's the Sea Breeze Motel (415/359-3903), right on the ocean at Rockaway Beach. As mentioned, self-contained RVs are sometimes allowed to park overnight at Pedro Beach. If you want RV camping with full hookups, check to see if Pacific Park for Campers (415/355-2112) is open at 700 Palmetto Avenue, Pacifica, CA 94044. Take Manor Drive, Palmetto Avenue exit off Highway 1, and go south two and a half blocks.

If you decide to forgo Pacifica, continue south on Highway 1. You'll swing around San Pedro Mountain past thick forests of pungent eucalyptus trees imported from Australia more than a century ago.

Soon the mountainside gets too steep for trees and you're at Devil's Slide, where Highway 1 hangs precariously almost over the ocean. At last report it hadn't dropped into the ocean, but who knows what Mother Nature has in store.

These bathers have chosen the clothing option at one of the three "clothing optional" beaches just south of Devil's Slide.

3

Approaching
Half Moon Bay

Highway 1 turns into a cliffhanger above crashing surf between Pedro Point and Montara; you're now at the dangerous **Devil's Slide,** which is waiting to send rocks crashing down. Drive slowly; the highway sags fifteen feet at some points and wrecks are commonplace.

During and after the winter into spring storms in the early 1980s, Devil's Slide had to be closed frequently, as huge hunks crashed into the ocean almost 1,000 feet below. After the 1983 winter storms, 400 steel rods were inserted into the roadbed to keep Devil's Slide from falling apart. Luckily no one was killed, but the inconvenience and economic hardship was considerable for those who depend on this vital route to get to and from the coastside; many folks wonder what will happen if there's an earthquake.

Because of the frequent slides, the twenty-six dangerous curves between Pacifica and Moss Beach, and the many accidents, years ago the Highway Department planned a Devil's Slide bypass. This

wider freeway was to run inland from one-fifth of a mile south of Pedro Creek in Pacifica to three-quarters of a mile south of San Vincente Creek near Moss Beach. The present scenic but dangerous portion—a long-time popular spot to dump bodies of murder victims—was to be turned over to San Mateo County, and it was expected that Devil's Slide would take over in the end. However, according to embittered local inhabitants, conservationists managed to block the bypass (approximately the same route Portola took on his jaunt north) and its future is uncertain.

On a clear day you can usually see the rocky Farallon Islands, twenty miles to the west. Avoid the steep paths down to the ocean that are marked "Hazardous." The signs mean what they say; swirling waters have trapped dozens of hikers here, and many have lost their lives.

Another hazard is the ever-increasing number of gawkers who park illegally on the highway right of

Travelers staying at the Montara Light Station, now a youth hostel, enjoy a panoramic view of the coast.

way, endangering themselves and others while they peer below at the couples and families enjoying **nude sunbathing** at the three small beaches just south of Devil's Slide. Back in 1979 the State Park Department announced public hearings on whether clothing should be optional at several state beaches. There was a loud outcry, and the frightened Half Moon Bay city council passed an ordinance banning sun-worshippers-in-the-buff from the seven-mile stretch of beaches within the city limits. The fine is $50 for the first offense and $500 or six months in jail for subsequent offenses.

Gray Whale Cove State Beach, the first nude beach, has primitive restrooms. Parking is available for a stiff fee at a lot across Highway 1 from the beach, but you have to cross the busy highway on foot. Gray Whale Cove State Beach is easy to get down to; the two tiny nude beaches further south are only for the agile. If you have the urge to indulge in nude sunbathing, do it here, at the private San Gregorio nude beach, or at those in Santa Cruz County farther south. Do *not* follow the example of thirty elderly nudists who stopped traffic by playing volleyball on Montara beach one sunny Sunday in 1984.

As its name indicates, Gray Whale Cove State Beach is an excellent place to watch the giant gray whales as they migrate south at the end of November into February and return in March and April. You can often spot them by their spout, or spume, a vapor they exhale before they dive. Several spouts in quick succession usually mean a long dive. You'll see them surface again at least 1,000 feet farther along if you wait patiently for a few minutes with your binoculars. See page 148 for more about these gentle giants.

The strange dirt and metal object looming up on a steep point just south of the three nude beaches is the aborted view-home of a Texan, who started to have the old coast fortification there bulldozed down. When the Coastal Zoning Act was passed, he gave up and returned to Texas.

Coarse, sandy **Montara State Beach,** next south, drops off suddenly under water, which means—according to fishing experts—that surf casting is good. Rockfishing is okay, but rocks are scarce here; most were brought in by truck to prevent erosion by waves churning and breaking wildly against this shore. Primitive restroom facilities and an easy entrance to the beach are just south of the Chart House restaurant (415/728-7366), which replaced the old Frank Torres restaurant. The state plans 260 additional parking spaces near here to make it easier to get to the beach, its restrooms, and twenty-five campsites.

Across the highway and on up over the mountains is the brand new addition to Montara State Park, the 625-acre McNee Ranch. Horseback riders and hikers (no vehicles!) are encouraged to use the trails which include the old county highway; the entrance is about 200 yards north of San Vicente Creek. Bring water, lunch, camera, and binoculars to enjoy the view from the top. Try to avoid the prolific poison oak. Eventually plans call for this park to be connected to the San Pedro Valley Park on the other side of the mountain. State park plans also call for a horse unloading pad and access trails.

Montara State Beach is a great place to picnic, but if you prefer eating at a table, try to find tiny Sharon's (415/728-5600), overlooking the highway inland at a cluster of businesses. Breakfast, lunch, or dinner are inevitably delicious. On weekends you can enjoy the food until midnight or after. The nearby Farallone Hotel (415/728-7817), 1410 Main, a wood building with balconies jutting out at various angles, advises reservations.

Farther south, just past a handful of private residences that flank Montara State Beach, is the **Point Montara Light Station.** The stark white buildings with their red roofs set against a background of dark green cypresses are a dramatic contrast to the crashing blue, green, and white surf and convoluted buff-colored coastline. This station went the way of many light stations (or lighthouses): A light and sounding device now operates automatically in the buoy, as on the Farallon Islands. Since a crew was no longer needed to tend the light and "fog howler," the buildings fell into disrepair.

In 1980 the abandoned Montara Light Station took on new life as a **youth hostel** for the "young of heart of all ages." The state defines a hostel as a place for travelers to sleep, eat, wash, and make friends. As in most other hostels, the guests provide their own food, sleeping bags or linen, and must do some chores. Men and women hostelers usually bunk in separate dormitories—six to a room at Montara. The hostel is locked in the evening for security and usually during the day from 9:30 A.M. to 4:30 P.M. Drugs, alcohol, and guns are forbidden. Hostels are certainly not for everyone, but the locations and the chance to meet fellow hostelers from all over the world (there are 5,000 hostels in fifty countries) make the stringent rules and lack of luxury worth it for many.

The Montara Hostel is a twenty-five-mile bike ride from the big International Hostel in San Francisco's Fort Mason. Within biking distance of Montara is the Pigeon Point Lighthouse Hostel, south of Half Moon Bay. In the planning stage is a hostel in the Big Sur lighthouse. The grand dream is to build a coastal hostel network from Canada to Mexico. The Montara Hostel is continually being improved. Eventually, if not sooner, the 1875 Keeper's Quarters will be restored to Victorian glory and will house staff, a small historical museum, and a dining and recreation area. For more information or reservations write the Montara Lighthouse Hostel, P.O. Box 737, Montara, CA 94037 or phone (415) 728-7177.

If you're a railroad buff, drive by the **Montara Ocean Shore Railroad Station,** now a private home. It's a block inland from Highway 1 on the corner of Main and Second streets. You can spot it by its two-foot-thick stone walls constructed with black mortar, sturdy enough to withstand the 1906 earthquake. The arched doorways and original beams remain as does the former railroad platform, now a patio, with big red letters spelling *Montara* in the concrete.

During those early days of the railroad, poet Joaquin Miller was invited to ride the first passenger train into Montara and plant a giant sequoia to inaugurate the expected growth of the town, which barely existed then. But the sequoia died and—when the railroad tore out its rails in 1922—so did hope for a boom town that might blossom into another Oakland.

Moss Beach, one mile south of Montara, is famous for the tidepool life on its three miles of rocky sea shelf. Many sea creatures have their young in the protected nooks among the rocks. However, too many tidepoolers have walked away with specimens, and many species have almost disappeared. There are enough left to be protected in San Mateo County's **James W. Fitzgerald Marine Reserve.** Take California Street seaward at a well-marked sign to the parking area by the information kiosk. You'll find restrooms and picnic tables under cypress trees, but no overnight camping. The reserve has produced an excellent booklet describing local marine life, and excerpts are on the walls of the information booth.

Start your tidepool-watching at a minus tide when the ocean has receded, so that rocks, seaweed, and sea life ordinarily covered by water are visible. A park

Tidepooling Along the Coast

Even the more common varieties of seaweed are beautiful.

One of the most popular activities along the Central Coast is to visit the plants and animals that make their home in tidepools. Along this shore you have a wide choice of these rocky catch-alls where you can learn how some fellow creatures adapt to incredibly difficult situations. (Consult the index for the tidepools nearest you.)

Start your **tidepool watching** at a minus tide when the ocean has receded, so that rocks, seaweed, and sea life ordinarily covered by water are visible; usually this is in the chilly early morning, so dress warmly. Also, remember, you'll be bending over a lot; so secure your wallet or glasses or anything that can fall off.

In high and dry areas where the beach is exposed at about a two-foot tide, you'll probably find periwinkles or a black turban snail, which will quickly withdraw into its shell, closing its horny door if you pick it up. If you are patient you're also likely to see little hermit crabs scuttling about in the shells they've stolen for homes. You may even see a covetous home-seeker try to evict another hermit crab by pulling him out of his shell.

Farther out at low tide you'll find sea anemones. They might look like squishy, sand-covered lumps, but then again they might open up like flowers to show off the pink or white stinging tentacles with which they paralyze small prey, such as worms. Algae causes the vivid interior color of the giant green anemones, which can live for more than seventy-five years. The mossy chiton, a flat, oval animal with eight plates down its back, clings to the rocks and feeds on algae at night or at low tide. When the giant (up to a foot long) chiton dies, the shells that wash ashore look like petrified butterflies. Sea urchins, the spiny, purple porcupines of the sea, graze on seaweed. Limpets, small soft-bodied animals covered by conical shells, cling tightly to the rocks until nighttime or until the tide is in. Then they creep along on a muscular foot to feed on microscopic algae attached to the rocks.

Multilegged, clawed crabs scurry about in areas containing small rocks they can hide under. If the crab you see rears up and brandishes its pinchers to protect itself, it's a lined shore crab. If it's flat, with antennae, it's a porcelain crab. If it's large, with big claws and red spots on its belly, it's a red rock crab.

In surf-swept areas you'll find barnacles attached to the rocks with a glue twice as strong as any made by man. You may also see California mussels, their blue-black shells attached to the rocks with strong whiskerlike threads. You may also see the common ochre starfish— which is often red or purple—feeding by wrapping its rays (or arms) around a mussel and inserting its stomach into the mussel's shell.

Seaweeds are crucial to the tidal ecology, providing shelter for shellfish, fish, and sea mammals. The names of many seaweeds suggest their appearance—for example, sea palms, which cling to surf-buffeted rocks; surf grass; Irish moss; sea lettuce; and feather boas. Bull whip kelp, a massive brown algae that can stretch more than fifty feet from the ocean floor to the water's surface, has air-filled flotation bulbs that pop when you step on them. Dulse looks like enormous flattened rubber gloves. Rock weed has olive-brown, flattened blades that exude a slimy mucilage to prevent drying.

To protect this fascinating tidal life, naturalists suggest that you always return rocks to their original position, remembering that seaweeds grow on the upper surface of rocks. They also stress: *Do not remove any plants, animals, rocks, or even empty shells.* These may be vital to the survival of some of these creatures, battling so hard to live. Besides, you'll want to leave them for others to enjoy, too.

naturalist, usually on duty from 8 A.M. to 5 P.M., can sometimes be persuaded to take groups on a lectured walk at low tide. Since these often occur in the chill of early morning, dress warmly. Page 20 describes the marine life you'll probably see here and at other tidepools as you comb the coast.

If you'd like to see a rare **earthquake fault** that draws geologists from all over the country, walk down the steps at the entrance to the marine reserve, turn right, and on the cliff face 100 feet north of the mouth of San Vicente Creek you can see the vertical trace of the Seal Cove earthquake fault. (Notice the nearby sign requesting that you refrain from disturbing the cliff's face.) A fault is a crack in the earth's crust along which there is relative motion on each side. Here 7-million-year-old siltstone beds have moved up against the lighter, sandy terrace, which is a mere 25,000 to 75,000 years old.

Near the entrance to the reserve, on Beach Street and Nevada, is Nyes Reefs II, a leftover from the days when Charles Nye ran The Reefs restaurant on a pier sticking out into the ocean. Nye entertained luminaries like Jack London and Luther Burbank, but the ocean unkindly swept The Reefs and the pier away. At the present rustic establishment nearby, open sporadically on Saturday and Sunday, you can drink beer and wine and indulge in nostalgia as you play tunes on the funky jukebox. Nyes Reefs II presently wears a for sale sign. If you can come up with half a million, you could dicker with Nye, who will probably throw in the abalone shells nailed the building.

Before you leave Moss Beach, drive along as close as you can to the ocean to view some of the old and contemporary homes and estates within constant sound of the ocean. In your brief tour, stop by the Moss Beach Distillery on Ocean and Beach. This establishment replaced the Galway Inn, named because the restaurant overlooks a pleasant cove that is supposed to resemble Galway Bay in Ireland. Galway Inn took over from the old Vic Torres place, which prospered during the bootleg-Prohibition era between 1919 and 1932. On the small hill nearby, lookouts would be stationed with lanterns to signal to smugglers in small boats offshore that all was safe and that they could bring in their cargos of Canadian whiskey.

Many coastside old-timers remember the Prohibition period as the Golden Era, and they proudly tell how they smuggled bootleg whiskey in huge apron pockets or under the coal or kept it behind revolving kitchen drawers. Business was rosy then, not only

Skin divers congregate on the beach at Montara's Fitzgerald Marine Reserve, where the rocky reefs offer excellent skin diving and tidepooling.

for the boat smugglers and operators of stills back in the canyons but for all their employees and hangers-on. Many of the tourists who flocked in for bootleg booze were also not averse to a good meal and perhaps a little red-light hanky-panky, so lots of people were kept busy. When Prohibition was repealed, this somewhat lawless prosperity vanished, along with the excitement of playing tag with the Feds, and the accompanying gunfights and chases at sea.

The trail to the old lookout hill near the distillery has been posted as dangerous because of erosion. Even if you can't climb the hill, the view from this windy bluff is great, especially at sunset or in spring when the banks are massed with wild iris. Look hard at a small rocky island offshore; you may see harbor seals there at low tide, but their color blends in almost too well with the rocks.

The Moss Beach Distillery Restaurant (415/728-5434) has changed hands, menus, and lifestyles many times in the decades since the Golden Era of bootlegging, but the view of the bay remains superb. The restaurant presently offers dinner daily at 5 P.M., brunch Saturday and Sunday from 10:30 A.M. to 2 P.M., and Mercedes sedans are now among the cars

in the crowded parking lot. At another old-time restaurant, Dan's Place (415/728-3343), up the hill at Etheldore and Virginia in Moss Beach, you'll find Italian food and lots of it.

For a change of pace, try Tillie's Lil' Frankfurt (415/728-5744) at 2385 San Carlos Avenue in Moss Beach, just across from the entrance to the marine reserve. The food is bounteous and modestly priced, and there may be an extra seasoning of excitement when Tillie, who actually is from Frankfurt and is not a fragile person, rolls up her sleeves to straighten out someone she believes is out of line.

If you prefer to picnic, all along this portion of highway are big and small delis. Many locals recommend Picnics (415/728-5300) in Moss Beach, which offers gourmet lunches for "2 to 200."

The **Half Moon Bay Airport** is used mainly by small private planes (it's home to 90, and there's an annual traffic of about 80,000), but medium-sized jets have landed here when the San Francisco Airport was socked in. You can sit in the small coffee shop and absorb the excitement of small-plane flying as you eat breakfast, lunch, or a snack, some prepared with a Portuguese flavor. Plane trips over the coastline to

San Francisco and back and whale-watching trips leave from here. Interested in flying lessons? On weekends an attractive woman schoolteacher is one of the instructors. In any case, you can't pick a much more beautiful area to fly over than this coastline.

The only industry in the vicinity, besides boat repairing and the care and feeding of tourists, seems to be candle making. You may not want to stock up on some of the flowery candles and holders at the Blue Gate Candle Shop on Airport Street, directly behind the airport, but if you hunt around you'll find bargains on utility candles and seconds, and the place smells nice. Open every day but Sunday usually; during the big pre-Christmas or warehouse sales, they're open on Sunday also.

On the inland side of Highway 1, just south of the airport entrance, a builder named Doelger imported suburban living to an artichoke patch. The development, Frenchman's Creek, sold out. Soon afterward, Doelger sold more than 8,000 acres to an outfit now called Half Moon Bay Properties, which put up expensive developments including the Half Moon Bay Golf Links.

To your right, jutting up on a spit of land, you'll see **Pillar Point** and its big radar installation, with its missile tracking dish antenna. Pillar Point is now treeless. In 1585, however, when he first sighted it, Francisco de Gali reported, "We passed a very high and fair land with many trees, wholly without snow." Driving to the top is off limits, but you can park below and walk up.

For a closer look at the ocean and tidepools, visit the three-in-one beach wrapped around Pillar Point. Drive past the Princeton Inn on Capistrano and continue west and north past many boat repair shops until you reach the forbidden road to the radar dish. Park and walk in; the potholes on the lower road would swallow an elephant. The first little squishy beach, in the arms of the Half Moon Bay breakwater, is calm enough for children to wade or paddle about in a rubber boat. Continue on to see interesting tidepools, less visited than the Fitzgerald tidepools that run into them to the north. If you have forgotten your rubber boots for wading around the tidepools, continue on out to where the ocean roars in like a squadron of planes. Many locals in the know bring their picnic baskets (of brie and champagne?) here, to avoid the bikers that whine and hiccup and throw up dirt and sand almost to this point.

The tourist's mecca, **Princeton-by-the-Sea,** snuggles along the water south of the airport and Pillar Point. The fishing boats bobbing in the harbor are protected on one side by a many-million-dollar breakwater, which will be increased, along with more docking areas and harbor facilities, if plans materialize. Also on the drawing boards is a projected building that will include shops and restaurants.

Right off Capistrano near the Princeton Inn, on Prospect, is Pardini's, a small stand open on Sunday that sells fresh peas, artichokes, and other vegetables in season. A word to the wise about the "fresh" crab that's advertised at some stands: It may be fresh-thawed crab, probably from Eureka.

The main lure of Princeton, besides boating, is fishing: from the pier, from private boats, and from the party boats that leave from the Pillar Point breakwater area at the south edge of Princeton. According to a Fish and Game survey, anglers on party boats caught an average of better than eight and a half fish per capita—not bad.

Two firms operate party boats here seven days a week if the weather permits. Captain John's (415/726-2913 or 728-3377) has seven boats from forty-five to sixty-five feet long. Check in time for those promising bottomfish is 6:45 A.M., and even earlier (5:30 A.M.) if you're taking the *Captain John* out to the Farallon Islands to view the many sea mammals and sea birds. Huck Finn Sportfishing (415/726-7133) has the *Huck Finn II,* the *Tom Sawyer,* and the *Mark Twain* for open boat or charter trips, including salmon-fishing and whale-watching excursions.

The fees for local fishing trips from Princeton are somewhat lower than in San Francisco, and both outfits offer special prices to senior citizens during weekdays. Prices do not include fishing equipment, bait, sinkers, sacks for your catch, or fishing licenses (available near the dock at additional cost). Nor do they include beer, seasick pills (take them half an hour before embarking), a warm windbreaker, a knife, or lunch.

The boats on the short-range trips chug back and dock at around 2:30 P.M., when an audience watches the passengers disembark—usually with gunny sacks loaded with bottomfish such as rock cod, bass, red snapper, lingcod, and so on, but rarely salmon. During the early 1980s many catches included halibut and other fish usually caught in warmer waters. Professional fish cleaners show up to clean and fillet the fish. This is a show in itself; the attentive gulls and occasional pelican think so, too.

Alongside the sportfishing outfits is a restaurant, Ketch Joanne, open Wednesday through Sunday. (There are many other restaurants away from the wharf area.) In the Abalone Shop at the end you can buy almost anything in season, from huge sea urchins to swordfish to salmon to freshly thawed

Fishermen wet their lines at Princeton Wharf against a backdrop of boats riding at anchor.

Princeton Wharf offers successful fishermen a convenient site for cleaning their catch.

lobster, but take out a bank loan first if you intend to buy in quantity. The owner of the Abalone Shop is Bill LaVey; he's the man with the big mustache wearing rubber boots and apron. On weekend afternoons there's often a demonstration of fish cookery plus Japanese sashimi and sushi, and you can sometimes buy walk-away seafood cocktails. If they're not too frantically busy, LaVey and his people will describe ways to prepare the less popular and, therefore, much cheaper fish and shellfish.

The Princeton breakwater area also boasts a place to launch boats, public restrooms, and a sizable parking area adjacent to Highway 1. Self-contained RVs can stay overnight for a modest fee, but the reason the fee is modest is that facilities are primitive.

Very important are the two long fishing jetties where families can try pier fishing. On the west jetty nearest Pillar Point, fishing buffs bring in kelp fish, greenling, striped sea perch, and other species usually found near rocks. White croakers, surf perch, and flatfish are caught mainly from the east jetty. (See the section on fishing on page 12.) The Pillar Point area is also popular with skin divers. Enough surfers to cast several Hollywood surfing movies show up at gently sloping **El Granada Beach,** next south, and wind surfers often ride the wind and waves out beyond the breakwater.

Feeling hungry? You have several choices as you start driving by El Granada Beach. Ida's Seafood Restaurant (415/726-2822) earned renown for its abalone, although prices for this seafood delicacy are now in orbit. At the Moon Garden, next door to Ida's, you can eat Mandarin Chinese food. There are other restaurants in Princeton that serve chowder, fish and chips, and so on. The most popular is The Shore Bird (415/728-5541). The lunch crowd leaves around 4 P.M.; the dinner contingent arrives about five-ish. Prices for steak, lobster, or seafood are not out of reach. The catch of the day is often the best bargain (don't pass up that shark). Touches include homemade salad dressing, hot sourdough bread, and a rose presented to you when you leave. Bonuses: The help is friendly, the atmosphere charming, and there's a small outside patio for sunny days. The hitch? You usually have to wait a long time for a table.

El Granada Beach runs into **Miramar Beach,** which blends into a series of state beaches. Since El Granada and Miramar beaches have no rock hazards, you can enjoy the safest ocean swimming available north of Santa Cruz; that is, if you can survive in the chill water, usually in the low fifties. That long stretch of sandy shore also attracts hikers and beach-combers. If you wait for a low tide and keep an eye on the surf, you can walk three miles of uninter-rupted beach from the Pillar Point breakwater to the end of the Miramontes Point Road at the southern boundary of Half Moon Bay.

Residences in the town of **El Granada** spill down the slopes east of the highway and are partially hidden by trees. Just off the highway and very visible is another old Ocean Shore Railroad depot. It now houses the Lane Realty Company, but about all that's left from the original depot is the red tile roof.

Where else but El Granada would you find a res-taurant flying the Union Jack that purveys authentic English farmhouse-style breakfasts, lunches, and teas? These include homebaked scones and pastries, or cucumber sandwiches or bangers; the teas are correctly served in pots wearing tea cozies. This bit of old England, called **The Village Green** (415/726-3690), is at the southern end of El Granada across from the post office at 89 Portola Avenue. Learning as they went along, two Englishwomen started the restaurant in 1968. One of the founders remains,

Susan Hayward, originally from Bath. She doubles as a ballet teacher when not working with her family at the restaurant. The Village Green now serves dinners on Saturday night, and Susan hopes to start a bed and breakfast inn in her old blue Victorian home in Montara some day.

Miramar has its own edge-of-the-ocean ambience, although the city of Half Moon Bay's borders enclose this tiny town. The Miramar Beach Inn (415/726-9053), easily seen from Highway 1, serves brunch, lunch, and dinner. There's live music and dancing daily from 9:30 P.M.; on Sunday after-noon bands with such names as the Hoodoos get the crowds moving.

Another spot where people get together to hear music is the nearby **Bach Dancing and Dynamite Society, Inc.** (415/726-4143). Why drive to Mon-terey for your day's entertainment by the sea? asks the society. On Sunday afternoon, usually at 4:30, jazz artists from saxophonists to singers to guitarists to combos show off their talents. The audience, which is allowed in at 3 P.M. to save their seats, can enjoy the program while they gaze out toward the ocean, sip wine, and munch on the food they have brought. The society was incorporated in jest in 1964 after jazz musicians began coming here to jam infor-mally. Since then it has expanded to include other kinds of music, classical to folk. Now on most Fridays there's a catered dinner by candlelight at 7 P.M. followed by a classical concert at 9. You're expected to bring your own wine and a healthy contribution.

A short distance south on Mirada Road, just before the road tumbles into the ocean, is one of the coastline's most unique structures, straight out of Hansel and Gretel. It's the **New Age Center,** also known as the Miramar Beach Health Club, designed by Michael Powers, a photographer turned sculptor. Powers and helpers assembled the buildings out of wood from nearby forests and recycled salvage materials. The main building, a five-pointed star, supports a huge carved angel on top plus three lesser carved female figures. A huge piece of redwood der-ricked in from the beach was placed in the center of the outside/inside area. A hexagonal building in the rear is leased to a holistic dentist. Michael has his bed, desk, and telephone in a beached boat within listen-ing distance of the surf. Eventually plans call for the cluster of buildings and garden to be covered by glass, creating a solarium. As with the Douglas beach setup that houses the Bach Dancing and Dynamite Society, Powers will rent out his center to interested groups (415/726-2748).

The eclectic New Age Center at Miramar is the studio-home of photographer Michael Powers.

The condition of Mirada Road is mute testimony to what happens when man tries to fool Mother Nature. In the years since the nearby Princeton breakwater was built, Miramar beach has been disappearing. Usually, sand drifts out in winter and returns in summer. Now not enough sand returns to the beach below the road; many feel it is trapped by the breakwater. The sea laps right up to the cliff under the road, and even though huge rocks have been placed along the ocean's edge, Mirada Road continues to crumble away.

Back to Highway 1, from this point on, you'll be driving by a series of entrances to the crescent of beaches that brings most people to this territory. The beaches are within the Half Moon Bay city limits, but that's just a technicality. The first, once called Naples or Roosevelt Beach, can be reached via Young Avenue. **Dunes Beach,** next, can handle 150 cars on a dirt and gravel parking lot. Both have flush toilets and there's drinkable water at Dunes. You can reach **Venice Beach** via Venice Boulevard. It has a fifty-car gravel parking lot and restrooms. State park plans call for Venice Beach to be developed with a new parking lot, picnic tables, and better restrooms.

An equestrian trail runs behind these beaches, and you can rent horses at two nearby stables. Friendly Acres (415/726-9871) is on the leeward side of the highway just past the entrance to Dunes Beach. Sea Horse Ranch (415/726-2362), farther south, is open daily, and also arranges hay rides. This is big horse country and you'll see strings of riders passing by on rented horses or on their own, which they board in the area.

The next beach, and the biggest and most popular, is **Francis State Beach** at the end of Kelly Avenue; turn seaward at the light. Francis has more than fifty camping sites and charges the same modest nightly fee whether you stay in your self-contained RV, pitch a tent, or put your sleeping bag out under the foggy night sky. If you're a hiker or arrive on bicycle, however, this is one of the campgrounds along the Bikecentennial Highway 1 route that lets you roll out your sleeping bag for only 50 cents a night. Day use costs $2 per car. You get a lot for your money: paved parking for 240 cars, picnic and firepit facilities, a sanitation dump station, and three restrooms. Beach access is easy, too. For more information or reservations on these or any of the state beaches in San Mateo County, call (415) 726-6238. Park headquarters, open Monday through Friday from 8 A.M. to 4:30 P.M., are at the end of Kelly Avenue. The rangers are friendly and knowledgeable, too.

Levy Brothers' Half Moon Bay store was at the hub of activity in the 1870s; of the three stores they closed down, one reopened in 1972.

4

Half Moon Bay
Itself

Half Moon Bay proper, the largest town on the coastside, has an official population of 7,500 (or less). On a summer or fall weekend, however, you'll probably assume that several times that number live here because of the throngs of visitors from "over the hill." According to one authority, tourists have replaced vegetables as the number two crop; the flower industry is still number one.

Even before you reach the outskirts of Half Moon Bay, you'll see acres ablaze with lilies, heather, or helichrysum (which can be turned into straw flowers: There's a straw flower factory in Pescadero and several gift shops and stands sell the products, as well as cut flowers and ferns). Or perhaps as you round a curve you'll see workers waist deep in fields of sunlit daisies. Many of these flowers end up far afield with flowers in other cities; some, of course, brighten San Francisco's famous flower stalls.

However, enjoy this acres-wide flower show only from the highway. Visitors are not welcome at big wholesale nurseries because of dangerous machinery and lethal sprays. A large retail nursery that welcomes you, the Half Moon Bay Nursery, is inland on Highway 92.

You're sure to notice Half Moon Bay's number one crop at Frenchman's Creek Road, which heads back toward the hills through fields of cultivated flowers near fields of upper bracket homes put up by developers. Frenchman's Creek was named for a legendary encounter between a Frenchman out hunting beaver who came across a grizzly bear. History doesn't report who won, so take your pick.

The late Galen Wolf, a well-loved coastside artist, lived near the end of the Frenchman's Creek Road. When Wolf first moved to Half Moon Bay, he used to tell visitors that he "painted clean rocks, clear beaches, and untouched hills covered with warm, golden grass." Doves nested in alders behind his home and mountain lions visited. "Then many birds and animals fled, and the beaches and streams were no longer clear."

But not all natural beauty has fled the coastside. Besides its beaches, in winter the inland hills are green with grass, in summer they're burnished yellow-gold, in spring the orange-gold poppies—California's official flower—put on a show, and all year long those miles of cultivated flowers are a delight.

Besides the acres of brussels sprouts, you'll also notice fields of artichokes (see page 98) and, in late summer, pumpkins. Artichokes and pumpkins are practically a religion along the coastside, and the biggest and most highly advertised pumpkin stand is Tom and Pete's, just off Highway 1 at Main Street and Highway 92. John Minaidis, Sr., the owner, is credited with starting the coastside pumpkin boom. Now, besides those turned over in his whopping wholesale trade, Minaidis sells more than 50,000 pumpkins a year. Every October busloads of children visit his colorful acreage and marvel at the pumpkins' size.

In October all roads leading into Half Moon Bay are usually clogged with cars carrying pumpkin seekers. The third weekend in October even bigger crowds jam in for the **Great Pumpkin Festival.** On that Saturday local bands and hundreds of children dressed as witches, goblins, pumpkins, or whatever their parents have dreamed up, parade down Main Street. There's a pumpkin-carving contest and a pumpkin-eating contest for children, a pumpkin-decorating contest for everyone, a pumpkin recipe contest, and a masquerade ball on Saturday night with prizes for best costumes. There's a haunted house to visit, plus several blocks of booths for arts and crafts and for food (the booths benefit local nonprofit organizations). To avoid the often bumper-to-bumper traffic, check with SamTrans (415/348-7325); they operate several tours.

Each year the suspense grows as to who has produced the biggest pumpkin. Although Half Moon Bay considers itself the pumpkin capital of the world, outsiders from Canada and even farther away have been known to win the annual contest. The 1984 winner weighed 614 pounds. Besides pumpkins (in the late fall), trucks and stands along the highway sell other local produce: artichokes, of course; peas; and zucchini squash all seem to be popular. A big

barn about a half-mile toward the ocean on Kelly sells freshly picked produce on weekends.

While produce is seasonal, the beaches are a lure all year. In fact, Half Moon Bay was named after its four-mile crescent of sandy beaches, described in the previous chapter. Back then the town was a cluster of adobes belonging to families who owned two big, adjoining Spanish land grands. More Spanish-speaking people drifted in, and the few Americans who arrived dubbed it Spanishtown. Next came clans of Portuguese. Even today many storekeepers find it helpful to know English, Spanish, and Portuguese.

Although its boundaries extend about five miles south from the edge of Miramar, Half Moon Bay's population of 7,500 is small for an area so close to San Francisco and the crowded Peninsula. If you add the population of outer Half Moon Bay, from Montara to San Gregorio, you still come up with only about 12,000 or so official inhabitants.

Half Moon Bay is famous for its Great Pumpkin Festival, but choosing your favorite pumpkin is fun, too.

At one time rumors flew of new industries coming, one manufacturing educational computers. But the area still hasn't licked its transportation problem. If the present two-lane roads leading to Half Moon Bay are vastly improved, rerouted, or changed into freeways, the coastside will explode for better or worse. If you're a land developer or a city father looking for added taxes, expansion may be for the better. If you're a taxpayer, providing schools, sewage, police, and other services for newcomers, it might be a headache. The battle is on, especially whether that bypass around Devil's Slide should be built; reading the battle reports in the *Half Moon Bay Review* is exciting.

Added to local tensions is the possibility that oil rigs will be permitted along this coast. Concerned groups and citizens, including the California Coastal Commission and the San Mateo County Board of Supervisors, oppose drilling along this "sensitive and treasured" coast. The project was dropped, then reactivated. Its future depends on which way the political winds blow.

Even with transportation, sewage, and water problems, the population of greater Half Moon Bay has increased slowly but inexorably. As families flee from cities "over the hill" to the ocean-washed air, new businesses have followed, mostly clustered in shopping centers. One big, conspicuous center— with Alpha Beta supermarket, service stations, chain drugstore, liquor store, and delis—marks the junction of Highways 1 and 92. Among the many establishments in this shopping center is Blanda's, a small haven of gourmet cheeses, lunch meats, and soup. You can eat there or order to go.

In this same center is Levy Brothers, who established a store in Half Moon Bay in 1872, later moved inland to San Mateo, and then returned to the coastside; their "new" store features clothing for the family. When it first opened, Levy Brothers sold mostly general merchandise—everything from hay, grain, and feed to furniture and root beer. Their stagecoach carried mail and passengers to San Mateo in three hours. Present mail, some natives say, now takes two or more days. Levy Brothers' telegraph station flashed orders to San Francisco, where fast teams of steam vessels brought merchandise to the coast within thirty hours.

Across Highway 1, the **Strawflower Shopping Center** has been enlarged. Now, besides eating, buying country clothes, art, real estate, or having your hair coiffed, you can shop at Safeway and other big chain stores. Another shopping center, **Shoreline Station,** is inland just off Highway 1 between Highway 92 and Kelly Avenue. The gray and white buildings house the popular German Bakery and Restaurant (415/726-3666), open daily from 7 A.M. to 10 P.M. There's a camera shop and the Bay Book and Tobacco Company (415/726-3488), which carries 20,000 titles. Kevin Magee, the affable owner, also doubles as an unofficial local information service. The real **Chamber of Commerce** (415/726-5202), in an old railroad caboose in this same center, is open weekdays. There are also stores on or just off Main Street and spilling over onto Kelly.

If you haven't been to Half Moon Bay for years, you will be pleasantly surprised at the way Main Street looks. In 1970 a committee voted to go ahead with plans for a general painting and restoration. Consultants were hired to draw up the overall plans. On a sunny weekend in May, local townspeople did the actual painting, planting trees and flowers, and changing signs. Old-timers, long-haired youths, and folks of every age between clambered over scaffolds with paintbrushes while others played music or prepared food for the paint crews.

As the years passed, more trees and flowers were planted, street lamps made to look like the original gas lamps appeared, and more buildings were Victorianized. The town's new look attracted more tourists. Not everyone approved, since inevitably, rents increased. One antique dealer, driven out by a rent increase, warned that Half Moon Bay was in danger of becoming "Carmelized." She reports that whenever an old-timer living on Main Street dies, the home becomes a shop to lure tourists.

Main Street at present is a mixture of old and new. Soon after you leave Highway 92 and cross the funky concrete bridge, circa 1900, you'll see the Creekside Mall, recently moved into a renovated old plumbing establishment. The Buffalo Shirt Company (415/726-3194), now in this new collection of shops, sells shirts, big canvas bags, brass objects, local Sonshine pottery, washable hand-knitted sweaters from Portugal, wood sculptures, windchimes, and more. The store is run by pleasant Bob "Buffalo" MacCall and his wife, Isabelle, an airline stewardess. The couple decided that Half Moon Bay—where life was more leisurely and the air still fresh—was preferable to San Francisco as a commute from the San Francisco Airport. The B.S.C. Annex features Coastside Creations' bags.

The Half Moon Bay Feed and Fuel (415/726-4814), next, not only smells of hay and wood but also carries almost everything a local farmer or rancher might want, from fly swatters to Greek purses to hand plows to coal. The store is also unofficial headquarters for exchanging, buying, or selling rabbits, horses, and other livestock. Around the corner a travel service also sells gifts and gadgets.

Across the street is the relatively new German Haus where you can stop for croissants, sandwiches, soups, and pastries. The beautifully restored Greek revival house at 326 Main, built of redwood in 1863, once housed Estanislao Zaballa, a native of Spain married to Dolores Miramontes, the daughter of a land grant owner. The house is now occupied by professional and business firms.

At the corner of Main and Mill streets is another of the Half Moon Bay buildings that has been tastefully restored, this to a mid-nineteenth-century ambience. It's the **San Benito House and Saloon** (415/726-3425), formerly Dominic's, and before that the Mosconi Hotel. Four local people joined together to give the drab building a facelift. Layers of old paint were stripped and new paint was added, along with flower boxes. Eventually chef/owner Carol Regan-Mickelsen hopes the building will be smothered in bougainvillea. Brass chandeliers now decorate the high ceilings of the dining room and French doors open onto a garden where guests can eat lunch on sunny days, Wednesday through Saturday. Dinner is served every night. Classic country French and Northern Italian cuisines feature local produce and seafood. Call ahead to find out the entree or entrees: perhaps freshly caught salmon or bouillabaisse or veal piccata. A hearty Sunday breakfast is served from 9:30 A.M. to 12:30 P.M.

Upstairs, the San Benito House follows the tradition of old country inns. The twelve rooms are somewhat spartan and the front ones occasionally noisy, but there are extra touches like bathtubs big enough for two, fresh flowers, antique furnishings, and fluffy comforters. Guests can also relax in a nonhistoric sauna bath or on a flower-bedecked deck, where they can absorb sun, if any, and chat. Carol says that guests may also use her busy kitchen as a home away from home. The saloon seems to be a gathering place for local workmen, each clutching a beer as he watches sports on TV. The restaurant crowd is quieter, and the men usually wear jackets.

There's a Bicyclery (415/726-6000) at 415 Main. You can get information there about the local bicycle club. The Bay Electric Company close by used to sell T-shirts with a motto: "Let us remove your shorts."

Now they sell this and other pithy iron-on mottos and refer you to a local shop to buy your T-shirt.

The building, circa 1900, housing Cunha's Country Grocery at the corner of Main and Kelly was once a general merchandise store and one of eleven saloons in town at the time. William Cunha moved his store here in the mid-thirties, and his family has run it ever since. Cunha's has excellent fresh produce and wines, lunch meats, and cheeses. The Nunes Meat Market, in the rear, still sells old-fashioned custom cuts. The G & J Market, a block east at Kelly and Purisima, has a similar meat market and also sells picnic supplies. An important addition to Main Street, at Kelly, is the mini-park, with belltower, restrooms, and benches and tables where you can picnic.

Another popular establishment on Main Street is in the next block across from city hall. (If the city hall is open, you can sometimes obtain an excellent map of the Half Moon Bay area.) It's the **Half Moon Bay Bakery,** which uses the original double brick ovens; loaves are still shoved into these ovens on long wooden handles. Every day you can pick up freshly baked French bread and, if you're lucky, delectable Portuguese sweet bread or focaccia, a delicious breadlike version of pizza. The bakery also sells sandwiches to go.

Next door is the old I.O.O.F. Hall, circa 1895, Much of the town's activity used to take place in the assembly hall here, including Benjamin's Medicine Shows, with free tooth pulling as an attraction. One of the present tenants, McCoffee's (415/726-6241), advertises its presence by the aroma of freshly ground coffee. From 9 A.M. to 6 P.M., it, too, is a popular gathering place. The local intelligentsia and others come in to chat and for tea, coffee, cheeses, pastries, and sinfully rich ice cream; a single scoop is more than adequate. Next door Peggy Eriksen frames pictures and sells photographs of the area. Her consistent best sellers are mood pictures, such as boats in a fog, fence posts, or indistinct hillside views. George's Toggery, across the street at 527 Main, is the oldest continuously run business in town. The only remaining hitching post stands outside the store. Coastside Books is nearby. The Saturday Thrift Shop still carries on its permanent flea market every Saturday at that sharp triangle where Main Street meets Purisima.

Nearer the Cabrillo Highway (1) are more establishments geared to tourists. At 648 Kelly, just off Main Street, a tiny gem of a place called Womany has an exquisite array of folk dolls, wool teddy bears, handworked linen and lace, aprons, paper collectibles, sachet, and a few surprises. The renovated **Alves House** at 520 Kelly just off Highway 1 has more shops, including Quilts West, which carries old and new quilts plus baby things. It was built in late Eastlake-style architecture with scalloped shingles and a polygonal tower, It's just one of the interesting and historic old buildings sprinkled throughout this small town. The active Spanishtown Historical Society, P.O. Box 62, Half Moon Bay, CA 94019, has put out an excellent Half Moon Bay Walking Tour with map. It's sold at both book stores, at Cunha's, at local inns, and other tourist-oriented establishments. Track one down; following the tour is a great way to spend a few pleasant hours. Here are a few highlights.

One of the oldest houses in the area, built in 1869, once belonged to Pablo Vasquez, scion of an early Spanish family. It's at 270 Main Street, just north of the old reinforced concrete bridge across Pilarcitos Creek. The first Vasquez home in Half Moon Bay, of adobe, was demolished to make way for this small cottage. Many adobes did not survive earthquakes.

Artist Galen Wolf recalls in one of his historical remembrances the thrill of seeing Pablo Vasquez, "slender, grave, with white head and beard, unbelievably poised and graceful on his golden pony. Little hooves flicking like white butterflies, golden

The Queen Anne–style Alves House in Half Moon Bay has been converted into an attractive shopping center.

skin polished and glinting in the sun. They pass. An era passes on those twinkling hooves." Some Spanish names that evoke the historic rancho era still appear in coastside phone books: Gonzales, Castro, Vallejo, and Miramontes descendants still live in the Half Moon Bay area.

The Methodist Episcopal Church, circa 1872, at Johnston and Miramontes, is one of the oldest and most interesting Gothic Revival Protestant churches in San Mateo County; its social hall, once part of one of Half Moon Bay's Ocean Shore Railroad stations, was moved here when no longer needed. A more complete reminder of the Ocean Shore Railroad is the Arleta Park Railroad Station at Railroad Avenue and Poplar Street. Drive toward the ocean along Poplar; it's in the southwest part of town among many other streets named for trees. You'll see the depot, now a private residence, to your left. The deep eaves of the roof once projected over the railroad tracks, but the tracks are long gone. (See pages 11–14 for Ocean Shore Railroad lore.)

Back to the main part of town, an interesting Victorian house, built in 1892, with beehive shingling and colored-glass borders around the windows, is at 505 San Benito Street at Kelly, near the old Methodist Episcopal Church. The two-story building at the rear once housed a bakery. A good example of nineteenth-century Victorian Gothic architecture is the small, well-maintained house with four gables at 546 Purisima Street, a block west of Main Street. Half Moon Bay also has excellent examples of Art Nouveau architecture, like the Dutra Funeral Home, circa 1928, at 645 Kelly.

The half-century-old Our Lady of the Pillar Cemetery, comparatively new as local cemeteries go, has an overall view of this essentially flat town. Instead of walking, you'll probably want to drive there. Go inland on Miramontes Street and take a sharp right immediately after crossing a small wooden bridge.

Unless you arrive by boat or helicopter or were born there, you can reach Half Moon Bay by two routes only: slow, two-lane Highway 1, which hugs the ocean, or Highway 92, another twisting two-lane road. Five miles inland, Highway 92 connects with even twistier Skyline Boulevard (Highway 35) and seven miles from Half Moon Bay with Highway 280, the six- to eight-lane freeway from San Francisco to San Jose.

As freeways go, Highway 280 is pleasant. Near the Highway 92 turnoff it parallels the San Andreas

The Methodist Episcopal Church, circa 1872, is on the historical walking tour of Half Moon Bay.

Lake and the Crystal Springs Reservoir; both follow the direction of the San Andreas fault, which was responsible for San Francisco's 1906 quake and fire. The area near the spring is a fish and game refuge, popular with deer, and you may meet one that has leaped over the fence onto the freeway. Some morning commute broadcasts routinely report that a buck or doe is blocking one lane.

What is there to see along Highway 92? As you're driving toward Half Moon Bay, about three-fourths of the way down the steep hillside, you'll usually see several cars parked and people waiting to fill containers with free spring water. Farther along, to your left, is the **Half Moon Bay Nursery.** The proprietor, Ronald Michelsen, is knowledgeable about planting in the area and has a large and rare cactus collection. Further on to your right, try to glimpse Anne Howe's House of Doors. The house, actually made of doors from the San Francisco Exposition of

1915, is jammed against a steep hill near a cascade of volcanic rocks on a dangerous turn. Keep a sharp lookout or you'll miss it.

Artichokes, peas, pumpkins, and flowers, when they're in season, are also attractions along Highway 92. After Halloween you'll see cows munching the leftover pumpkins. Several produce stands are open on the south side of Highway 92 during peak tourist periods. Among the signs along the way is one advertising well-diggers, "Digges and Son," plus several promoting tree farms where you can cut your own Christmas tree. (Digges has a tree farm, also.) As the holiday season nears you may be surprised to see Santa himself stroll out on the highway to entice you to his tree farm.

A winery in Half Moon Bay? A few curves later, to your left, you'll spot a sign on the bottom of a wine cask that reads, **Obester Winery.** This small and charming family winery and tasting room is run by Paul and Sandy Obester. In their previous lives Paul had a high-powered electronics job in Palo Alto, where they lived. Then, at the age of ninety, Sandy's grandfather sold out his winery in Mountain View and moved in with the Obesters. Still lively into his late nineties, he taught them the techniques of winemaking, in the garage. The result is their winery and home by the side of the road overlooking a field of Christmas trees, where they enjoy country life. However, the Obesters have discovered that running a winery is around-the-clock work, even with the help of their boys, David and Doug, and their dog, Angelica.

Since Half Moon Bay's climate is not the best for grape growing, the Obesters travel to vineyards in other counties, including Monterey, Sonoma, and Mendocino (where they hope eventually to have a winery and vineyard). They walk through the vineyards row-by-row, selecting. The grapes they choose are picked in the early morning, crushed immediately, poured into a special portable tank, and brought to Half Moon Bay before the day heats up. There, according to the Obesters, the cool climate provides an ideal, energy-efficient environment for fermentation and oak aging. Visitors can talk wine philosophy with the Obesters and sample their handful of wines—some already prize winners—Saturday and Sunday, many Fridays, and some holidays between 10 A.M. and 5 P.M.. You'll see a big sign telling you they're open if they are. If you can't make it on their listed days, call (415) 726-WINE for a special appointment.

Just past a big lumberyard, to your left, is the

rustic **Spanishtown Arts, Crafts, and Antique Center** (415/726-9971), where you might see artists at work. Spanishtown, which opened in 1969, still attracts passersby, although more accessible collections of galleries and shops have opened since in Half Moon Bay. The center was started to solve the perennial problems artists face in displaying their wares. Seven people set out to locate a place with low overhead where they could combine the advantages of a small shop with the atmosphere of a small studio. They finally decided to construct their own. The big gallery at the rear has a representative selection of paintings, sculpture, and pottery, with emphasis on well-known local artists. People with steady weekday jobs run most of the other Spanishtown shops—juvenile probation officers and teachers are in the majority. You'll see shops featuring sea fantasies, wallhangings, glass, treasures, and trinkets; one shop is called Wonderful Clutter. You'll find it hard to get away without succumbing to at least one purchase.

The Hilltop Mobile Home Park, is on top of a small hill, as its name implies, barely outside the main section of Half Moon Bay. It is one of the few commercial places on the coast south of San Francisco where some trailers or campers can find space by the night or week. Check at the Hilltop Store across the highway. Here you can also buy groceries, fishing gear, and pick up tide tables early in the year.

Also on Highway 92, almost opposite the turnoff to Half Moon Bay, are the aging wood signs and the dark cypresses of the **Pilarcitos Cemetery,** established in the 1850s. The I.O.O.F. cemetery is behind it; its eastern portion is for men lost at sea. Tombstones in both pioneer cemeteries bear mute evidence to the varied ethnic inheritance of the coastside.

The Portuguese influence is evident during the **Annual Holy Ghost and Pentecost Festival,** a colorful import from the Azores. In May—usually seven weeks after Easter—the section of Half Moon Bay around the I.D.E.S. Hall comes to life. On Saturday night and again during a doubleheader parade on Sunday, you'll see dozens of reigning, future, and past festival queens and princesses, each with a sizable coterie. After the Saturday night procession, there's a feast and dance. On Sunday morning at about ten, the many queens plus marching bands parade down Main Street, turn at Kelly, and end up at Our Lady of the Pillar Church for Mass. Just when you think you've seen the current queen clad in pastel, another group marches by and you're not sure. You can spot the real newly crowned queen by her magnificent velvet train and by the heavy, ornate silver crown made of melted silver dollars, which is carried by one of her coterie.

The fiesta, like the one that usually takes place a week earlier in Pescadero, originated centuries ago in the Azores. The legend is that when the people on the island were starving, the Holy Spirit miraculously intervened and sent a foreign ship loaded with food. The ship's master fed the people and refused any pay, hence the free barbecue now. Queen Isabella of Portugal herself led a procession through the streets to celebrate the delivery of her island people—thus the parade and the "royalty."

Other events, besides the Pumpkin Festival already mentioned, include a Coastside County Fair and Rodeo during the July Fourth weekend. If you like crowds and heavy traffic, fine. If you prefer to enjoy peace and quiet on the beaches, try to visit Half Moon Bay when there's no big event taking place.

Where to eat and stay? Besides the German House and its cousin, the German Haus, a small Garden Deli adjoins the fancy San Benito House restaurant. You can eat your soup, salad, and sandwiches inside or in a picnic area behind. If you like Mexican food and aren't in a hurry, walk through a pool hall to the small enclosed dining room for dinner at Santana's, 400 Main. Ricci's on Main Street attracts many local working people who come for the conversation as much as for breakfast and lunch. Ricci is fast with the pun, serving, for instance, a Papal breakfast with Polish sausage. The Happy Cooker in the Strawflower Shopping Center has modestly priced meals for the budget-minded and attracts many locals. Restaurants at the south edge of town are described in the next chapter, as is the newly enlarged Half Moon Bay Motor Lodge.

Besides the San Benito House on Main and Mill, a new bed and breakfast inn, the Mill Rose (415/726-9794), has opened on 615 Mill Street. You'll recognize it by the sea gull weather vanes among the many varieties of rose bushes in the garden and yard. Eve and Terry Baldwin, the owners, plan to increase the present two rooms to at least six when an addition they have designed and built is ready.

The James Johnston House, built in the early 1850s at the south end of Half Moon Bay, is one of the first Yankee-style houses in the entire Bay Area.

5

Mid-Coastside: South of Half Moon Bay

INCLUDING SAN GREGORIO, PESCADERO AND BIG INLAND PARKS

≈≈≈≈≈≈≈≈≈≈≈≈≈≈≈≈≈≈

The area south of Half Moon Bay is comparatively isolated and little known; these are just two of its charms. Before leaving town, gas up if you need to; there are no services directly on Highway 1 for twenty-five miles, although you can get gas until 6 P.M. in San Gregorio. Also watch out for posted speed limits; traffic fines are a popular way of filling Half Moon Bay city coffers. If hunger pangs strike, unless you have brought picnic supplies, try to hold out until you reach Santa Cruz.

For those who like quiet, bucolic scenery, the Higgins-Purisima Road, which starts where Main Street joins Highway 1, loops inland through rolling farmland and hillsides, returning five miles later to Highway 1.

This road passes Half Moon Bay's proudest historical site, the **James Johnston House,** also known as The White House of Half Moon Bay, easily visible on a sloping hill to the east of the highway. This was not only the first Yankee-style house near Half Moon Bay but also one of the oldest in the Bay Area.

Johnston, born in Scotland but reared in Pennsylvania and Ohio, joined the California Gold Rush in 1849. With money earned from real estate and part ownership in a San Francisco saloon, Johnston bought 1,162 acres here from the Miramontes and mortgaged this land to buy almost 500 acres more. He dispatched his brother, Thomas, back to Ohio to purchase 800 head of dairy cattle. The livestock was driven across desert and wilderness to Johnston's new ranch land, where grizzly bears finished off most of the newborn calves.

Starting in 1853, Johnston erected his once elegant home for his Spanish bride, Petra d'Jara. Since there was no loading dock in the early 1850s, much of the redwood lumber brought in by ship was dumped overboard into the ocean on an incoming tide and picked up along the beaches as it washed ashore. The house, painted a dazzling white and richly furnished, was a center for much of the refined social life in the area. (A descendant of Thomas Johnston tells of how the ship carrying his grandmother, on her way to California to work as a governess, rounded the Horn and sailed up the coast. Because of heavy fog, the ship remained out of sight of land, but then the fog lifted and her first sight of California was that white house high on a hill in a field of golden grain. She knew then that she must visit this house as soon as she could. The result? She met and later married Thomas, James Johnston's brother.)

James Johnston's life and his white house gradually turned gray. His Petra died in 1861. In 1878 the bank foreclosed, leaving only the house and fifteen acres. Johnston died soon afterward. The slowly disintegrating house survived sharecroppers; the 1906 quake; squatters; harsh weather; vandals; and even, at one time, cattle living in the lower level. Finally, in 1972, a group of concerned citizens united to save this site. By November 1976 they had raised enough money to elevate the house and pour a new foundation. Against the advice of old-timers, one side of the house was removed.

Then it happened.

One Saturday, strong winds completely flattened the half-dismantled house. Luckily, 98 percent of the materials survived the storm. A consultant to the Smithsonian Institute was called in to supervise. Each piece was labeled, and restoration experts reassembled the house as if it were a giant jigsaw puzzle. They used the original mortise and tenon construction, refitting each timber and beam, only adding new material when it was really needed. For added strength, the house was sheathed in plywood. A redwood shingle roof was added and the building was once again painted gleaming white.

The Johnston House is now listed on the National Register of Historic Places. With the help of grants and donations (Box 62, Half Moon Bay, CA 94019), the Half Moon Bay Historical Society hopes to furnish the entire interior as it was during the gracious period of the 1860s.

Soon after James built his house, his brother, William Johnston, erected another house across the road, using wooden pegs instead of nails. William's home, presently in private hands and housing migrant farmworkers, has survived in good shape. Even the shutters are the original ones.

Continuing south on Highway 1, the Redondo Beach Road wends its washboard way to a bluff, where there's a steep path down to the ocean.

Next are the green, landscaped **Half Moon Bay Golf Links** (415/726-4438) surrounded by Ocean Colony Estates homes, definitely in the higher income brackets. The 72-par, 18-hole golf course, which overhangs the Pacific, is supposedly the third toughest in Northern California (and perhaps the windiest) after Monterey Peninsula's Pebble Beach and San Francisco's Olympic Club. (The P.G.A. pro, incidentally, is Moon Mullins.) Contoured greens are kept green with water from the course's own wells plus recycled water. Bonuses include a championship view and fat, iridescent ducks that sit on the fairways.

Just south of the golf course entrance is the blue and gold **The Swedish Place** (415/726-7322), which serves Scandinavian lunches and dinners every day but Monday, and breakfast on Saturday and Sunday. The next turnoff south, the bumpy **Miramontes Point Road,** leads to another high bluff and beach past the Canada Cove Mobile Home Park (adults, permanent only). The Pelican Point RV Park (415/726-9100) at the end has full hookups for seventy-five RVs. It's a pleasant campsite; the proprietors are friendly and knowledgeable, and there's a small store, laundry room, and meeting room, all overlooking the blue Pacific.

The point to the north of the Miramontes Point Road is full of paper streets and twenty-five-foot-wide lots, the residue of when the long defunct Ocean Shore Railroad expected the area to boom. It didn't; there is only one house here now. The optimists who bought lots here decades ago have mostly sold out to the state, but no one is sure what will happen to this relatively untouched area where whales occasionally come in to visit and pelicans and cormorants sit on offshore rocks.

Returning to the highway, another sign that this area—so close to crowded cities—still retains some of its natural wildness is the hawks who find it profitable to sit on telephone wires overlooking the fields. Watch for them.

The **Half Moon Bay Motor Lodge** (415/726-9000) (Best Western) is just south off Highway 1. Most rooms and suites have balconies and overlook the golf links and ocean. Reservations are needed for weekends.

Soon after you pass this area, just off the highway you'll see a sign reading, **"Scenic Route,"** showing a golden poppy waving against a snow-capped mountain under a blue sky. An official scenic route is a road whose surroundings are so unique, beautiful, or historic that it has been put under state protection.

Highway 1 has improved since this photograph of a stagecoach was taken at Tunitas Creek in 1873.

Only a fraction of California's roads wear these golden poppy signs, but at least a few miles of *this* scenic coastline are now officially protected.

The Higgins-Purisima Road returns to Highway 1 at the ghost town of Purisima, where you'll see a small, white Victorian farmhouse with fish-scale shingling and an original waterwheel. About the only reminder of the past population remaining, since the schoolhouse burned, is the old cemetery — overgrown with weeds and poison oak — on a knoll on the southeast side of the intersection.

There's a small waterfall at the south end of Purisima Creek, but you may not feel it's worth paying admission to the now-private area and the struggle to get in to see it. Better rent a plane at the Half Moon Bay Airport and see it from the air.

The **Lobitos Creek** cutoff is the next road to the left, about a mile further south. The cutoff and the **Lobitos Creek Road,** just inland, connect with the beautiful, narrow **Tunitas Creek Road,** flanked by redwoods and hideaway cabins, that finally twists its way up to Skyline Boulevard.

The many tall poles on the seaward side of the Lobitos Creek Road still service the Marine Bureau and Radio Station of I.T.T. World Communications, Inc., and the small building is jammed with equipment for communicating with ships at sea by Morse code, a dying art, according to employees. The men report proudly that they still, on occasion, intercept messages of distress from small freighters or ships without fancy communication equipment, perhaps on the other side of the world, and relay the S.O.S. signal on to the nearest rescue operation.

Probably the most photographed farm along the coastside, especially during pumpkin season, is nestled in the Lobitos Creek Valley on the landward side, just south. In October, drivers often stop their cars along the highway and snap color shots of the white farm buildings, the grazing animals against the deep green hillsides, and the rows of orange pumpkins on the black earth. The road here loops back and connects with Verde Road. All these backroads are pleasant for biking, as well as driving.

In the slower paced days of horse and buggies, the town of Lobitos and many other areas next to creeks along the coastside were the sites of anticipated villages. In 1892, Lobitos was called "headquarters for oil wells," representing the acme of inflated hope.

Several structures were actually built here, unlike in other "paper towns" that never existed.

Martin's Beach, next south on Highway 1, charges a toll and closes at sunset. It's a handkerchief-sized beach chock full of cars, picnickers, transistors, and fishermen. A small store peddles such beach equipment as beer, suntan lotion, and hotdogs daily in summer and weekends in winter. The steep dirt slope to the beach is peppered with small cottages owned by the residents, although they do not own the land. You might bring or rent a two-man jump net and try surf netting for smelt here from spring into November.

Next south, **Tunitas Beach,** straddling Tunitas Creek on both sides of the small bridge, was once a transfer point for the defunct Ocean Shore Railroad. It was here also that Alexander Gordon—trying to make a port where none existed—built Gordon's Chute at a 45-degree angle from the 100-foot bluff to rocks constantly battered by waves. The chute was supposed to shunt produce from land to ships waiting below, though ship captains hated to anchor in the roiling surf. The friction of the long slide usually burned holes in the produce bags, which often burst open when they hit the deck. In 1885 a storm demolished the bankrupt enterprise. Now only the eye bolts are visible on the few occasions when the rocks are uncovered at low tide. There's a legend that a sea monster resides in a cave in the turbulent area between these rocks and Martin's Beach, but the only verifiable big sea creatures seen in this water are mother whales and calves returning in spring from their annual migration south.

Note and warning: Tunitas Beach can be reached only through private property rampant with fences, locked gates, dogs, poison oak, and no-trespassing warnings. To get to the ocean, pay the fee at Martin's Beach to the north, or at Nude Beach directly south, or wait for San Gregorio State Beach, about a mile and a half farther south.

Nude (or Bare-Bottom) Beach, next south, charges a small fee for the privilege of baring all while you enjoy the sand and surf. This two-mile-long beach is free in the sense that no holds are barred; dozens of small planes buzz the stretch on weekends to take in the sights. At very low tide curiosity seekers wade around the rocks at the south end. According to the annual Nude Beaches edition of the *San Francisco Progress,* gays used to be the main participants, but now they share this opportunity to develop an all-over sunburn with straights. The road leads in to Nude Beach just north of San Gregorio State Beach.

On sunny weekends the official non-nude **San Gregorio State Beach,** eight and a half miles south of Half Moon Bay, is usually packed with people who pay a small fee to use the beach and restrooms. A truck is often on hand to sell snacks; there's a lagoon that's warm (well, not freezing), and high bluffs partially protect the sand from winds. Extensive camping and picnic areas on the landward side of Highway 1 are still in the planning stage.

Just outside the park, across from the turnoff to the town of San Gregorio, is a state marker in honor of the Portola Expedition, which camped nearby on its bedraggled march north in 1769.

San Gregorio, population about 150, is about a mile inland; the turnoff is directly across from the beach unless you've taken the short tag end of Stage Road about one-quarter of a mile north. The town itself, surrounded by green hills, looks as if it were straight out of New England, but it was actually part of the original Rancho San Gregorio. Later, at the turn of the century, before the redwoods were logged out, this community was a popular resort. Now, like other small towns in the vicinity, it has shrunk, which makes most of the locals happy. Note the nostalgia-evoking one-room schoolhouse, now empty, on your right.

South of Highway 84 on the Stage Road, behind a service station with rusty pumps, you'll see an old hotel with full-length balcony and the inevitable wooden water tank nearby. Originally called the **San Gregorio House,** it was built in the 1850s and people with nationally famous names sometimes stopped for hunting and fishing. Now the once popular resort hotel is a private residence, and on sunny days old men sit outside on benches and reminisce about the early days when a stagecoach line ran here from San Mateo.

The main action takes place daily from nine to six at the hub of the town, the **Peterson & Alsford General Store** with its tiny adjoining post office. Don't miss it. You'll find almost everything you need and more: saddles, saws, clothing, wine, hardware, pot-bellied stoves, licorice sticks, old fashioned bean pots, nature books, cards, and—you name it. You can sit at the small bar and exchange gossip with the local artichoke and sheep farmers, and—if you're there before the 7 P.M. closing time on Friday—you might get in on an impromptu party around the piano.

The store was built in 1889. In 1930 Eric Alsford, the spirited pioneer who ran it along with family members, watched it burn to the ground. The "new" rebuilt version continues its tradition as the area's

The non-nude part of San Gregorio Beach attracts picnickers and beachcombers.

social headquarters. After Eric died in his late eighties, George and Joey Jacobs Cattermole, from over the hill in Palo Alto, eventually ended up as owners. In their previous lives George was a professor at Stanford; he now teaches part time. Joey was a full-time attorney; now that their two children are in school, she is slowly returning to the field. The two have kept the store's traditional ambience; "It's a good life," George commented. "I think the best thing is the air—so fresh—and we hear coyotes at night."

They have added conveniences like a gourmet-quality deli which serves homemade soup, sandwiches, salads (try the German potato salad), and cheeses. A few tables encourage weary travelers to sit down and eat or play checkers, write postcards, or just chat. The Cattermoles have an unlisted phone because so many people were calling to find out what the weather was like.

You can follow the route of the old stagecoaches to Pescadero south on Stage Road, which you'll probably share with bicyclists. This is a beautiful but lonely backroad with quiet farms and occasional glimpses of the ocean. About a mile before you arrive at Pescadero, at an L-shaped turn, is a farm with barn and animals that will make you nostalgic even if you didn't grow up on a farm. You can buy peacock feathers here, an enterprise handled by the farm's children.

At the apex of a triangle with San Gregorio and Pescadero at its western edge is **La Honda,** population 525. It's an easy nine miles inland on the San Gregorio turnoff from Highway 1, or what seems like forever, when driving on Skyline Boulevard. Early pioneer Nellie Hedgpeth reported from La Honda several decades ago: "The second story of the hotel was full of guests, and the woods around were filled with campers . . . very festive, with strings of Japanese lanterns and flags." One camp was called Up-Enough because of the steep climb the horses had to face.

The hotel is no longer, nor is the old "Bandit-Built Store"—supposedly built with the help of the Younger Brothers, who later hooked up with Jesse James. (This is a bit hard to believe, since the Younger Brothers were safely behind bars before the store was started.) Many towering redwoods (some second growth) are still left to attract tourists.

In addition to gazing at the big trees and enjoying the usual sunshine (sometimes too much) you might canvas the town's bars. Boots and Saddle partially burned in 1984, but may have reopened when you arrive. Apple-Jack's, originally a blacksmith's shop, is delightfully old and seedy and a pleasant place to

Enough towering redwoods are left to attract campers to La Honda.

tarry: outside on log chairs when it's hot, inside near the fireplace when it's chilly. La Honda, like the towns all along this mountain redwood area, attracts a smorgasbord of types, including author Ken Kesey in the 1960s, and presently cowboys—fact or fantasy; young people with bare feet; and family groups attending religious goings-on (there's a big religious institution in La Honda). As for feeding the inner man, woman, or child, if you're wearing shoes and a shirt, you're welcome to eat chili, homemade soups, and entrees or pancakes at Roger's Back Yard Restaurant.

About the only big annual event in town is the La Honda Days Celebration put on by the fire brigade in the middle of July. Then flags blossom along the highway and there's a barbeque and other festivities.

Most tourists who drive along Highway 84, the La Honda Road, are on their way to one of the big redwood parks within easy driving distance.

The 870 acres of steep **Sam McDonald County Park,** three miles west of La Honda on Pescadero Road, are to be enjoyed on foot. The northwesterly acres are mainly covered with lush redwoods. The other portion is mostly open ridge; you can see the sweep of the Pacific Ocean as you hike along the four-mile Ridge Trail. The Towne Trail leads from park headquarters to the **Pescadero Creek Park,** 6,000 acres of redwood forest strictly for daytime hiking. One and a half miles along the Towne Trail is a Danish designed wood hiker's hut erected by the Sierra Club, where you can reserve overnight bunk spaces by calling (415) 327-8111 on weekday afternoons.

The original portion of this park was donated by the late Sam McDonald, the son of slaves, who saved enough money from his groundskeeper's job at Stanford University to buy 400 acres here. McDonald wanted his bequest used as a park for young people, and it is. Most of the park's campgrounds are for organized groups who want to get away from a parking lot full of cars and campers; preference is given to San Mateo County organizations. For information on camping, call the Park Supervisor at (415) 727-0403.

If you just want to picnic, you'll find a few facilities near the park headquarters. Before you leave, be sure to visit the **Heritage Grove** with its magnificent old-growth redwoods. The grove is on Alpine Road, one mile west of Pescadero Road.

San Mateo County Memorial Park is probably the most beautiful of the inland coastside parks. Drive south a half-mile from La Honda, where signs clearly direct you left on Alpine Road, then right on the Pescadero Road for about six miles.

Memorial Park has over 100 overnight first come, first served campsites among sun-dappled redwoods; additional campsites can be opened for crowded weekends. For reservations call (415) 363-4021. Fees are moderate and there's plenty of outdoor recreation. A large, dammed-up swimming hole has a sunny edge of sand for sunbathing. The creek is often stocked with rainbow trout during tourist season, and in winter, steelhead trout spawn in Pescadero Creek. Everyone can enjoy the lovely hiking trails that vary from short nature trails with wheelchair access to longer hikes that loop into adjoining parks. There's also a full schedule of nature films and campfire programs, and an unofficial program of watching bluejays steal food during the day and raccoons thieve at night.

Portola State Park, at the bottom of a twisting, narrow road, is almost ten miles from La Honda and a good twenty-two miles inland from Pescadero. You can also reach this park by driving west from Redwood City on Highway 84, south on Highway 35 (Skyline Boulevard) for seven miles, and then west on scenically spectacular Alpine Road. The park has fifty-two overnight campsites, plus three hike-in group camping areas that can be reserved by calling (415) 948-9098. Redwoods are the big attraction in Portola, and the many miles of hiking trails include a self-guided sequoia nature trail that leads you past an old redwood whose heartwood has been burned out after many fires but whose top is still green.

Butano State Park is probably the least visited of the inland parks in this area. It's near the coast, five miles south of Pescadero and three miles east of Highway 1 on Cloverdale Road. This 2,200-acre redwood park has forty campsites. Because you have to park and walk in to nineteen of them, the surroundings are exceptionally quiet. Indians first picked the area as ideally beautiful for gatherings. There are fifteen miles of hiking trails. One trail leads to an overlook with a panoramic view of the ocean and Año Nuevo Island. You'll enjoy this view, that is, if there's no fog billowing along the shore. Nothing is perfect, however, and Butano Park is inclined to be dusty. Call (415) 879-0173 for information or reserve through your local Ticketron office.

Besides the huge redwoods and Douglas firs at all these parks, especially near streams, you'll probably see western azalea, California blackberry (delicious when ripe), and the infamous poison oak with its three shiny leaves and the ability to present anyone who touches it with days of agonizing itching.

You're also sure to see at least some of the following coastside animals. The brush rabbit, small and brown, with short ears, usually hops about in thick underbrush at twilight. The raccoon, a gray bandit with a black mask, explores garbage cans or your food containers at night. A striped or spotted skunk is better seen than smelled. Gray foxes, with white under their necks and black tips on their bushy tails, are quite common. Merriam chipmunks, with rusty-colored sides and white bellies, will probably accost you. When they scold, their tails jerk. You're also sure to see a western gray squirrel, gray with a white belly and a large bushy tail, scuttling among the large trees. Harvest and deer mice are common (ask anyone with a cabin in the area). So are wood rats. You can often spot the huge wood rat nests of twigs in the branches of trees or shrubs. You can sometimes see

Plants to Avoid (and Some to Look For)

Leaflets three, let this plant be! Beware the deceptively beautiful poison oak, green in spring, red in fall.

Do not touch poison oak. Before you venture out of your car, be sure that you know what this poisonous vine or bush looks like or you may end up with days of itching misery. Notice its three slightly lobed, shiny leaves per branch. Poison oak is vivid green in spring and can turn red in summer or fall. If you touch some, wash it off immediately with strong soap and water.

Nettles have four-cornered stems and stiff hairy leaves that sting like fire for a while after you brush against them.

You will find some of the following edible plants along the coast. Sea spinach, also called New Zealand spinach, often grows at the bottom of ocean bluffs. You'll find watercress back on the shores of streams in early spring. California blackberry trails over the ground or up trees. Avoid the thorns (and any nearby poison oak) and have a feast when the berries are ripe in the summer. Wild strawberries hug the ground and are well worth the effort of looking under each tiny, shiny red or green leaf to hunt the berries.

black-tailed deer, and pocket gophers advertise their presence by mounds of dirt. The Virginia opossum is gray, with a white face and a naked scaly tail. A bobcat—if it's really a bobcat and not a domestic cat gone wild—has a reddish body, white belly, and a small bobbed tail. At dusk you often see the California myotis bat, a mouse-size mammal, whizzing by to catch insects.

Meanwhile, back to combing the ocean shore, Pomponio State Beach, one and a half miles south of San Gregorio, charges $2 a car for day use. This fee gives you access to 410 acres of protected recreational area, paved parking for eighty cars, picnic facilities, and restrooms (but no drinking water). The beach was named for a renegade Indian who terrorized the coastside during the mission days. According to some historians, Pomponio felt justified in his activities. After he escaped from a mission which he felt had kept him and other Indians in virtual slavery, the only occupation open to him was bandit.

Some artists consider Pomponio, with its marshy lagoon and high bluff, the most paintable beach along this stretch. Wildlife—besides man—still prowls at night in Pomponio Canyon. As late as the early 1980s ranchers reported seeing coyotes, bobcats, and foxes; there are still rumors of a mountain lion farther back in the hills.

Pescadero State Beach, about three miles farther south, is long and lovely with enough variation to please everyone, and there are a few primitive restrooms. To the north, you can slide down sand dunes, and there's a creek big enough for children to play in. A favorite sport is to float down to the mouth of the

creek on rubber rafts. Right at this location, where the creek meets the ocean, steelhead runs occur every year. To the south is a rocky area with excellent tidepools. Although Pescadero State Beach is popular, you can usually find a semisecluded nook behind a dune or rock.

Inland, across Highway 1, along the road to Pescadero, is the 555-acre **Pescadero Marsh Natural Preserve.** Stay on the trails that wind through it on dikes and enjoy this placid panorama of nature without, however, dogs or horses—they are banned. Besides the distant, wide-angle view of Pescadero, you might glimpse deer, raccoons, foxes, skunks, and rare birds like the kite.

Farther back, great blue herons nest in eucalyptus trees and stalk fish in the shallow waters of the swampy area. Among frequent visitors, besides the great blue herons, are the crested white herons (also as tall as six feet) and the shorter egrets and ibis. This set seems to favor standing on one leg. You'll probably see the pair of resident marsh hawks circling above, reddish-backed cinnamon teal cutting through the water, and perhaps bitterns fluffing out

A birder enjoys close-ups of birds at the Pescadero Marsh Natural Preserve; in the background is a wide-angle view of the town.

their feathers. Add to this background music, as the yellow throat, the Bay Area's only resident warbler, pours out its song.

Mallard and pintail ducks visit, and red-winged blackbirds are usually around, along with so many other species that the National Audubon Society helped add 340 acres to the original 215-acre preserve. For information on occasional birding excursions and other activities in the midcoast area, contact the Sequoia Chapter of the Audubon Society at (415) 344-4577.

A mile east of the turnoff to Highway 1 is an antique emporium run by Tony Oliveira, who once shined shoes in Santa Cruz to acquire enough money to buy collectibles. Eventually he parlayed his money into a shopping center in Aptos. In 1978 he decided the Santa Cruz area was becoming too crowded, so he bought sixteen acres in Pescadero and remodeled an old barn to house his antiques. He is usually open Friday, Saturday, and Sunday from 11 A.M. to 4 P.M. You'll find a wide gamut of collectibles inside, including Indian blankets, handicrafts, and baskets; old Depression glass; antique tins and boxes; and a whole barnful more.

Tony's sixteen acres are the site of Pescadero's Annual Artichoke Festival, held on Labor Day. Besides artichoke T-shirts and French-fried artichokes, you'll probably see everything from antiques to pottery to plants to art.

Pescadero has two stores along its main street, the Arcangeli Grocery with an old-fashioned butcher shop, and the Williamson General Store, circa 1885, which probably carries more than you'll ever need. It's a gathering spot for many old-timers, and you can find out a lot about the area from Harriet Dias, who helps to run the store.

Harriet is also impresario of the parade for the quaint **Festival of the Holy Ghost, the Chamarita,** which takes place on the sixth Sunday after Easter. (See page 35 for origins of this folk festival.) The parade marches to the Catholic Church at 10 A.M., then retraces its steps to the main highway after noon. High-school bands, former queens, horsemen, wandering minstrels, the newly crowned queen, old queens, and future royalty all march proudly by. Afterwards everyone is invited to a free barbecue. The queens are royally treated; one sign along the main street reads, "All queens admitted free."

Duarte's is another unofficial headquarters for locals, partly because it's the only restaurant-tavern for miles around, although Dinelli's, a small fast food outlet, offers French-fried artichokes and other viands kitty-corner across the highway. But it's Duarte's that's famous for its food: artichoke omelets and soup, seafood quiche, grilled fresh fish, and homemade olallieberry pie. The tavern was begun in 1895 when Frank Duarte asked a friend to bring back a barrel of whiskey from Santa Cruz. Frank set the barrel on a plank and was in business. In the mid-thirties, Frank, Jr. and his wife, the late Emma Duarte, started the restaurant, which appealed to the local dairymen and farmers; when Emma died the flag on the tall pole south of the highway flew at half-mast. Now open seven days a week, Duarte's is usually jammed with locals and city-folk, although prices have risen since those early days. Cioppino feeds are held every other Saturday during crab season, but they're so popular reservations are necessary (415/879-0464).

The Pescadero Country Store (415/879-0541) in back of the Duarte's parking lot sells Western clothing and gear as well as delightful nature-oriented pottery, carvings, and art. (The ceramic otters on their backs are hard to resist.) Phylis Gandy, one of the owners, has taken over the old carriage house at 292 Stage Road; her shop, now named The Whaling Company, features antique-oriented imports.

It's worth a few minutes to take a look at some of the old buildings and water towers in this quaint town with its population that speaks English, Spanish, Italian, and Portuguese. Straight ahead on Stage Road, Pescadero Street, or Main Street (they're all the same), you'll see the big tower and spire of the **Pescadero Community Church,** started in 1867. Built of white wood, the siding simulates stone. If you're in the area on the first Friday and Saturday of December, take in the church bazaar where you'll find handiwork and handicrafts, homebaked bread, and other delectables.

Farther ahead on a lopsided hill is the **Pescadero Cemetery,** with its nostalgic record of the past. One side is called Mount Hope, the other Saint Anthony's. Walk up to the top for a panoramic view of the village and rolling farmlands. The cemetery is at its spectacular best in late summer, when it is covered with hundreds of vivid rosy pink naked ladies (*Amaryllis belladonna*).

Saint Anthony's Catholic Church, built in 1870, is on North Street (North Street is north of the Pescadero Highway). Opposite the church is a typical and well-maintained house of the same period.

The log cabin on nearby Goulson Street was not built by some early pioneer but was erected within the last fifty years as a Boy Scout headquarters.

The Alexander Moore house, the first frame house in Pescadero, used to be just outside the present city limits on Pescadero Creek at the Cloverdale turnoff. The son of the city's founder built the house in 1853 using timbers brought from Santa Cruz by ox cart. The home has since been destroyed by vandals and then a fire. The Weeks home, also on Pescadero Creek Road, is still standing. When it was built in 1856 it copied the general plan of the Moore house.

En route to the Weeks home, on Pescadero Creek Road, you'll see fields of flowers and the **strawflower factory** of John Dias and Sons. Women take the flowers home to wire; you'll see them in yards around town. The flowers are then dried in ovens for twenty-four hours, sorted into bouquets, and packed. So many visitors asked to be shown around this colorful factory, interfering with business, that tours are no longer given. However, anyone may look out over the fields of flowers waiting their turn to be dried.

The family-operated **Tom Phipps Ranch** (415/879-0787), one mile east of town on Pescadero Creek Road, can definitely be seen; look for the huge American flags waving at each end. Prices may be slightly higher than at your local supermarket, but the home-grown produce has probably been picked that day. From June through August, you can pick your own strawberries, raspberries, and olallieberries. If you enjoy herbs and potpourri, check the fresh and dried herbs for cooking and decoration, most grown and gathered by Tom's wife, Valerie. After you've stocked up, stroll through her flower gardens stretching along the creek. There are picnic tables; one particularly beautiful spot is over a small wooden bridge near the end, where you can eat your lunch with doves cooing in the background. The Phipps Ranch also has a Critter Corral, with a few small farm animals, and gives guided tours for a small fee. Perhaps in a few years the Tom Phipps Ranch will be on the way to becoming another Knott's Berry Farm.

The youth hostel at Pigeon Point makes use of the lighthouse buildings and benefits from the spectacular location.

6

Coastside South San Mateo County

Pebble Beach, one and a half miles south of Pescadero Beach on Highway 1, is famous for agates, jasper, carnelians, and other small sea-polished stones; this tiny beach also has a rocky area that the sea has pummeled into free-form sculptures. But the pebbles draw most people.

Back in 1867, a reporter wrote that wagonloads of guests were taken to Pebble Beach daily from the thriving Swanton House hotel in Pescadero.

At the beach they pass the day buried in pebbles. From the cliff above a full view of the scene may be had, which is ridiculous in the extreme. Imagine a dozen females, some in bloomers and some without, some with long, some with short dresses, high boots and low-cut gaiters, straw hats, green veils, bandannas, and the inevitable Shaker—lying about in every conceivable position, some on their knees and hands, others flat on

their stomachs, with hands busy, feet stretched out and heads half buried in holes they have made in the beach.

Since that festive time the supply of pebbles has diminished and it is supposed to be illegal to take any now. One good thing: in concentrating on pebbles, people have refrained from stripping the nearby tide-pools of their sea inhabitants. If pebbles don't interest you, try surf casting, rock fishing, or—if you are a determined optimist—abalone picking.

Bean Hollow Beach, also known as Arroyo de los Frijoles, one mile south, is actually two pleasant, small, but sandy beaches with good tidepools nearby. Try rock fishing, surf casting, or abalone picking. If you like driving pleasant, noncongested backroads or are biking or hiking, investigate the Bean Hollow Road to Pescadero.

Pigeon Point, with its lighthouse looking like a lighthouse should, is about three and a half miles farther south. Besides being so photogenic a bank uses it in commercials, Pigeon Point is a favorite with skin divers, and you can also surf cast, rock fish, and pick abalone. With binoculars you can sometimes see a group of albatross out at sea. At low tide the tidepools are worth a look, and sea mammals hunt for dinner in the turbulent water below the cliffs. One old sea lion called Charley often hauls up on the beach north of the lighthouse and chases away any dog that tries to menace him. You don't even have to get out of your car to enjoy the sights and sounds; park, along with some self-contained campers, along the private road that hugs the beach. However, there's a catch to this wind-blown Eden. There are no—emphasis *no*—public restrooms.

The **lighthouse,** built in 1872 with bricks brought around the Horn, has a base six feet thick. The powerful lens, made of 1,008 pieces of glass, was used first in New England and later at Fort Sumter in South Carolina, where it was buried in sand to protect it during the Civil War. A weight and cable originally operated the lens. The rope was wound by hand, so if power failed, the lens could still be used.

At one time Pigeon Point could nearly have been called a port town. It boasted a whaling station plus a dozen cottages for the Portuguese whalers. In a small cove on the side, ships could be warped and loaded by means of cables, and later by a wharf with a swinging chute.

For a close-up panoramic view of the sea and surf, follow the picket fence to the cliffside where there are benches and a wooden platform that hangs out over the ocean. As you look at the surf churning over the reefs, it is easy to see how the clipper ship *Carrier Pigeon* hit the rocks and broke in two in 1853—a ship, the *Seabird,* sent from San Francisco to conduct salvage operations also fell victim to the raging sea. Leaking badly, the second ship was grounded at Año Nuevo, farther south. In 1868 the American sailing ship *Hellespont,* carrying a cargo of coal, crashed off Pigeon Point. Portuguese whalers helped to rescue the 7 who survived out of a crew of 190. In 1929 an oil tanker rammed the passenger steamer *San Juan* off the point. Forty-two were saved; 87 perished.

As with the Montara Lighthouse, farther north, the buildings are now used as an **American Youth Hostel** (415/879-0633). If you can do without alcohol and don't mind sharing a room and bath, this is a dramatic place to stay, and the price is right. The hostel is comfortable, with a kitchen in each building, plus a large recreation room and all that ocean

around you. You can also walk just a few feet to treat yourself to fresh oysters at the oyster farm next door—if they're open.

Gazos Creek Access State Beach, two miles south, has grass-covered dunes, picnic tables (a few protected from the blast of the wind), and primitive restrooms. This provides the only legal access to Franklin Point, farther south, but stay between the ocean and the high-tide line. Because it does require walking to get to, this beautiful beach is rarely crowded, even though surf fishing is often good. This means you might find some beachcombing treasures. You can continue on south into Año Nuevo State Park, but to protect the sand dunes and the elephant seals that now stay all year, a permit is required to go farther than halfway to Año Nuevo Point.

Small streams wind down from the mountains to the Pacific all along the coastside, but good catches of fish are rare after the beginning of the trout season. An exception is **Gazos Creek,** which is occasionally stocked with rainbow trout. Salmon and steelhead used to enter several coastside streams to spawn— that is, those that escaped the seals and sea lions lying in wait outside the streams' mouths. With the increase of dams, pollution, and other dubious benefits of civilization, these fish rarely venture into streams and rivers on their own any more. Recently, yearling silver salmon were planted in Gazos Creek, in the hope that they would migrate to the ocean and return to the stream to spawn two years later. To establish self-perpetuating runs, the planting was done for three consecutive springs.

The Gazos Creek Beach House (415/879-0125), on the landward side of Highway 1, has a bar where many locals gather and a restaurant where you can get breakfast and lunch daily and dinner on weekends. There's also a service station that sells gas (usually).

Deserted Gazos Ranch, next south, has buildings dating from 1862, and the room at the rear of the two-story main house was built in 1896 of lumber salvaged from the wreck of the *Columbia*. The Indian museum and beach facilities once located here are no more, but the beautiful beach and sand dunes are still in their natural state because zoning regulations stopped plans to put in recreational facilities.

If you want to turn back toward the north and don't mind getting your car dusty, you might enjoy the old farmhouses and quiet scenes along the **Gazos Creek–Cloverdale Road,** which goes inland at

Butano Park and ends near Pescadero. Staying on the Gazos Creek Road to its end, however, is only for the hardy.

Franklin Point, named after another famous shipwreck, is south of Gazos Creek, where there is access. Most fishermen and beachcombers who visit the point now are unaware that the remains of the ship and part of her crew lie beneath the dunes. Until recently, shifting sands occasionally uncovered a headstone reading:

> To the Memory of Edward Church of Baltimore, Md. Age 16 years, and the ten other seamen lost on Ship *Sir John Franklin* January 17, 1865.

The headstone has not been seen for several years; perhaps it was stolen.

What exactly happened on January 17, 1865? The clipper ship *Sir John Franklin* of Baltimore was proceeding up the California coast by dead reckoning. The ship passed rocky Año Nuevo Point, but hit the rock ledge that juts out at Franklin Point and broke in two. Survivors claimed that so much cargo was strewn about that they could run along the tops of the boxes. Years later, pioneer Pablo Vasquez recalled that the beach was covered with boxes, wagons, pianos, and some of the 300 kegs of spirits the ship had carried. He insisted, however, that he and the others were most delighted with the cans of turkey, chicken, lobster, oysters, and other tasty foods that washed ashore.

One of the oldest homes on the coastside, built in 1851 by Isaac Graham, a relative of Daniel Boone, still stands on **White House Creek Road,** surrounded by eucalyptus trees.

Green Oaks Ranch, four miles south of Gazos Creek, was donated to San Mateo County as a recreational area and historical site by Mrs. Catherine Steele of the pioneering dairying family. However, the county did not have the money to restore the old 1863 ranch house, the barn built without nails, and the trophy room, to say nothing about maintaining the acres of gardens, orchards, and streams. Since this is a banana belt and the weather is sunny most of the year, plants, trees, and flowers flourish—especially roses and rhododendrons. Mrs. Steele became dissatisfied, so the property was returned and sold to Dr. and Mrs. George Griffin, who hope to convert it to a bed and breakfast inn with eight guest rooms.

In addition to its view of crashing surf and coastside mountains, **Año Nuevo State Reserve,** just north of the Santa Cruz County line, is probably the most interesting natural area along the entire San Mateo coast. Yet before 1970 few people had sampled its windswept attractions.

> "And how far is it to Point Año Nuevo?" a traveler near Pescadero asked an old Indian.
>
> "Oh, señor, it must be a very long way, I think it is in the neighborhood of the other world" (Albert S. Evans, 1873, in *Alta California*).

You do not have to travel to another world, however, to enjoy acres of wildflowers, deep sand dunes that may cover Indian shell mounds, and ocean beaches that vary from rocky to sandy to sea-debris covered. The main attraction is the noisy collection of sea birds and sea mammals within camera range. The featured players in this wild menagerie, the gigantic elephant seals—the world's most improbable animals—battle, mate and have their pups right on Año Nuevo Point.

If you miss the main elephant seal action, from December 1 through March, there's still plenty to see and do to make the modest admission fee worthwhile. If the wind isn't whipping sand and fog into your face, you can sunbathe and picnic on the first long beach, which is sprinkled with rocks and fossils. (Don't pick up any fossils from state beaches; it's illegal. Leave them for others to enjoy, as you did.) Surfers usually find the waves off the point to their liking, especially in the summer when other beaches may be disappointing. And, if you're interested in geology, you'll pass over five earthquake faults from the hill at New Year's Creek to the end of the point. You can identify the faults by the wide streaks of ground-up rocks they produce; it's easier to spot them from the beach.

Año Nuevo State Reserve has a lot of history going for it, dating from the time of Vizcaino who named it Punta del Año Nuevo because he sailed by on New Year's Day, 1603.

Ever since then, because of its hidden reefs, heavy fogs, and turbulent waters, the point has claimed many lives, some involving lighthouse personnel. The steamer *Los Angeles,* passing in April 1883, noticed that the lighthouse fog signal was not operating and that the ensign was flying upside down as a signal of distress. They found that the station crew had been drowned off a dory; only wives and children were left.

A surfer rides a wave at Año Nuevo Beach.

Many ships have been wrecked here, and you might uncover some of the debris as you're walking along the shore. After the 1983 storms, for instance, a hiker discovered the wrecked hull of the well-crafted old lumber schooner, the *Point Arena,* which had been blown into the rocks by heavy winds and swells in 1913. Luckily, the crew was saved.

On April 10, 1887, the *H. W. Seaver,* a twenty-seven-year-old sailing ship whose rotten hull had been painted over, went aground. Three crewmen died. Seventy-eight years later a man strolling on the beach after a storm discovered a rusted bowsprit band. He searched through records at the San Francisco Maritime Museum and found that the *H. W. Seaver* had disappeared mysteriously from official records in about 1887. Further searching turned up an account of the wreck in Santa Cruz weekly newspaper.

The old light station is abandoned now. While it was still occupied, the keeper complained that young sea lion pups were overrunning his house. On one occasion a killer whale stirred up the mammals so much they forced their way into every room. When the lighthouse crew left, the sea mammals moved in permanently. One official still recalls the odor of a 600-pound sea lion who had expired in the bath tub.

According to the late historian, Frank Stranger, when the foghorn of the first light station first blasted in May, 1872, all the cows on the neighboring Steele ranch stampeded down to the beach. Mrs. Steele commented that the cows must have thought there was a very wonderful bull down there.

In 1869 eleven well-kept-up dairies in the area were operated or leased by the Steele Brothers and their families. Against advice, the Steele clan first dairied at cold, windswept Point Reyes. This venture was so successful they bought similar land, part of the original Rancho Punto Año Nuevo, from Loren Coburn. Isaac Steele started his home at Green Oaks in 1862, and cousin, R. E. (Renneslear) Steele built in Cascade Creek that year, and the dairy empire was on its way. One brother became a general in the Union Army, but the Steeles were most famous for the cheese, nearly 4,000 pounds and twenty feet in circumference, that was auctioned off in San Francisco for the benefit of the Union Army.

Long before the Steeles settled and before the Spanish explorers and missionaries arrived in the 1700s, thousands of Indians lived near or visited Año Nuevo Point and Island. You'll see evidence of their activities when you reach the sand dunes near the point, for these cover Indian shell mounds, or dumps, where Indians threw away mussel, clam, oyster, and abalone shells from their daily fare. Archaeologists who excavate such mounds, which they call kitchen middens, can date the layers by the implements and ornaments they find. You can see fragments of the shells today, and when the wind whips enough sand off the mounds it may uncover fragments of stone arrowheads or stone tools. Other finds, some major, have been made here. In 1983 storms uncovered a rare fossilized tusk and teeth of a mammoth, a huge, elephantlike creature that lived 12,000 to 20,000 years ago. Note and warning: Digging in shell mounds on Año Nuevo Point park is illegal. If you uncover a rare scientific find, notify the authorities.

Almost every variety of offshore fishing is excellent off Año Nuevo rocks and beaches. The seals and sea lions are aware of this, as are the party boats from Santa Cruz. This is also one of the few coastside spots where you can scratch for littleneck clams at a minus tide, although state park officials frown on clamming.

As for animals, you're sure to see cotton-tailed rabbits and you may disturb some mule deer or perhaps a coyote. Look closely at the tracks of birds and animals—besides those of homo sapiens—in the dusty paths and sand dunes.

In spring the yellow and purple lupine, orange-gold poppies, and other wildflowers put on a spectacular show, but even in a parched late summer, the flowers and plants are interesting. Since the area is usually extremely windy, you can admire the methods the plants use to adapt. The coyote bush, for instance, has small tough leaves, as do the lupines. Where the wind is fierce, plants like the wild strawberries hug the ground. The "live forevers" have fuzzy leaves to catch moisture in the fog. Where the sun can be intense among the sand dunes, plant leaves may be almost silvery to reflect away the heat; the leaves of verbena attract sand to help retain moisture. Almost all plants in these arid areas have taproots at least ten feet long, and many produce seed pods that explode. The sea rockets, with their small lavender flowers, go further, producing two-stage rockets containing seeds that can survive in saltwater for up to eleven days after they are shot out.

Gradually, with the help of the willows that are growing near the man-made pond, enough plants are taking root to indicate that the sand dunes will eventually be stabilized. Other plants include the Indian paintbrush, with its red flower from which love tea can be made. The showy Hooker's primrose has big yellow flowers, and the "pearly everlasting" has dense white flower heads—its dried leaves are used for medicinal purposes. English plaintain—which springs up in walked-on areas—has longitudinal ribs and small flowers. You can eat its seeds, as you can the spicy wild radish.

As for feathered vertebrates, Año Nuevo is a bird-watcher's paradise. Soon after you start along the path from the parking area, you'll see cormorants, pelicans, and pigeon guillemots sitting on the weirdly shaped rocks in the ocean (one rock looks like a submarine). You can identify the guillemots by their bright red feet and clownish behavior. In the spring and summer you'll glimpse cormorants nesting on the sides of bluffs so steep it's hard to see how they and the babies don't fall off. Besides these birds and the usual gulls, plovers sit in the sand, swallows dart after insects, sparrows sing, and a pair of live-in marsh hawks circle above looking for field mice. (You'll see many mice burrows along the way.) Coots bring up their families in the pond, which was put in by the Steeles when this was working farmland but which is now a crucial part of the area's ecology and an attraction to many birds. Even in the prepond era, Año Nuevo was on the flyway; rangers report that almost every sea bird that migrates has been spotted here and many land birds as well—a total of more than 230 species!

Even non-bird watchers should be impressed with the number of varieties that have winged over this area. Some of the rarest include the golden eagle, the magnificent frigate bird, the American redstart, the red phalarope, and the whistling swan. Birds that breed on Año Nuevo Island include black oyster-catchers, Brandt's cormorants, western gulls, and house finches.

Many species of birds breed on the mainland: belted kingfishers, black swifts, pelagic cormorants, pintails, common teals, ruddy ducks, marsh hawks, American kestrels, California quail, pigeon guille-mots, American coots, snowy plovers, kildeer, marbled murrelets, rock doves, barn or great horned owls, black phoebes, swallows, chickadees, bushtits, wrentits, house wrens, mockingbirds, and California thrashers, hermit thrushes, loggerhead shrikes,

Seals and Sea Lions You'll See and Hear

What sights will you find most interesting along that beautiful sliver of coastline south of San Francisco? According to state park officials, the most popular attractions—far ahead of redwoods, bent cypress trees, or crashing surf—are warm-blooded, intelligent **sea mammals.**

Starting at Cliff House and all down the coast—usually at rocky intervals—the marine

Elephant seals are a gregarious lot; here mothers and pups relax on the sand.

mammals you'll see the most are seals and sea lions. These "cousins" are pinnipeds—mammals with flippers—that eat flesh.

Unless it is late June or July when they have gone to offshore islands to mate, you will mainly meet sea lions or, at least, hear their wet, deep barking. The black mammals that you'll see draped on rocks off Cliff House are actually California sea lions, the very same "seals" that cavort around in circuses and zoos. These particular pinnipeds are more agile than seals because they can rotate their hind flippers. The flippers of a true seal are fixed behind like a tail so the animal has to undulate and flop forward like a worm. Another tip: If you see external ears, it's a sea lion, not a seal.

Boisterous Steller's sea lions, usually tawny in color and bigger than California sea lions (bulls can weigh a ton), also have those outside ears. The smallest and shyest pinnipeds, spotted harbor or leopard seals, prefer protected waters, although a few may haul themselves out on small rocks further south. Their shyness is really caution; on shore they're clumsy and vulnerable. If you do spot any, chances are their big, liquid brown eyes will be regarding you with as much curiosity as you show gazing at them.

Probably the most exciting pinnipeds along this coast are the mammoth elephant seals, "the world's most improbable animals." Bulls can weigh over three tons, and the male's elephant-like proboscis, or snout, helps him give out a bellow you can hear for miles. You'll meet him close up at Año Nuevo Point; farther south, almost at the Santa Cruz County line; and occasionally ashore at isolated locations, usually at the foot of steep cliffs along the Big Sur. A blow-by-blow description of the elephant seal action during mating season is given on page 57.

Many visitors who comb the coast south of San Francisco rate seeing marine mammals the highlight of their trip. The exciting thing about this shoreline is that in any season you're almost sure to see these fellow mammals, especially if you use the index in the back as your guide.

If you come across a distressed sea mammal (or sea bird) the California Marine Mammal Center suggests these rules: 1) Do not touch the animal; some mothers abandon babies because of the human scent. 2) Call a wildlife rehabilitation group immediately. 3) Observe the stricken animal from a distance and keep others away while you're waiting for the rescue crew. 4) If possible, stay to assist the crew.

Here are some organizations that may help:

California Marine Mammal Center
Fort Cronkite
CA 94965
(415/331-7325)

Peninsula Humane Society
12 Airport Boulevard
San Mateo, CA 94401
(415/340-8430)

Wildlife Rescue, Inc.
4037 El Camino Way
Palo Alto, CA 94306
(415/494-SAVE)

Native Animal Rescue
2200 Seventh Avenue
Santa Cruz, CA 95062
(408/462-0726)

Monterey S.P.C.A.
Monterey-Salinas Highway
(408/373-2631)

This elephant seal, his number — 605 — daubed on with Lady Clairol Blue hair dye and peroxide, chooses to ignore human interlopers in the background.

red-winged and Brewer's blackbirds, American goldfinch, rufous-sided or brown towhees, and dark-eyed juncos. The many sparrows include house, Savannah, white crowned, and song sparrows.

When you reach the tip of Año Nuevo Point, after floundering through, or preferably by, the sand dunes — one of the last remaining active dune fields on the California coast — adjust your binoculars so you can enjoy the antics of the seals and sea lions on Año Nuevo Island. However — a warning! Many people have lost their lives trying to make it out through the treacherous surf at minus tide. If the day is at all clear you'll see and certainly hear plenty from shore, even when many of the elephant seals are off somewhere else.

In the Indian era, wolves, mountain lions, and grizzly bears hunted down most visiting seals and sea lions. These local predators, along with the Indians, are gone now, although reports continue of mountain lions back in the coastal hills. The result? Today's

visitors can see anywhere from a few hundred to thousands of pinnipeds clustered on Año Nuevo Island or swimming in the turbulent waters offshore. Perhaps you'll watch adolescent elephant seal bulls testing their prowess for battle. Or you may see California sea lions, often erroneously called seals, happily body surfing. (Remember, unlike the sea lion, a seal has no ears, and because its flipper is fixed behind like a tail, it has to flop or undulate forward like a worm.) You may glimpse a few smaller (up to 500 pounds) harbor seals out on the rocky shoals. They're also known as leopard seals because of their spots. Rarer are fur seals and hair seals which have hairy front flippers.

You're almost sure to see and hear the tawny-colored Steller sea lions on the island. They're bigger and noisier than California sea lions and have smooth, sloping brows plus, of course, those external ears. Steller sea lion bulls can weigh a ton.

It's the elephant seal crowd, however, that steals the show at Año Nuevo beaches, especially since they now carry on right on the point. The bulls arrive in early December to stake out their territories. The females join them in late December. Pups from last year's matings are born in January. When the babies are weaned in February, the new matings commence with much sound and fury.

A full-grown elephant seal bull can weigh from two to four tons. He's quite unattractive, a dirty gray color with a thick cracked neck and a snout, or proboscis, that helps him let out a bellow that can be heard for miles. That sound is hard to describe—it's something between an elephant's roar and the echo of a hollow log being struck in a deep tunnel. The fawn-colored females are docile (or lazy?), and much smaller, with large liquid, long-suffering eyes. When dozing away, side by side, the females look like oversized cigars, and the babies—actually called weaners—could be nicknamed weenies.

The bulls put up prodigious battles to keep other bulls out of their territories so they can mate with these listless females. When challenged, the big males heave their massive cracked heads, trumpet that uncanny sound, and start to pummel each other with their heads and snouts. The loser shrivels up his nose and retreats. The ultimate winner of a series of battles may end up with a harem of fifty or more cows and is known as the alpha bull. All the time these activities are going on, the elephant seals don't eat. The bulls are afraid to leave their territories and the females are afraid their pups may be lost or squashed by a big bull.

When you see hundreds of elephant seals crowding the island and dozing on point beaches, it's hard to realize that before the turn of the century these ponderous mammals were hunted for their blubber to the edge of extinction. A few survived on a lonely island off Baja California, and these finally spread up the coast from isolated Southern California rookeries. Now Año Nuevo is the only place in the world where hundreds of visitors a day can see elephant seals close up. How this came about is a saga of trial and error.

Because so many ships were wrecked off the island's rocky shoals, the government bought Año Nuevo Island in 1870 and erected a lighthouse which was abandoned in 1948. In 1958 the State of California purchased Año Nuevo Island and enough of the mainland to provide access. When the importance of this isolated area as a natural habitat for pinnipeds was realized, the state, in 1967, officially declared the island a scientific and scenic reserve.

To help protect the animals, the University of California at Santa Cruz was designated as a responsible lessee. When the waters were calm enough, a few professors and students of marine biology at the University would put out to the island in a rubber boat to study the animals from blinds. To make spotting easier, the huge animals were daubed with identifying marks—a mixture of Lady Clairol Blue hair dye and 30 percent peroxide applied with a stick. As the elephant seal population exploded on the island, a few bachelors swam ashore to the mainland, then called "Loser's Beach." By 1973, thirty-eight elephant seals, including several battling bulls, had moved to the beach.

In December of that year, Sunset Magazine recommended this spectacle to readers. Suddenly hundreds, and then thousands of people trampled their way through the fragile dunes to the point beaches, milled about the seals within biting distance, and threw rocks at sleeping bulls to get action photographs.

The state had to do something to protect both seals and people, but what? The reserve couldn't be placed off limits; there weren't sufficient funds or personnel to close it and police it. Finally, Roger Werts, who took over as head of the Northern San Mateo Coast State Parks, worked out a way for students from West Valley College in Saratoga to take part in a ranger trainee program. Werts also asked the University at Santa Cruz whether students might be interested in assisting the park ranger staff in explaining and protecting the seals, flora, and other fauna.

A young cow elephant seal poses daintily for her portrait.

After intensive training, a few student guides helped out in early 1976. Now guided natural history walks are conducted daily throughout the elephant seal season by student and community docent tour guides, and the reserve hopes to continue this program if enough volunteers are available. Docents also frequently staff the nature center in the weathered but sturdy old barn that housed dairy cows in the late 1800's. The tours now start from there.

Reserve early through Ticketron to get in on these tours; they're usually filled before November ends. For more information, phone Año Nuevo State Reserve at (415) 879-0227 or (415) 879-0595. If reservations are filled, all may not be lost. SamTrans may once again run Elephant Seal Special buses from mid-December to early March, which guarantees you'll be admitted to the state tours. Check with them by writing SamTrans, 400 South El Camino, San Mateo, CA 94402 or look up the phone number in your area. The Santa Cruz Metropolitan Transit district (408) 425-8600 also may again start up elephant seal tours. The address is 230 Walnut Street, Santa Cruz, CA 95060.

Whether you go at the height of the winter elephant seal breeding season or in late spring, summer, and early fall when the crowds are small, put this 1,252 acres of natural wonders on your list of places you must visit.

A wind surfer struggles with her sail on the wide sandy beach at Waddell Creek, just south of the Santa Cruz County line.

7

North Santa Cruz County

Waddell Creek, with its wide, attractive beach, is just south of the Santa Cruz County line and the chalk mountains. Before Highway 1 was scraped out of these steep, crumbling bluffs, stagecoaches had to wait for low tide before they could race across the sand. Because slides cut off this route so often, Pescadero seceded from Santa Cruz County and joined San Mateo County. Waddell, an early pioneer, erected a wharf at Año Nuevo as a shipping point for lumber from his mill, but met an early death in an encounter with a grizzly bear.

Inland, on the south side of Waddell Creek, is the Theodore J. Hoover Natural Preserve, which includes a marsh, all now part of the huge **Big Basin Redwoods State Park,** which stretches for miles up into the mountains. You can hike from park headquarters on a rough but scenic drop all the way to the ocean. The Sempervirens Fund, which was largely responsible for this breathtaking trail has maps that

describe the trail's many attractions. Write them at P. O. Box 1141, Los Altos, CA 94022, enclosing $2 and a self-addressed envelope.

The trail often skirts the creek and there are waterfalls; you can sit in some, a refreshing sensation. If you're quiet and patient, you might see a water ouzel or dipper, a chunky little bird that walks under water and nests behind waterfalls. Three backpack trail camps serve the lower Waddell area; make reservations through Big Basin State Park (408/338-6132). If you end your hike on Highway 1 at Waddell Creek, you can take the Route 40–Davenport bus back to Santa Cruz.

On Waddell beach you can beachcomb and surf cast. This is also popular as a launching place for wind surfing, on breezy afternoons you can sometimes see dozens of these graceful craft gliding over the waves. The bluffs north of the creek's mouth are used by hang-glider enthusiasts, so you can sometimes get in on a double feature. Although Waddell Beach is not an official state campground, self-contained RVs have been known to stay overnight.

You can see a sampling of inland mountain scenery on the way to the Big Creek Pottery, a gallery and live-in pottery school run by Bruce McDougal, who lives here year round with his family. The gallery is open by appointment (408/423-4402). Turn sharply inland on Swanton Road just south of the Big Creek Lumber Company. If you reach Greyhound Rock you've gone too far, but don't worry. Since the turnoff is so sharp many drivers prefer to turn around at Greyhound Rock. Drive up about a mile on the corkscrew Swanton Road until you spot the cluster of beautifully remodeled old redwood buildings and the yellow Renaissance flag. One of the buildings, dating from the 1860s, was once used to produce cheese.

As you go up Swanton Road, watch for the several abrupt changes of vegetation, from low-lying shoreline shrubs to great redwoods. You might glimpse some of the wild animals that still roam these comparatively isolated mountains. Do your looking mainly from the road; much of this country is on private property, strictly fenced off. Swanton Road continues through more forested territory until it eventually rejoins Highway 1 farther south.

Greyhound Rock, a state fish and game reserve, is the next access to the ocean on Highway 1. On weekends the parking lot is usually jammed with the cars and campers of rock fishermen; some stay overnight. The area has primitive latrines and a scattering of overflowing garbage cans. Besides rock fishing, surf netting and skin diving are popular. Dress warmly if you plan to fish; that wind off the ocean can cut like a fish knife.

The small town of **Davenport** is next. You know you're getting near when you see the huge smokestacks of the cement plant that utilizes a limestone quarry nearby. For sixty-five years, from miles away you could see the pall of cement dust that belched from these smokestacks to cover fields, cars, and roofs. After antipollution officials got tough, the factory spent a lot of money for a cure, and housewives can now hang out their wash. Some people insist that even the weather has improved.

Davenport and Davenport Landing were famous decades ago for whaling. The whalers are gone, but the whales return each year for their migration, usually from the last of November into February. The high bluffs overlooking the ocean here are excellent vantage points for watching these huge mammals. Many Portuguese who live in Davenport are descendants of early whalers. Theirs was a tense occupation. When a whale was spotted, small double-ended boats, like those still used in the Azores, were launched through the surf and directed by spotters on the cliff top, who ran signal flags up a flagpole. After the whale was harpooned, it was dragged ashore and the oil extracted right there.

Businesses in Davenport strung along Highway 1 include a gas station; a saloon; and a country store, which sells fishing gear, food, beer, and other necessities. It also calls itself a delicatessen from 10 A.M. to 4 P.M. The **New Davenport Cash Store** (408/426-4122), actually a restaurant–pottery shop and gallery, occupies the corner where the original Davenport Cash Store once served as the hub of social and business life until it burned down in the early 1950s. The current store, started by the McDougals of Big Creek Pottery, sells craft and gift items—many from Mexico—and pottery, some made on the premises. The restaurant is usually crowded; it's the only one for miles. The McDougals also started the New Davenport Bed and Breakfast Inn (408/425-1818) in the balconied rooms above the store; it became so popular they added an annex next door.

Besides being a beehive of potters, Davenport is home base for other artisans, and there's even a T-shirt factory. David Boye (408/426-6046), a knife maker who will etch your knife handle on request, is at 17 San Vicente. He is also author of a book on handmade knives. The Davenport Mill (408/423-8577), 433 Marine View Avenue, does large custom woodwork, including doors and table tops. The shop's sizable collection of antique woodworking tools is worth a look. The nearby Lundberg Studio (408/423-8577) produces such blown-glass items as lampshades, paperweights and goblets. Many of the studio's iridescent wares go on sale the three weekends before Christmas.

The **Aeolus Boat Works** (408/423-5681), also nearby, on this dusty cul-de-sac about two blocks down on the Old Coast Road, is run by Bill Grunwald, an ex-fisherman. The shop is named after the Greek god of winds and specializes in mahogany dories. You can buy anything from a do-it-yourself kit for a few hundred dollars to a gentleman's rowing yacht of the Victorian period—for the person who can afford to row first class. This enterprise, in a building erected at the turn of the century, welcomes visitors Monday through Saturday and is sometimes open on Sunday. You can find out about the dan-

This isolated beach, just south of Davenport, is easier to reach now than when Portola and his party struggled through in 1769.

gerous and exciting recreational rowing regattas at the boat works.

Downtown Davenport is so compact that even from the highway you can't help but notice the rustic St. Vincent de Paul Church, built of local cement in 1915. Another civic sight is the old restored jail.

Just south of Davenport, a bluff above a small beach across the railroad tracks has a photogenic view. Some historians think that this gully is the one where, on its march north, Portola's expedition lost a mule and many pots and pans. The drop to the beach is steep enough to make you believe that a mule might have trouble, too. Fishing from the south end of this beach is recommended at low tide only.

As for the famous **nude beaches** of Santa Cruz County, one mile south of Davenport, where the **Bonny Doon Road** starts up to Felton and other mountain towns, you'll see coveys of cars parked. From roughly this point on Highway 1 to the edge of Santa Cruz, cars parked with nothing in sight are usually signals that a clothing optional (nude) beach

is nearby and, also usually, hard to get to. Here you walk seaward across the railroad tracks and down the steep path to a wide and occasionally gusty beach with caves at the north end.

Some people spend all their recreation time at the sea; others head for the mountains. Around Santa Cruz you can enjoy both, for redwood-jacketed mountains start just a few minutes up and away from where surf laps or crashes against the shore.

If you prefer investigating backroads, take the Bonny Doon road that connects with the Felton Empire Road to **Felton,** where you can get on Highway 9 and the Graham Hill road. Actually, driving is easier and faster to this mountain area if you continue on Highway 1 to Santa Cruz and take Highway 9 or the Graham Hill road north from there. What's there to see? Redwoods! Most other tourist attractions are included in the Santa Cruz Mountain Visitors Guide distributed free at the Santa Cruz Chamber of Commerce and other places that cater to tourists.

Coast Redwoods — Sequoia sempervirens

From the time the first explorers discovered these trees of "tremendous girth," coastal redwoods, like these after a rain, have awed generations.

Some of the redwoods you will see in coastal mountains and parks can grow to over 360 feet and live more than 2,000 years. The thick bark on the older trees protects them against most fires; in fact, when the bark is peeled off and shredded it makes excellent insulation. *Sempervirens* comes from the Latin, meaning "ever living," and redwoods can live to almost forever if protected from their worst enemy: man—species lumberman. Redwood lumber is coveted because it lasts so long and is resistant to insects and rot.

Redwoods prefer canyons or protected hillsides with plenty of rain, back from the coast but close enough for frequent fog. Another reason for their long survival is that they can replenish themselves not only by the tiny shreds of seed in their cones but also by underground sprouts that grow out around the tree; this creates the "cathedral grove" in Henry Cowell and several other redwood parks. The mother tree is gone, but the circle of trees that grew out remains to awe us and other generations to come.

In recent years—barely in time, according to many—redwoods have become valued as much for their visual magnificence as for their lumber. It is difficult to imagine not feeling awe when in a cathedral grove of these ancient trees.

Felton does not cater to tourists but does have interesting spots; one is the **covered bridge,** built in 1892, a short distance east of Highway 9 across from a shopping center near the Zayante and Mount Hermon roads. This is now a small county park; the county has plans for picnic tables and other amenities. Park and walk (you can also bike or ride a horse—but do not drive) out onto the bridge. All you will see are the shallows of the San Lorenzo River, but how many covered bridges have you walked through lately?

Nearby, actually next door to Henry Cowell State Park, is the **Roaring Camp and Big Trees Narrow Gauge Railroad** (408/335-4484), a nostalgic reminder of the past when trains carried lumber, lime, blasting powder, and tourists through the mountains and down to Santa Cruz. Train buffs can admire the five well-maintained steam locomotives and other railroad apparatus. Even if you're not a railroad fanatic, you can't help but feel a thrill when the tiny train comes puffing and tooting into the station of the immaculate Roaring Camp town, with its gift shop and snack bar. When the train toots as you're riding in an open car through the redwoods, needles fall like feathers into the hands of eager children. The five-mile ride goes up and around, through a big redwood grove purchased in 1867, and over a trestle, pausing at a sunny picnic area where you can get off and take the next train back. Near here a conductor-guide leads passengers into the Cathedral Grove of redwoods in Henry Cowell Park for a lecture on these huge trees. The owner of this tiny railroad recently

Magnificent stands of redwoods enhance the five-mile run of the Roaring Camp and Big Trees Narrow-Gauge Railroad.

bought a regular-gauge historic rail line to carry passengers and freight nine miles starting from the Santa Cruz boardwalk, through the park, to Felton.

The 4,082-acre **Henry Cowell Redwoods State Park,** on both Highway 9 and the Graham Hill road, is upriver from the San Lorenzo Valley, somewhat optimistically called "America's Little Switzerland" (the peaks are not nearly as high as the Alps and it rarely snows here). This park was once part of the huge Henry Cowell ranch. Some of the most impressive old-growth redwoods along the entire Central Coast are here; they survived because logging machinery was too crude to cope with them in early lumbering days. The Rincon Trail starts from a parking lot alongside Highway 9 at the park's south end and passes by the Cathedral Redwoods, a ring of trees growing from a single base. Redwood Grove, the most visited site in the park, has a self-guided nature path. Another remnant of early days is the **dawn redwood** growing behind the ranger's office at the day-use kiosk off Highway 9. Thought to have died out 20 million years ago, a few dawn redwoods were discovered in China in 1944, and seeds of this ancient tree, which loses its foliage during the winter, have been planted in many moist areas like this.

Near the redwood grove the picnic grounds overlook the **San Lorenzo River,** popular with swimmers during summer and with fishermen during the fishing season from mid-November to the end of February. When the winter runs begin, the banks are crowded with anglers going after steelhead and silver salmon.

The southern unit has fifteen miles of hiking trails through redwoods and ponderosa pines. One hike climbs to an observation tower where you may glimpse Monterey Bay while you catch your breath. A gift shop and other amenities are near park headquarters, along with many picnic sites and 113 developed camping sites.

The second and newer 2,335-acre **Fall Creek** unit is for day use only. You park on the lot just off the Felton–Empire Grade Road and walk in to the deep canyon shadowed by redwoods, maples, and fir. Some trails lead to historic old lime kilns, one goes to a barrel mill and, of course, there is the cool, cascading Fall Creek itself.

On narrow, winding Highway 9, which follows the San Lorenzo River high into the mountains, you'll be on intimate terms with the big trees and may be tempted to stop at the string of small rustic villages along the way: Glen Arbor, Ben Lomond, Brookdale, and Boulder Creek.

Highway 9 was built for the narrow cars of another era, but the scenery is worth the effort of driving. The area is thick with summer cottages among the redwoods, retirement hideaways, restaurants, real estate offices, souvenir shops selling redwood artifacts (including redwood burls), resorts, and commercial campgrounds. One is Smithwoods Resort (408/335-4321) with 136 sites. Bear Creek, which joins the San Lorenzo River just above Boulder Creek, was named for the vicious grizzlies that roamed this area long after they were shot or poisoned elsewhere.

If you've driven this far (and the drive is almost as difficult if you start south from San Francisco on Skyline Boulevard), you should continue on to **Big Basin Redwoods State Park,** established in 1902 and probably the best known and certainly the oldest California state park. Watch for signs, and turn off Highway 9 onto State Road 236 the last few miles. If you can see only one redwood park, this is the one! It's tucked among impressive redwoods; deer come up to eat out of your hands, although the rangers frown on this practice. The heart of the park, at the bottom of Big Basin, has a nature lodge with historical and natural science exhibits. The lodge and the many waterfalls and wide variety of natural environments are just part of its assets.

The fact that you can visit this beautiful redwood park is due to the inspiration of photographer Andrew P. Hill. When trying to photograph some giant redwoods in 1899, Hill was stopped by the owner of the property. Incensed that trees of this magnificence could be off limits to the public, Hill helped start a club, now called the **Sempervirens Fund,** so that these trees, "among the natural wonders of world," would be saved for posterity.

Over 150 picnic sites with tables and stoves are scattered throughout the park, available on a first come first served basis for a small fee. Make reservations for the 188 overnight car camping sites through your local Ticketron office. From late spring to early fall, things get busy; it's a good idea to be sure your family has a place to camp after that long, tortuous drive. To reserve one of the 7 trail camps (with 6 sites per camp), contact the park rangers at (408) 338-6132.

At present hikers have sixty-five miles of hiking trails, and more are being built. Many follow streambeds through deep redwood forests; others climb the ridges to vista points. One popular trail loops along past several waterfalls, including the clear, sixty-five foot high **Berry Creek Falls** that emerges from the forest, sparkling clear against the deep green moss.

Berry Creek Falls is on one of the alternate trails that leaves the park headquarters and continues all the way to the ocean. Good hikers can make the trip in five to eight unforgettable hours. (Take bandaids and camera along.)

If you haven't made the inland detour and are still heading south on Highway 1, you'll pass three small creeks that meander down to the ocean south of the Bonny Doon Road: Laguna Creek, Majors Creek, and Baldwin Creek. According to Santa Cruz publicity, all three may contain trout, crappies, bluegill, black bass, and catfish. Most angling along this section of coast, however, is rockfishing, but getting

Big Basin's Berry Creek Falls is on a trail that leads from park headquarters to the ocean.

to the ocean through the acres of brussels sprouts is a problem and the beaches at the bottom of high bluffs may be hazardous as well.

Beaver or **Red, White, and Blue Nude Beach** (408/423-6332), is exactly three miles south of Davenport. After you park and pay your fee, an easy trail leads to a wide, sandy beach with plenty of private nooks for the modest nudists. There are other advantages to this beach that's been attracting old-time, over twenty-one, and family nudists for almost two decades. Besides the inevitable volleyball facilities there are restrooms, picnic tables, fire pits, and hot showers; cameras, guns, and dogs are not allowed. You can camp overnight, also, but it might be a bit chilly in the buff. Open from 10 A.M. to 5 P.M. or 6 P.M. in the summer.

Although part of the state park system, **Four-Mile Beach,** actually just a mile long, is officially "not open for public use." The quarter mile of brussels sprouts en route to the beach have been sprayed with so many pesticides that hiking along here is considered possibly hazardous; plans for a youth hostel were also put in limbo. Another disadvantage—too many hikers, nudists, and surfers have left beer cans and other trash on this beach. You'll find it by the clot of cars jammed in a dirt parking lot. If the state manages to carry out plans, the beach will eventually have facilities which might include camping upland.

This was once the Wilder Ranch, and the grounds still contain an adobe built in 1781. Candida Castro, a daughter of Joaquin Castro, and her Russian husband, José Bolcoff, who left a Siberian whaling ship in Monterey, lived long happy lives in this adobe with their large family.

Natural Bridges State Park on Natural Bridges Drive is definitely open to the public. Turn in near the Wrigley Gum Factory. Eroded rock arches give this park its name. Some wags now call it "Fallen Arches" because the biggest arch collapsed in 1980; appropriately, a wake was held. Pelicans, cormorants, gulls, and other sea birds congregate on the fallen arch, and the waves still thunder in to continue the erosion. If it's too windy, you can watch from your car on an overlook just outside the entrance to the park.

The park, open for day use only, is a small fifty-four-acre sanctuary of nature, from its small ocean beach with tidepools to its three-fourths-mile nature trail, which leads back to a spot where you can imagine yourself to be hundreds of miles from civilization. You even pass a secret lagoon on this trail,

Monarch Butterflies

Beautiful gold and black Monarch butterflies congregate by the thousands on specific "butterfly" trees at Natural Bridges State Park or in Pacific Grove.

From mid-October through mid-March, especially at Pacific Grove and Natural Bridges State Parks, you can see the beautiful orange-and-black **Monarch butterflies** that may migrate up to 3,000 miles at speeds as great as thirty miles an hour to hang in golden clusters from the branches of special trees. You may even see them en route. The thousand or so that cluster together on a three-foot branch look like dead leaves when it's foggy or rainy. When the sun comes out, they fly about to eat and mate. One female may lay 300 pale green eggs on milkweed plants, a ready-made food supply for the black-and-white caterpillars that soon hatch. A month later they're full-fledged Monarch butterflies, a beautiful sight. Luckily, they're distasteful to birds because of their diet.

No one knows for sure why Monarchs fly so far to hang from favorite trees. Since their life cycle is only nine months long, the ones that leave their special trees for the trip north will never return. But in some mysterious way, the instinct—or whatever—to return to these same trees is passed on to following genera-tions. Perhaps it is the residue of the smells of the Monarchs of years past that draws the new generation to the same Monterey pine or euca-lyptus trees that have sheltered this royalty of butterflies for decades.

Naturalists have conjectured Monarchs take readings from the sun and the temperature. They also utilize air currents and layers of air temperature to aid their flight; this they must do in the daytime and do quickly to stay ahead of falling temperatures. If the temperature falls below forty degrees, Monarchs can't fly.

These suburban homes have a great view of Natural Bridges State Park, named for its eroded rock arches, one of which is now, unfortunately, a fallen arch.

where mallard ducks may be cutting a smooth, dark swath through the green water. And there are restrooms and picnic tables.

The main attraction from mid-October through mid-March is a grove of eucalyptus trees that lures the beautiful orange and black **Monarch butterflies** from as far as 3,000 miles away. Some contend more arrive here than in Pacific Grove. To honor the return of these colorful animals with velvet wings, the park usually holds a Welcome Back Monarchs Day on the second or third Saturday in October. Call (408) 423-4609 or 688-3241 to verify.

In the same general area and also well worth seeing is the **Long Marine Laboratory** (408/429-2464), or University of California Center for Coastal Marine Studies, near the corner of Delaware and Shaffer Road. From Highway 1 turn west on Western, again at the Wrigley Gum Factory to Natural Bridges Drive, then right on Delaware to the entrance, just past a mobile home park. You'll spot it by the tall concrete tank beyond fields of brussels sprouts.

The center, on a cliff overlooking Monterey Bay, is open daily, except Monday, from 1 P.M. to 4 P.M. There's a gift shop, and often student docents lead tours. You'll see a small aquarium of local marine life and tanks where sharks and other sea animals are studied. There's a "touch tank" where children and blind visitors can feel some of the smaller marine creatures. One highlight of the center is the skeleton of the largest creature ever to live on earth, the blue whale. The skeleton is of an eighty-five-foot long, fifty-year-old female that washed ashore near Pescadero several years ago. Native plant enthusiasts can also check out the small demonstration garden of coastal dune and bluff plants at the center. If plans materialize, new bioresearch and teaching facilities plus a new visitors center will go up where there are now just hopeful signs.

One of the many sights at the Long Marine Laboratory just north of Santa Cruz is the skeleton of a blue whale, the largest creature ever to live.

The **University of California at Santa Cruz (UCSC)** is just outside the northeast corner of Santa Cruz on 2,000 acres of meadow and redwood forest overlooking the city and Monterey Bay. The campus is also host to grazing cows, black-tailed deer, raccoons, coyotes, great horned owls, and one bobcat. Turn inland at Bay Street, drive up and zig south on High to Bay. Other alternatives are to continue on Highway 1 and turn at Bay, or to go farther and turn north on High. The weathered buildings near the main entrance on Bay are nearly a century old, relics of when the property was part of the Henry Cowell Ranch. Now the barn is a campus theater and the other buildings are all in use. Stop at the kiosk near the entrance for maps, one a guide to the campus and one showing the extensive hiking/biking/jogging trails and par course. Also pick up a one-day parking permit at the red Cookhouse and check the calendar of the many special events. If you visit the campus on a weekday, you can leave your car and hop on and off the open-air shuttle bus, the Banana Slug, that slowly wends around the campus.

The university, which is geared mainly to undergraduates, once expected to enroll 25,000 students by 1990. At present eight colleges are open, and enrollment is about 6,000, including some older students attending through a reentry program. The colleges—in clusters with open land between—are the basic units of the campus. Each college is a self-contained complex of classrooms, meeting rooms, a dining hall, and residences for both students and faculty, a west coast version of Oxford University. Certain facilities, such as the library, are used by all. Each college has its own style and lifestyle. The theme of Kresge College, for example, is man and his environment; other colleges are becoming more problem-oriented, with some trying to solve problems of nearby communities. Some permanent members of the community, off the hill in Santa Cruz, are not happy about students who become liberally active, vote in "pie in the sky schemes," and then graduate, leaving the community to follow through. Other people in the community like the leavening effect of the students.

If you enjoy wandering through gardens, visit the campus arboretum, off Empire Grade, for perhaps the best display of Australian and South African plants outside those countries. There's something blooming all year round, but March to May are good months to visit because you may see the King proteas, about a foot across, blooming then. Docents are usually on hand to answer questions, and you can buy plants Wednesday and Sunday from 2 P.M. to 4 P.M. College Eight at UCSC operates a seventeen-acre farm and a five-acre garden. Both projects make use of organic gardening techniques, free from chemical products. Most of the produce helps supply the campus's unique **Whole Earth Restaurant** (408/426-8255) off Height Drive. Besides this, there are many other coffeehouses and restaurants on the campus, all open to the public.

The 2,000 acres on which this top-of-the-world campus sits was a gift of the Cowells. The property was once part of the Henry Cowell ranch, which was originally part of a Mexican land grant dating from the early 1840s. Henry Cowell, who arrived during the Gold Rush and acquired this ranch and miles of other property up and down the coast, became immensely rich. On many of his mountain property sites, he quarried and refined so much limestone that he became known as the Limestone King of Santa Cruz.

Cowell's huge hilltop home still stands near Bay and High streets in Santa Cruz. The five Cowell children attended a nearby school, but the family stayed almost too closely knit: Henry, Sr. frowned on any of his children marrying. One son, Ernest, did wed a girl he met at the University of California at Berkeley, but the family ostracized him and the childless marriage soon ended. One daughter was killed in a runaway carriage. The last living child, Samuel Henry, known as Henry Cowell, died in 1955 at the age of ninety-four, and the dynasty ended. Before his death, the son Henry established a foundation that helped fund health centers at several universities. The foundation also deeded 1,500 acres to the state for Henry Cowell Redwood Park. So the name Cowell remains, and—according to student legends—so does the ghost of the Cowell daughter who met her death in that runaway carriage.

This lovely old house, built circa 1893, on West Cliff Drive, is only one of many in Santa Cruz.

8

Santa Cruz City Highlights

All year long sun-hungry tourists by the thousands pour into **Santa Cruz.** They come to relax on its wide, sandy beaches lapped by mostly safe surf and to swim without turning purple from the cold, and some come to escape the heat of their inland towns or farms. Young actives arrive with surfboards to ride the waves or attach themselves to roller skates or bikes. Many come to sample the fishing. Others come to ogle at the Miss California State Finals in June; protests have made this activity more exciting than originally intended. Many— sometimes too many on a Sunday—come to take in the amusements and thrills along the famous boardwalk. Some slip in for a romantic weekend that may include sampling fare at some of the 175 or so restaurants in the area. Others head directly for the small boat harbor or to the Pacific Avenue Garden Mall with its laid-back coffee shops; often tasteful boutiques and stores; and its free, informal entertainment.

Santa Cruz has something for everyone: students to laborers to bearded intelligentsia. You'll see all kinds, from little old men and ladies in tennis shoes to the yachting set to the last of the old-time hippies wearing overalls or paisley bedspreads. Wherever *you* fit in, you'll find bushels of free folders on everything to do and see that's legal at the **Convention and Visitors Bureau** (408/423-6927) in the Civic Auditorium at Church and Center streets. It's in the next block from the city hall, which has a beautiful Spanish-style garden that's in colorful bloom all year.

The bureau is open from 9 A.M. to 5 P.M. on weekdays. In addition to folders listing places of interest, including restaurants, lodging, fishing, and other sports, be sure to pick up the folder describing the four walking tours to some of the town's beautifully restored Victorians. The small "Coastal Guide" has capsule tips on what to do and see. You can sometimes pick up a copy of *Good Times* here or at newsstands; the in or far-out crowd swears by it. Within its pages you'll discover which rock groups are in town and pore over classified personal ads such as: "Bisexual w/m wishes relationship with local couple to enjoy afternoons of experience sharing."

A few backroads less traveled wander into Santa Cruz, but three routes carry most of the traffic: Highway 1, which mostly parallels the coast; Highway 9, which goes into the mountains; and busy Highway 17 from Los Gatos, San Jose, and Oakland, which arrives over the Santa Cruz Mountains. As you maneuver around the steep curves on Highway 17, hoping your radiator won't boil over, you see acres of huge trees. Near the summit they are often touched with fog and, on rare occasions, with snow. Then it's down to Santa Cruz. After crossing Highway 1, you're deposited on bumper-to-bumper Ocean Street, which crosses other crucial thoroughfares like Water Street and Soquel Avenue.

If you've driven south on Highway 1 you can still postpone being thrown into heavy traffic. After you leave Natural Bridges State Park, continue south on **West Cliff Drive** (or turn west off Highway 1 at Swift, Fair, or Almar), a route that winds for several miles along the edge of high bluffs above the water before dropping down to the Santa Cruz Pier and Boardwalk. En route, you'll want to stop at several overlooks to take in the panoramic views. If you're on a bike or on foot, there's a path just for you seaward of West Cliff Drive.

Before making that final turn down to the boardwalk, pause at the New England–style brick **Mark Abbott Memorial Lighthouse** on the official dividing line between the Pacific Ocean and Monterey Bay. This is the only lighthouse ever built with private funds. It was donated to the Coast Guard by Chuck and Esther Abbott, who had it built in memory of their son, Mark, killed in a body-surfing accident. The lighthouse contains a tiny museum, open Saturday and Sunday afternoons, but you'll probably want to stay outside to snap pictures: of the coast to your right, and the pier and boardwalk to your left; of boats and ships of every variety; and of the noisy herd of sea lions just offshore on Seal Rock. There's plenty of free parking (rare in Santa Cruz); it's a great spot for a picnic, and there's a public restroom.

Another pleasant stopping-off place before you reach the crowded tourist meccas is **Neary's Lagoon Park and Wildlife Refuge.** If you've stayed on Highway 1, which becomes Mission Street, turn right on Bay and continue to California. If you've taken West Cliff Drive, turn left on Bay to the park entrance, across railroad tracks. There are a children's playground, tennis courts, picnic tables, a beautiful lagoon with the inevitable ducks, and swallows darting over the surface after insects. You can also get to the lagoon off Laurel and Felix streets, but you have to walk through the fancy Cypress Point housing complex to reach it.

Possibly even quieter, **Evergreen Cemetery,** designated as a Point of Historic Interest, adjoins **Harvey West Municipal Park.** Take the Highland turnoff sharp north off Mission Street, or you can walk over on a concrete overpass from School and High streets, near the Santa Cruz Mission. Dappled sunshine lights on the gravestones, some dating from the 1850s. The White Lady, Santa Cruz's favorite ghost, may no longer haunt the cemetery, but the gravestones call up other colorful residents. There's a small section for Civil War dead. Gun-toting Isaac Graham is here, along with a freed slave, a pioneer school marm, Santa Cruz's first judge, Chinese coolies, a prostitute, paupers, children, and many others. The grounds are not manicured; native plants, a scattering of weeds, and many trees wander up a steep hillside toward giant redwoods.

There will probably be more action at neighboring Harvey West Park on Evergreen Street. Here you'll find displays depicting early California, a free train ride, a swimming pool and playground, picnic grounds, barbecue facilities, a snack bar, and restrooms.

Whatever offbeat locations you visit, you'll inevitably also check out the mile-long **Santa Cruz Beach and Boardwalk,** anchored on one end by the Cocoanut Grove casino, which recently had its face lifted, and—silhouetted against the sky—the humps, bumps, and corkscrew turns of the Giant Dipper. Is it all slightly archaic and declassé, or camp? Or is it exciting fun for the whole family? After all, can a century of eager tourists—two million a year—be wrong? All across the country, amusement parks and boardwalks have become dingy and turned out their lights and locked their gates. But the Santa Cruz Boardwalk remains clean, painted, picked up, and well lit. It still attracts throngs on weekends from Labor Day to Memorial Day and every day after that through the summer. Usually during the summer the boardwalk offers special-savings tickets on Monday and Tuesday. On any day, you can buy a ticket for just one ride or a pass for unlimited rides all day. For the year's schedule of rates, phone (408) 423-5590.

What's there to do on the Boardwalk? You have a choice of over twenty rides, and numerous games of skill including a miniature golf course and a shooting

The handcarved merry-go-round at the Santa Cruz Boardwalk has a Ruth Band organ with 342 pipes.

gallery. The climax of all the rides is that big wooden **Giant Dipper,** built in 1924 and given top rating for screaming chills by roller-coaster aficionados. Less harrowing and more appealing to the romper set is the classic **Merry-go-Round** with its sixty-two horses and two Roman chariots hand-carved by a Danish wood carver, and its Ruth Band organ with 342 pipes. As the music blares happily, youngsters still grab at the gold ring as they swing by.

Besides older visitors reliving childhood thrills, the Penny Arcade now attracts a young crowd that has never seen the likes of the vintage machines: the Moviola, the Peep Show with its circumspect unclothed ladies taking a dip, the Lovemeter, or the tinkling player piano. The fortune-telling machines, many built at the turn of the century, are popular. A benign Grandma Fortune Teller tells you, "You are going on a short trip," then, "If you desire more information, please put in another coin." So many people put coins into these museum-caliber machines that they often bring in more revenue than the electronic games that create such a din. If you tire of the games you can buy a fluorescent seashell ash tray or

T-shirt in one of the many shops, munch a burger or cotton candy, or sip a beer while you people-watch. That's a popular occupation.

The **Cocoanut Grove** casino draws a different crowd which has come to "experience yesterday's carefree atmosphere." As many as 850 people can dance to the old-time big bands that occasionally still play in the tradition of Glenn Miller. (New Year's Eve is sold out long in advance.) The $10 million restoration includes convention facilities, and a bay view lounge and room where you are surrounded by the "rich blue rolling seas of the Monterey Bay." The sun room has become so popular that reservations for the Sunday champagne brunch sometimes have to be made months in advance (408/423-5590). This spectacular 6,000-square-foot room, with the ambience of a New Orleans courtyard, has a curved glass roof that can be rolled back to admit the sun or offshore breezes.

Most visitors insist that the main magnet in Santa Cruz is that mile-long stretch of sand and easy surf fronting the boardwalk. Many parents have discovered that they can escape to the beach by giving the kids a book of unlimited rides. Because this beach faces due south and is sheltered at either end by steep bluffs, the sun shines here when fog may hang dankly along the coast on either side.

The number of beach enjoyers is so large that some retired people living nearby earn extra money by using a metal detector to discover coins and other objects the crowds have left. If you feel it's too jam-packed, **Cowell Beach,** just west of the pier, caters mainly to surfers, and you may have more room to put down your beach towel. At the opposite end of the beach, where the San Lorenzo River flows into the bay, you'll find more sandy space, and the kids (or you?) can often wade in the shallows of the river. But watch out for the signs, "Danger: contaminated water," that appear on occasion.

For an overall view of the Santa Cruz beach and boardwalk and the string of enticing beaches to the south, walk over the San Lorenzo River on the trestle and then out to **San Lorenzo Point,** a long, narrow promontory at the foot of East Cliff Drive, which juts out into the bay. Walk over from the boardwalk if you can; parking space is usually rare near the point.

If you can tear yourself away from the beach, what other tourist spots does the Chamber of Commerce recommend? The **Roaring Camp and Big Trees Narrow-Gauge Railroad** at Felton (408/335-4484) is one (see page 63). Another that may attract a more limited audience is **The Last Supper,** life-size wax figures in the manner of da Vinci, in the Santa Cruz Art League Galleries (408/426-5787) at 526 Broadway. There's no admission charge, but donations are expected. There are paintings here, too, mostly of pastel sunsets and surf.

One of the most publicized tourist lures is the **Mystery Spot** (408/423-8897) on Branciforte—*not* North Branciforte. The route is hard to follow. Market Street turns into Branciforte and you drive on a twisting road shadowed by redwoods to reach this Mystery Spot. For your admission fee, you walk up a steep path to a cabin tilted at an unhappy angle. According to the guide, the earth's gravitational pull is awry here, perhaps because a huge meteorite is buried in the hillside. Plumb lines and standing visitors appear to rest 17 degrees off normal, a phenomenon discovered in 1939 by the new owners, who intended to build a summer cabin on the site. The various other oddities, like golf balls appearing to roll uphill and people seeming to change heights while standing on a level board, may be somewhat suspect in or near that wildly tilting shack. Encouraged by

the guide, however, many visitors speak of a "force" or "heaviness," and some become dizzy and upset. Return the way you came or turn left and take the Glen Canyon backroad that winds a few pleasant miles up to Highway 17.

If you prefer a longer drive, major tourist attractions are marked on signs posted along a twenty-nine-mile scenic Tree-Sea Tour that goes all the way to Felton and Aptos. The tour includes the well-preserved **A. K. Saltz Tannery** (408/423-1480), built in 1861 and still flourishing. You can take a tour and sometimes pick up buys in scrap leather; it's on River Road, just north of the junction with Highway 1.

Not all Santa Cruz attractions charge admission fees. Walking or driving out on the **Santa Cruz Pier** is free, although the parking meters must be fed seven days a week. The pier, or wharf—over half a mile long—is often lined with people fishing and has several bait shops. There's also a fish market so that you can carry home just-caught fish even if you've been unsuccessful on your own. If you're an early riser and don't mind spending money to practically assure yourself of catching fish, C. Stagnaro (408/423-2020) on the wharf has a large fleet of charter boats. You can also rent sixteen-foot sea skiffs with outboard motors from Santa Cruz Boat Rentals (408/423-1739).

Besides fish-oriented activities, there's the usual array of souvenir shops and restaurants, one after the other. Malio's advertises panoramic views, but Stagnaro's or the Dolphin, at the outer end of the wharf, have even more degrees of view. If you've brought your lunch or are just looking around, stroll out to the end, sit at a picnic table, and enjoy that view and the antics of resident sea lions, who often help themselves to the crabs and fish caught by people fishing. When the tide is high, some of these noisy mammals rest on the cross-planks under the pier. When the tide goes down, there they are, high and dry, and people who peer down at them through the wells wonder how in the world they got there.

Another popular gathering place for locals as well as tourists is the tree-studded **Pacific Avenue Garden Mall,** started as a do-it-yourself redevelopment program by the late photographer, Chuck Abbott, and his wife. Abbott decided to retire in Santa Cruz in the mid-sixties, but his idea of retirement was to work full-time trying to improve his adopted town. Downtown business was a disaster and the area looked it. The Abbotts presented color slides to civic groups to show what other cities had done to spruce up their deteriorating areas. Finally 70

The mouth of the San Lorenzo river is great for swimming or floating on a rubber raft.

percent of the downtown property owners signed a petition to tax themselves for the mall, and construction was begun in July 1969. A *Monterey Life* writer interviewed one civic leader who worked with Abbott: "Chuck Abbott took all this on when he was nearly eighty years old and he was tireless," the man commented. "He'd keep going when the rest of us had had enough. But by the time we finished the

mall, we had become an inspiration for other cities facing similar problems."

Ever since the mall put on its first Spring Fair, with an ecology motif, the crowds have grown every year. With its pleasantly artistic shops, restaurants, and whatnot—even the banks look artistic—the mall is a far cry from the vegetable gardens planted for early mission consumption on the muddy old street at the turn of the century. Now there are paved walkways, occasional places to sit, and a rare collection of trees. Three gardeners work full time to keep the flower boxes always in bloom and the place clean, so it's a continual showplace. To really enjoy it all, you must walk; only a trickle of traffic is allowed through.

You'll have no trouble spotting the mall's mile-long swath of plants and shops. It's about as downtown as you can get in this city of twisting streets. You can park on nearby streets and in free public garages. One end starts at the old restored Town Clock at North Pacific and Water streets. While you're there, notice the life-size sculpture of Tom Scribner playing a saw in the tiny **Scope Park.** When city fathers discovered that Scribner was a long-time dedicated member of the Industrial Workers of the World, the Wobblies, they weren't too happy about donating space for his statue, but there it is.

The mall is a beehive of activity, somewhat reminiscent of Telegraph Avenue in Berkeley. The clientele includes barefoot youths with beards and knapsacks; families of tourists; and a sprinkling of eccentrics, mild to wild. You'll still see an occasional senior citizen trying to soak up sun, but they have mostly given way to the street people. Entertainers usually run to guitarists, but you may catch magic acts or juggling or dancing of almost every variety; a band of cleanly scrubbed people singing the praises of Jesus has also been sighted.

One center of mall activity is the **Cooper House,** the county seat in olden days, now filled with three stories of shops and restaurants. Outside, you can sit in the crowded sidewalk cafe listening to a lively local band as you watch the passing people-parade.

Another gathering spot where you can mingle with the local intelligentsia is the **Bookshop Santa Cruz** (408/423-0900) at 1547 Pacific Avenue. It's a warm, wonderful emporium that calls itself "California's Complete Bookstore" and quotes Walt Whitman: "Any friend of books is a friend of mine." Daytime, evening, or both, you're invited to browse. To facilitate relaxed, unhurried browsing, chairs and benches are provided. At one time you could recline on a waterbed.

Behind the bookshop is a delightful open court with shops and the small Caffé Pergolesi (408/426-1775), with paintings on the walls. Seating is inside or outside in the sunshine where you can sip your espresso, beer, and wine; munch your light food; and enjoy the relaxed atmosphere. Warning:

Santa Cruz is a haven for bakeries, and you may not be able to resist the enticing scent of freshly baked croissants or other sinfully rich delectables emanating from Kelly's French Pastry in this same courtyard. Nearby, at 1545 Pacific, is Lulu Carpenter's, voted the best bar in town; the munchies are good, too, and Lulu serves hearty soups, sandwiches, and more for weekday lunches.

Beer is no longer fifteen cents, as it was when the psychedelic generation quaffed it in the old Catalyst on River Street, but the "new" Catalyst (408/423-1336) at 1011 Pacific Avenue still packs them in. Besides beer, you can buy sandwiches to eat among the palms and ferns, while you sit and discuss life and art. Now, however, the Catalyst emphasizes its bar and features entertainment, including various rock bands; there's a bouncer, too.

Just off Pacific at Front and Cooper streets, but a decided contrast to the buzz of people on the mall, is the **Octagon House** (408/425-2540). The century-old structure was built to house county records and is now a very quiet historical museum. Be sure to ask for the free flyers describing the four historical walking tours in town.

You can spend an hour or all day poking about the mall and environs. Notice the many murals and off-beat signs for some of the shops. Sorry, folks, but the sign over the United Cigar establishment shows a whale smoking. In the long, narrow **Artisan's Cooperative** (408/423-8183) at 1364 Pacific Garden Mall, thirty-five artists and craftspeople show their wares. Besides art to hang, you'll see handwoven wearables and rugs, ceramics, leather handbags, and more. If you're looking for a book on almost any subject for almost any age—tots to teens to "not telling"—you'll probably find it (plus bargain books and posters) in the tastefully decorated 8,000-square foot Paper Vision–Plaza Books (408/525-1111), at 1111 Pacific. They've been in business since 1910, and the present owner is Hal Morris.

Shops, restaurants, cafes, and galleries have spilled over from Pacific Avenue to nearby streets, especially onto Cedar. The Cedar Street Gallery is in a small Victorian, circa the 1860s, at 411 Cedar, near the south end of the mall. This gallery is somewhat subdued compared to the **Santa Cruz Art Center** (408/429-1188) at 1001 Center Street, which jogs off Cedar. In this big, rambling conglomeration of gallery space and open studios created out of a cavernous, dusty fireplace factory, you can often chat with and watch potters, weavers, jewelry-makers, clothes designers, and glass artists at work. The Center

A concrete replica of the adobe mission Santa Cruz sits on a quiet hill at Emmet and School streets.

Street Gallery here shows works of two dozen artists. In back of the building is the Center Street Clayworks. The center is a potpourri of cooperative art well worth investigating; even the inside mail box is a whimsical ceramic piece of art.

The India Joze Restaurant (408/427-3554) adjoins. It's another favorite gathering spot for real or intended artists to drink espresso, eat an Asian dinner, or sip beer and wine. The restaurant has the unique distinction of fostering perhaps the world's only **Annual Calamari Festival.** Co-owner Tom Brezny, who disliked cleaning these slimy, inky squid, once fantasized about such an event. He joked about it so constantly that his artist acquaintances started turning out pottery, T-shirts, glassware, and jewelry featuring the squid. At the first early fall festival in 1980, Brezny and Friends of Calamari expected 200 or so participants. Instead, 2,500 showed up, some in tour buses.

Other shops and galleries away from the mall include the Unicorn Pottery Studio at 1013 River Street; they feature traditional, functional pottery including stoneware sinks. Farther away at the western edge of Santa Cruz on 1642 Mission (alias Highway 1) is the Santa Cruz Potters' Co-op (408/426-8711). In this old brick building, which was once a Chinese grocery store, potters are hard at work turning mostly functional pottery, and you can buy some.

Many public buildings also have pockets of fine art. At the University of California at Santa Cruz (408/429-0111), you can check the changing displays at the College Five Gallery; the Smith Gallery, at Cowell College; and at the Stevenson College Gallery. The tiny newish **Art Museum of Santa Cruz County** (408/429-3420) shows an exceptionally high caliber of art. It's upstairs in the library building at 224 Church Street.

As for antiques and collectibles, over forty shops are scattered throughout Santa Cruz County, mostly in the mountains and in Soquel, Aptos, and Capitola, but they're sparse within the Santa Cruz city limits. You'll also see some historic mementos — including a few rare artifacts of coastal Indians, as well as stuffed animals and birds, unusual seashells, and specimens of sea life—at the small **Santa Cruz City Museum** (408/429-3773) at 1305 East Cliff Drive. The museum is also the site of the Santa Cruz Fungus Fair, in which hundreds of native wild mushrooms are on display when the fungus is at its best; in the spring, the museum holds a wildflower show.

Unlike Monterey, Santa Cruz has few historic sites remaining from its early Spanish-Mexican past. A shrunken concrete replica of the adobe **Mission Santa Cruz** sits on a quiet hill at Emmet and School streets, overlooking the tangled concrete of the present day. The original Mission de la Exaltación de la Santa Cruz, established in 1791, collapsed with a loud crash in 1857 (or in 1856—accounts vary) after an earthquake damaged its walls. The only known picture of the original mission, painted by a French scientist who visited it in 1853, aided the 1931 design of the mission replica. The Frenchman, Jean de la Perouse, foresaw that the mission system would fail as it "did not develop self-reliance in the neophytes." He was correct. Spanish control gave way to Mexican, which was later seized by American settlers. By 1890 less than a handful of Indians were left.

As for remaining adobes, the **Neary guardhouse,** probably built in 1810, survives nearby on School Street, as does the lived-in Rodriguez House, joined to it by an adobe wall. The Branciforte Adobe, at Neary and Branciforte Avenue just north of Highway 1, is now a private residence.

Even before the earthquake, the Santa Cruz Mission fell on bad times, especially in 1797 when 200 Mexican colonists—many exconvicts and derelicts—arrived to set up the Pueblo Villa de Branciforte on a height across the San Lorenzo River from the mission. Once again it was the church versus the secular world. The colonists, while waiting for housing and farming supplies, whiled away their time drinking, gambling, and roistering. Branciforte Avenue, where they held horse races, still remains, as does the **Branciforte Plaza.** This restored building, with its gardens, patios, and views, was started in 1797 by the Spanish. It was a schoolhouse from 1896 to 1920, then a hospital, then a rest home. Now the original Villa de Branciforte lives again. However, instead of Spanish officials and Mexican convicts, the building houses a restaurant, shops, and firms. It's at 555 Soquel Avenue.

In 1818, frightened that the Argentine privateersman Hippolyte de Bouchard, who sacked Monterey, would do the same to Santa Cruz, the padres fled to the Santa Clara Mission. They left the colonists to protect the mission, which was like asking a wolf to protect a flock of sheep. The padres returned to find the mission heavily damaged and their stock of aguadiente (spirits) gone. The church's decay was speeded up after it was secularized in 1834.

In 1886 Santa Cruz City was granted a charter, but it wasn't until 1907 that it swallowed the Branciforte settlement. Slowly the population grew. Ships stopped to pick up supplies and a few industries started up. Limestone was one, and in 1843 Elihu Anthony's foundry turned out iron picks for miners and plows for farmers.

Another industry, the Powder Works—the West's first munitions plant—started up in Felton in 1864, during the Civil War. Accidents were frequent; one shattered glass miles away in Santa Cruz, another blew out every window of a passing passenger train. Packed with gunpowder or blasting powder, trains made frequent trips down the steep mountainside and through Santa Cruz to the wharf, often with the powder kegs on open flatcars behind engines spitting sparks. In retrospect, it's a miracle Santa Cruz wasn't blown sky high.

The *big* industry was lumbering. Lt. Pedro Fages, who headed an expedition into the area in 1717 along with Father Juan Crespi, noted trees of a red color with "girth so great that eight men placed side by side with extended arms are unable to embrace them." These same redwoods, once popular as masts for sailing vessels, were responsible for the lumber boom.

Seemingly endless miles of thick virgin forests were logged. Back in the mountains you can still find shacks where the loggers lived. (New second-growth redwoods cover some of the denuded landscape.) At first, part of the San Lorenzo River was diverted into an eighteen-mile flume to wash down lumber and redwood logs from the mills to the railhead at Felton. Adventurous youngsters who grabbed a ride on a log had a never-to-be-forgotten thrill. The lumber and logs were then loaded onto a narrow-gauge train for the remaining journey. Compared to the powderkeg trains, these trips were tame. Nevertheless, trestles collapsed and tracks broke under round-the-clock use, engines and equipment were toppled, and brakemen lost control on the steep grade. One train was brought to a halt by several exhausted brakemen only instants before it reached the end of the Santa Cruz wharf.

Before the turn of the century, with the fortunes that were made until the forests gave out, lumber barons and other prominent Santa Cruz inhabitants erected huge homes, mainly in the Victorian and Italianate styles. Whether they are the ultimate in conspicuous consumption or the ultimate in crafts-manship, many survive.

Two or three decades ago, however, most of these grand old ladies were in a genteel state of collapse. Chuck Abbott, instrumental in the success of the Pacific Avenue Garden Mall, and others concerned about inner-city decay and lack of student housing started to buy up and renovate some of these struc-tures. In 1960 a plan to slice a freeway through a neighborhood crowded with historic buildings was defeated. "Historic preservation used to be known here as a radical cause," a young city planning com-missioner commented. "Now business people have realized it's good for tourism," which also means you and me. Soon an ordinance putting teeth into preservation efforts was passed. Today the owner of a pre-twentieth-century Santa Cruz house would feel ashamed if he, she, or they didn't renovate, paint, and decorate according to the manual provided for that purpose.

The results are a must to see. The Convention and Visitors Bureau, other tourist centers, and some com-mercial maps have brief descriptions of four suggested **Victorian Walking Tours,** each covering eight to ten of these well-preserved structures. Although each group is a manageable hike from the Pacific Avenue Garden Mall, you may prefer to drive to the various clusters. When you arrive, park and walk the few blocks with your camera; you'll savor more.

The **Mission Hill Tour** is the most historic; just drive to the top of Mission Street. It includes the mission replica; the Neary-Rodriguez adobes; and the oldest frame house in Santa Cruz, built in the 1850s, at 109 Sylvar Street. On this tour, don't miss the houses on nearby Green Street, a quiet cul-de-sac. They, the plantings, and view are especially charming.

The **Ocean View Tour** takes only fifteen minutes and covers eight houses from 235 to 412 Ocean View Avenue. The **Beach Hill Tour** includes the board-walk, a house at 912 Third Street rebuilt from the remains of a beached ship, plus some stately Queen Anne–style homes. The **Laurel Area Tour** takes thirty-five minutes. At 413 Lincoln Street you'll see a house whose backyard has the distinction of being the site of the last hanging in Santa Cruz. The tour also includes the oldest existing church in Santa Cruz, at 532 Center Street. It's the Calvary Episcopal Church, built between 1864 and 1865, which features an unusual curved apse. And do visit the nearby Civic Center gardens.

If you've exhausted all the historic, well-publi-cized, and offbeat possibilities in Santa Cruz and still want something to do, the **Nelson Community Center** (408/429-3504), at 301 Center Street in downtown Santa Cruz, may be your answer. Nelson was a freed slave who donated his estate to Santa Cruz. The center hums with activities for every age group from children to seniors: classes for baton twirling, gymnastics, bike racing, various varieties of art, and cooking. The latter class has a tasty spinoff, for the students occasionally put out a dinner for the public for a modest fee. This center may also help if you're visiting with children and want some time off. Its Popcorn Palace features inexpensive movies for children aged five to twelve which should entertain them from 1 P.M. to 3 P.M. on Saturday. Ask about the weekday childcare center (408/425-8668) for chil-dren aged two and a half to five.

As for **sports,** whether you like the indoor or outdoor varieties, you'll probably find what you're looking for (except for snow skiing) in this sunny area where ocean, bay, and mountains meet. Golf? De Laveaga (408/423-7212), a municipal course, is in the 540-acre **De Laveaga Park,** which also contains archery and handgun ranges, bridle paths, barbeque pits, picnic tables, and a children's playground. Pasatiempo 18-hole championship golf course (408/426-3622) is off Highway 17; there are also courses in Aptos and Boulder Creek.

Some of the young crowd likes to get around Santa Cruz via roller skates or skateboards, although this is forbidden on the boardwalk itself. If you want to give it a try, Go Skates (408/425-8410) at 118 Riverside carries surfboards as well as skates.

This is definitely bicycle country, from weekend pedaling to long, arduous trips. Extensive bike routes throughout the county are shown on the free bicycling guide available at the Santa Cruz Public Library or from the Santa Cruz Convention and Visitors Bureau. You can pedal along the bay from Natural Bridges State Park to Capitola, then go slightly inland along San Andreas Road until you're deposited again by the briny deep. Other bike routes climb up into the Santa Cruz Mountains along Empire Grade, Graham Hill Road, Frontage Road, and Glen Canyon Road. Another cluster of routes on moderately flat ground includes the many backroads by orchards and farms in the Watsonville area. Some-what hilly but providing great views is the Univer-sity of California at Santa Cruz (UCSC) campus. Dutchman Bicycles has three branches and rents bikes from 1325 Mission Street (408/426-9555), 3961 Portola Drive (408/476-9555), and in Scott's Valley. If you bring your own bike, the Santa Cruz yellow pages in the telephone directory lists dozens of shops where you can get service and advice.

Besides yachting, the Santa Cruz Small Craft Harbor offers wind surfing lessons, fine restaurants, and pleasant views.

Santa Cruz is made for **strolling.** The Victorian walking tours and a walk down the Pacific Avenue Garden Mall are two choices. It's only about half a mile from the mall to the waterfront, where you can walk north or south along interesting shorelines. As for long **hikes** complete with boots and knapsacks, most start or end in the Santa Cruz Mountains with its wide collection of redwood parks (see previous chapter or contact the Sierra Club at (408) 426-4453, P. O. Box 604, Santa Cruz, CA 95060).

Water-oriented sports are popular, and no wonder. **Swimming?** It's usually sunny and safe enough for children to swim in front of the boardwalk and in Capitola. **Surfing?** From sunup to sunset, near Lighthouse Point to the north and near Pleasure Point to the south, dozens of surfers wait to catch the waves. O'Neill's Surf Shop (408/475-4151),

1149 Forty-First Avenue, Capitola, is headquarters for surfers.

O'Neill's also has a yacht center (408/476-5200); dive shop (408/475-4151), and sailboard shop (408/462-5036) at the busy **Santa Cruz Small Craft Harbor,** south of the boardwalk off East Cliff Drive (which turns into Murray). Here you'll find other sailing schools, a diving school, and boats for charter or for sale. Even if you don't intend to board a boat, this harbor is a fascinating place to watch the small craft as they come and go. Notice the creative names on many. There are several restrooms, but most are reserved for the yachting crowd.

You can watch the passing parade of boats outside on the deck or inside at the Crow's Nest, perched at the edge of the entrance to the harbor. This restaurant is a favorite with locals; even with the new second story, you may have a wait. You can't reserve for lunch, but you can for dinner (408/476-4560). At Aldo's Harbor Restaurant (408/426-3736), 616 Atlantic Avenue, west of the entrance and directly across from the Crow's Nest, you can also enjoy this nautical spectacle, but only at breakfast and lunch.

Perhaps the activity you enjoy the most (second most?) is eating—which brings up a question: How can you choose among almost 100 restaurants in the wider Santa Cruz area? Ask a local, if possible—even a police officer will do—where he or she eats. If you're not the questioning type, comb through the lists put out by the Santa Cruz Chamber of Commerce or in tourist papers like *Good Times*. You could even check the yellow pages of the telephone book. A sampling follows of the various establishments in Santa Cruz city that haven't been mentioned.

In the quiet coffee shop category is the Caffé Domenica (408/427-3520), 418 Cedar, where you can actually hear your luncheon companions. Nearby at 320 Cedar is the Bagelry, selling many varieties— plain to poppyseed to yogurt-dill—of this object loved by New Yorkers. This enterprise and a branch at 1634 Seabright Avenue is run by ex-UCSC students who wanted to stay on but didn't know how to earn a livelihood in this resort town. Their quest ended when they found a secondhand bagel machine for $200. The Poet and Patriot Irish Pub (408/426-8620), in this same plaza, specializes in beer and fun and also serves hearty Irish stew and Cornish pasties.

For more conventional dining, the Santa Cruz Hotel (408/423-1152), downtown at Cedar and Locust, believes in hearty Italian meals, and the price is right. The Santa Cruz Bar & Grille (408/429-1000), at the same address, is over 100 years old and stresses its Victorian heritage. Adolphs (408/423-4403), 525 Water Street, is popular with local professional people who like family-style Italian dinners. Portola House (408/476-2733), 3326 Portola Drive, serves the more conventional steak and seafood daily from 5:30 P.M. At the Broken Egg, 605 Front, from 7 A.M. to 4 P.M. you can create your own omelets to eat along with fresh cider or coffee, and fresh fruit.

Where to stay? As in most well-publicized areas, prices for Santa Cruz motels are higher than you'd like. The Chamber of Commerce has a list of approved motels, although prices seem to rise before the ink is dry. Generally, the closer to the beach, the higher the tariff, although many of these motels run to plastic decor. Then there's the big Dream Inn (408/426-4330), 5175 West Cliff Drive. If you can do without the ocean every instant, check the smaller

motels on Ocean Avenue just as you turn off Highway 1 or 17; they're often more modestly priced. The rustic old St. George Hotel (408/423-8181) on the mall at 1520 Pacific Avenue rents most of its rooms to retirees but might have a few extras. Prices are low, but this isn't the Ritz and the bathroom may be down the hall.

The Santa Cruz American Youth Hostel is still in the future. However, they do furnish temporary facilities (but no kitchen) from June 15 to August 20. Write Santa Cruz Hostel Project, P. O. Box 1241, Santa Cruz, CA 95061 or call (408) 423-8304; try evenings.

As might be expected in a place brimming over with big old houses, the bed and breakfast industry is booming in Santa Cruz. After all, as Democritus said in 450 B.C., "A life without festivity is like a road without an inn." Cliff Crest (408/427-2609), 407 Cliff Street, is on Beach Hill in the former home of William Jeter, who was lieutenant governor of California in the 1890s. Chateau Victorian (408/458-9458) is a block from the beach at 118 First Street and features queen-sized beds. One of the fascinating old inns is Babbling Brook Inn (408/427-2437), 1025 Laurel Street. Originally it was an old Indian fishing site, then a log cabin, then the location for many early silent movies; later it was bought by a countess. Now there are twelve rooms with fireplaces, each decorated with country French antiques. The grounds are beautiful, with gazebos and paths along Laurel Creek and a waterfall and pond. If you can hold out until Aptos or Capitola, you'll find other distinguished bed and breakfast inns.

If you're on a really meager budget, try camping at the New Brighton, Sunset, or (perhaps) Seacliff state beach parks below Santa Cruz, or at Henry Cowell or Big Basin Redwoods state parks in the mountains. Reserve through your local Ticketron office. Most of these parks have facilities for cyclists for a tiny fee.

In addition to the several commercial camping and RV parks mentioned in the Santa Cruz Mountain areas, there's the Santa Vida Travel Park (408/425-1945), 1611 Branciforte Drive, which has tent sites as well as RV hookups. The Santa Cruz KOA (408/722-0551) is at 1186 San Andreas Road, south of Santa Cruz—almost to Watsonville—but near pleasant beaches. They have 242 sites and allow tents. The Seacliff Center Trailer Park (408/688-3813) at the entrance to the park has complete hookups for RVs. There are also many beautiful camping sites in state parks south of Santa Cruz—*if* you reserve early enough.

Capitola's last fling with summer is the Begonia Festival, when boats and floats covered with begonias parade down the creek.

9

Santa Cruz to Edge of Moss Landing

CAPITOLA, SOQUEL, APTOS, RIO DEL MAR, AND WATSONVILLE

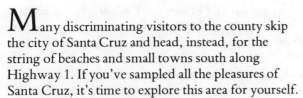

Many discriminating visitors to the county skip the city of Santa Cruz and head, instead, for the string of beaches and small towns south along Highway 1. If you've sampled all the pleasures of Santa Cruz, it's time to explore this area for yourself.

You can start at **Twin Lakes State Beach** (408/688-3241), on East Cliff Drive at Seventh Avenue, a pleasant place to picnic or fish. It curves into **Schwans Lagoon,** a popular stopping-off spot for birds, as is **Corcoran Lagoon** even farther south. On a field trip one February at Schwans Lagoon, a local club spotted fifty-eight species of wild birds—thirty-five during a leisurely walk on the wooded path around the park and the others in the tidal lagoon or lake. Get out your binoculars and you may see the pied-billed grebe, which looks like a chicken that learned to swim; or the lanky black-necked stilt in his impeccable tuxedo; or the more casually attired long-billed curlew and marbled godwit, more at home in the mud. You may hear the eerie, yodellike laugh of the loon. The rusty orange marsh grass is alive with the chirps, peeps, squawks, and wing-flutterings of countless birds, many migratory.

If you continue on south—East Cliff Drive becomes Portola Drive—you'll arrive at the charming but crowded town of **Capitola.** You can also reach Capitola from the freeway, as you can Soquel, further inland and also adjoining Santa Cruz, but, since Capitola is on the bay, why not enjoy the sights and sounds as long as you can?

Capitola calls itself the oldest seaside resort on the Pacific, and it still retains some of its longtime prestige. When the railroad was built in the 1860s—the high trestle is visible from almost everywhere in town—the town became a fashionable watering place for the elite of San Francisco, some of whom stayed at the Capitola Hotel. Those not lucky enough to have reservations there or to own one of the ornate homes, some of which remain, vacationed on the strand in rented tents.

The Capitola Chamber of Commerce suggests that, in the interest of saving gas, you make Capitola Village your home base: Five miles southeast of Santa Cruz, "this charming amalgam of beach, winding streets, restaurants, galleries, and shops is so compact that your car will seem blessedly obsolete during your stay," they tell you. What the Chamber of Commerce doesn't say is that once you park, that's it. If you leave your parking space you may never find another one, especially on summer weekends. To help alleviate this problem, the Santa Cruz Metropolitan Transit District (408/425-8600) provides a parking lot and a free beach shuttle. Take the Capitola exit from Highway 1 onto Bay Avenue, go one block west to Hill Street, take a left, and follow signs.

The **Capitola Village** center is at the beach near the mouth of Soquel Creek; the town then spreads on either side of the creek back into oak-dotted hills. The area where the creek meets the sea is great for driftwood hunting after winter storms. In calmer weather, it's heaven for kids of all ages. Little children can wade or paddle about in rubber rafts or inner tubes, near the always-present ducks. Bigger kids can play volleyball on the sandy beach or ride surfboards offshore, and everyone can fly kites. And there's the **Capitola Fishing Wharf** where you can buy bait, dangle your line, or rent a boat.

Besides investigating the beach, you'll want to browse through some of the many art galleries, antique emporiums, or craft shops along Capitola Avenue from the edge of Soquel Creek to under the trestle near the **Little Red School House.** This small, sprightly building has a Chamber of Commerce (408/475-6522) sign in front but is rarely open. The entrance to the Craft Gallery (408/475-4466), which also functions as an information center, is just off Capitola Avenue at 126 San Jose Avenue. Here you'll find an outstanding array of pottery, paintings, and handicrafts, most turned out by local artists. At Latta's Jewelry as Art (408/475-1771), a tiny gem of a shop off the main street at 120 Stockton, you may see Jay Latta crafting jewelry on his forge. He also shows a few paintings by local artists.

The Capitola Camel at 202 Capitola is somewhat funky. The Artifacts Gallery at 602 Capitola has tribal crafts and folk art from forty countries. Then there's the Capitola Mercantile, just off the beach, whose dozen little shops include That's a Hell of a Note (selling greeting cards) and Grandma's Buffalo Cookies. Besides the many other shops and boutiques in Capitola Village, you'll also find galleries,

gift stores, and grocery markets in the huge shopping center inland at Forty-First Avenue and Capitola Road. This includes the Capitola Mall Shopping Center with over forty shops in the enclosed climatized mall; there's free parking here.

Capitola is probably most famous for its begonia gardens. At **Antonelli Brothers' Begonia Gardens** (408/475-5222), 2545 Capitola Road, in a 10,000-square-foot display greenhouse, the whole roof is aglow with hanging baskets of begonias from June into November (peak season is August and September). There are coleus, Boston ferns, other hanging foliage, and the floor is crowded with cactus, azaleas, rhododendrons, camellias, and more indoor plants. You can also see prize-winning orchids and buy orchid kits to grow your own at Shaffer's Tropical Gardens (408/475-3100), 1220 Forty-First Avenue; exit off Highway 1 at the Forty-First Avenue exit, then go three-quarters of a mile to your right.

Capitola's big event of the year, usually in early September, is the **Begonia Festival.** During this last fling with summer, there are barbecues, fishing derbies, sailboard races, aquatic shows, the crowning of a local queen, and a parade of boats and floats covered with thousands of begonias. On Friday before the parade, participants start building their floats at twilight all along Soquel Creek; some work all night long.

Where to eat in Capitola? The Shadowbrook (408/475-1511), on the river (or creek) at 116 Wharf Road, is probably the most famous of local restaurants. You take a cable car to get there, and you need reservations. The Edgewater Club & Restaurant (408/475-6215) at 215 Esplanade is right on—almost over—the water and has an all-glass greenhouse patio with a retractable glass ceiling. Besides lunch and dinner, on Sunday you can brunch at the water's edge and wash your meal down with champagne. Modestly priced but without a view is the Pelican Cafe, 207 Esplanade; they specialize in omelets.

If you decide you just have to stay in Capitola, where do you? The Capitola Inn (408/462-3004), 822 Bay Avenue, has kitchen units; the Harbor Lights Motel (476-0505) is by the beach. The funkiest and hardest to reserve is on the beach where the river meets the sea. The Capitola Venetian Hotel (408/476-6471), 1500 Wharf Road, is a cluster of stucco buildings with a faint Italian air, which started life as a motel circa 1920, gradually ran down, and then was sufficiently renovated to attract devoted guests, especially those with sizable families. Since every unit has a kitchen, lucky guests can cook fish dinners with perch or flounder caught practically out their window. If you enjoy bed and breakfast establishments, the Summer House (408/475-8474) is on Depot Hill at 216 Monterey Avenue overlooking the village and bay.

New Brighton State Beach, adjoining Capitola, is the first regular camping park directly on the ocean south of San Francisco. You'll see the exit signs about four miles south of Santa Cruz on Highway 1. The curving, sandy beach is protected by headlands, so it is often bathed with sunshine; fishing is usually interesting, and there are interpretive nature trails. You can also enjoy the many species of wild birds that live or visit here: western meadowlark, red-tailed hawk, valley quail, goldfinches, and white-crowned sparrows, as well as other migratory species. More than 100 camping sites are located in the sixty-five-acre park on a high, wooded plateau cut off from the beach. One bonus is a magnificent view of Monterey Bay on clear nights; another, if you can turn your eyes away from the bay, is the fossils in plain view in the sides of cliffs. Reserve through your local Ticketron office or call (408) 475-4850 for information.

If you look at a Santa Cruz County map you'll wonder why the boundaries of Santa Cruz, Capitola, and **Soquel** are such a jigsaw puzzle. Soquel is inland and you can reach it by taking Highway 1 or, preferably, slower-paced Soquel Drive. As you reach the village, huge oak trees crowd up to the roadsides, and the old white steepled church where Soquel Drive crooks is straight out of New England. This is the Congregational "Little White Church in the Vale," founded in 1868. Just off Soquel Drive up the hill on Center Street is another charming old structure. Now in private hands, it was the parsonage, built at the same time as the church. Soquel's small pockets of nostalgia are worth a stop. No wonder movie crews have used the church and vicinity as locations for movies.

Antique hunters can have a field day in Soquel and in Aptos, the next town. Across from the church in Soquel, twenty-two small shops are clustered in a quonset hut called the Trader's Emporium (408/475-9201) at 4940 Soquel Drive. A sign outside warns: "Unattended children will be towed." After Effects, another antique shop, is next door. The Square Nail (408/475-4393) at 5870 Soquel Drive has twelve showrooms—an acre of antiques and collectibles from many historic periods—in a garden setting. And that's just a sampling of the places where you'll find antiques. The Collectors' Gallery (408/475-4091) at 2315 Soquel—still in Santa Cruz—has over a dozen shops. It's across from the Skyview Flea Market, which takes over the Skyview Drive-In Theatre during daylight hours on the weekend and charges for parking. Some hard-core flea market buffs make good buys early here; others contend it carries too many hub caps and used or reused tools.

A pleasant interlude in Soquel is to sample wine at Bargetto's Winery (408/475-2258), 3535-A Main Street. Just follow the signs to the tasting room, which overlooks the creek and displays old winemaking tools. If you're a purist you can bring bread cubes or crackers to nibble on to clear your palate (and head?) between nips of wine.

Where to eat in Soquel? For steaks, the Grapesteak (408/475-4635), 621 Forty-First Street, lets you broil your own. Many locals swear by the food and service at 2525 Main Street (408/462-2525) for lunch, dinner, or Sunday brunch. The Courtyard Restaurant (408/476-2529), 2591 Main, overlooks Soquel Creek. If the weather cooperates, you can eat lunch, Sunday brunch, or dinner outside. In the Greenhouse Restaurant at the Farm (408/476-5613), 5555 Soquel Drive, you can eat seafood or steaks as you look outside at the tidy farm that grows many of the vegetables served at your table or at the salad bar. There's a nursery, bakery, and gift shop here, also. If you're more interested in a picnic, Maddock's Bakery, 4628 Soquel Drive, specializes in old-fashioned bakery goods such as crusty bread without preservatives baked in a sixty-year-old hearth oven.

Between Soquel and Aptos on both Highway 1 and Soquel Drive, you'll pass **Cabrillo College,** whose architecturally unusual buildings overlook Monterey Bay. The college sponsors many lectures as well as the prestigious Cabrillo Music Festival in August. A semisecret is that gourmet meals, open to the public, are cooked and served by students of master chef Tom King. For information on dates and times of these moderately priced repasts, call (408) 425-6259.

Aptos, on the landward side of Sunset State Beach, has two modern shopping centers. There's The Village Fair Antiques is in an old apple shed at 417 Trout Gulch Road. In a couple of dozen shops, each operated by an individual dealer, you can look for bargains in everything from secondhand household items to fresh produce, but mainly antiques. Across Soquel Drive, a small string of shops carries antiques and gifty items. Nearby at 8041 Soquel Drive is the Bay View Hotel (408/688-1928), built in 1870, which still contains most of the original fur-

The Art of Beachcombing

Since almost everyone likes to **beachcomb,** here are tips on where to find seashore treasures and what to do with them. Driftwood hunting is best after winter storms in areas where a creek or river empties into the ocean. But at any time of the year occasional freak winds and currents bring in driftwood, bottles, and fishing floats. Sometimes your booty is covered with gooseneck barnacles. If they don't add to the appearance, scrape them off or let them dry up in the sun.

The tools you need are a creative eye, a rope, perhaps a shovel or small saw to help liberate the big pieces, and a knapsack to carry away the smaller ones (even tiny pieces can be interesting in mobiles). To clean driftwood, remove fragments of bark with a screwdriver or dull-edged knife. Use a sharp knife or icepick to pry out knots or embedded rocks (although they're often an asset). After you cut off frayed ends, use a file or rasp to weather the cuts. Clean off your prize with a brush soft enough to leave no marks, unless you want a grained effect. If the piece isn't weathered or light enough to suit you, leave it in the sun and water it daily for a few weeks. For quicker weathering, use a commercial wood bleach and brush on neutralizer when the wood reaches the shade you want. Finish the piece with a clear wood preservative or varnish sealer, or paint on a thin coat of shingle or siding stain. Some purists insist on merely rubbing in clear furniture wax with a clean shoebrush. It's also amazing how rubbing driftwood with just a rock makes it gleam.

Many dedicated rockhounds turn up their noses at beach pebbles, but they can be beautiful. Most are in the quartz family and are not pure minerals but aggregate rocks. (One reason for the confusion of names is that people picked up pretty pebbles and gave them names before scientists came along with their classification systems.) Hunting is best at low tide, especially in winter or early spring when deposits of sand on the beaches are low. You can often find translucent pebbles of pure quartz. Agates of various types—quartz banded with impurities of different colors—are also common. So is jasper, an opaque quartz that ranges from rich red or yellow to dark green. Chances are that the "jade" you pick up will actually be jasper or serpentine, although you can find the real thing at the south end of the Big Sur.

As for polishing pebbles, tumbling can take weeks. A quicker way is to use an emery cloth and scouring powder followed by a thin coat of colorless lacquer or hair spray with a lacquer base. This treatment saves time but may add a faintly yellow glint.

Although it's illegal to take them from state beaches, you can find fossils, often shells of clams, snails, cockles, scallops, and occasionally abalone. Whalebone fossils are very heavy. Sometimes fossils are in hunks of sandstone that have broken off cliffs. If they start to disintegrate, scrub away dirt with a soft brush and coat them thinly with lacquer.

Although this coast is not noted for seashells, you should find a few, probably shells of ur-

A beachcomber's collection of prizes may include sea shells, floats, driftwood, lures, and barnacle-encrusted bottles.

chins; snails; mussels; clams; abalone; and tiny "jinglies" with their iridescent underside and hole so you can make a mobile, tinkly wind chime, or necklace. Do not take away rocks or empty shells from tidepools. These may be vital to the survival of creatures in the pool.

On sandy beaches, you'll probably find **sand dollars.** Living sand dollars breathe through and travel on hundreds of short, tubular, velvety legs. They live below the tideline in sheltered sand flats in bays or out beyond the force of the waves and browse along, chewing the algae off sand grains; they may actually gnaw the sand into finer particles. The sand dollars you find will probably have lost their purple or greenish color and be bleached white. After they've dried out, break one gently and release the tiny dried objects inside, each scarcely larger than a grain of rice. Then decide: Do these small pieces look like doves of peace or angels?

Don't turn up your nose at fishing lures. They can be beautiful (and sometimes reusable), and you may find old wooden lures from Japan. As for fishing floats, right after a storm you should find cork or plastic floats, sometimes enmeshed in a net. The most prized are glass floats that may have drifted over from Japan or Russia. They are occasionally found on isolated beaches immediately after a vigorous spring storm, often in March. However, since the advent of plastic, about the only place you'll find glass floats soon will be in a souvenir shop; many of them have never been dunked in any ocean but were made to sell.

Bottles etched and frosted by sand and sea may not be valuable to knowledgeable collectors, but they are still finds. If they are turning an iridescent purple, they are antique bottles. Other things that may prove a bottle's age are mold marks that don't come to the top, indicating that the lip was added later; on spirits bottles, a lack of the embossed warning, "Federal Law Forbids Resale"; and pontil marks, the roundish marks left on the bottom of a bottle by the iron or steel rods used for fashioning hot glass.

Beware! Bottle collecting can become addictive. Some avid collectors pore over old maps and pick the brains of old-timers to discover dumps or sawmill sites where they might find bottles under debris or brush. The Santa Cruz Mountains are full of old lumbering sites. Some dedicated bottle buffs dig at the sites of old privies on the theory that someone's great-grandfather may have tossed empty whisky bottles in the privy rather than have great-grandmother catch him with the forbidden evidence.

nishings and has gone the bed and breakfast route. The restaurant serves lunch and dinner—emphasizing Creole cuisine—and Sunday champagne brunch.

If you prefer Mexican food and modern art on the walls, try Manuel's (408/688-4848), 261 Center Street, at the entrance to Seacliff State Park. The Cookbook Restaurant (408/688-2800) at 207 Searidge Road is open from 7 A.M. to 9 P.M. every day for breakfast, lunch, and dinner; seniors get a discount. If you decide to linger on in this beautiful, wooded town, here are two bed and breakfast inns to consider: Apple Lane Inn (408/475-6868), in a secluded 1870s Victorian farmhouse offers cider and breakfast in the parlor and a dart game in the old cider room. It's at 6265 Soquel Drive. You can enjoy British hospitality at Mangels House (408/688-7982) on four acres of lawn, orchard, and woodland on Aptos Creek Road, nearby 10,000 of redwood park and trails.

The **Forest of Nisene Marks State Park**—a huge, almost 10,000-acre semiwilderness—is directly north of Aptos Village Park on the Aptos Creek Road. The hard-to-find road is across the railroad tracks opposite a gas station by a grapestake fence. Bear right through stone pillars and drive in about one and three-quarter miles to the official entrance. A gift from Herman Marks and his brother and sister, the forest was named in honor of their mother, Nisene, who hiked here into her late nineties. The park is intended to remain largely undeveloped, a place of refuge and solitude for hikers in an essentially primitive redwood landscape. Over thirty miles of trails have been opened up. Some are in cool redwoods by wandering creeks that have uncovered ancient fossils. Some go up to the dry, warm hillsides where you may find sweeping views. Other trails approach an old mill site, pass by abandoned loggers' cabins and trestles, and lead onto old railroad beds. Walking all these trails should take about twenty-three hours. You can't do it all at once because the forest is open only from 6 A.M. until sundown, except for a primitive trail camp that has to be reserved ahead (408/335-5858). If you come in to hike or picnic, bring water or other appropriate liquids and enjoy a forest so quiet that the whisper of a falling leaf seems loud. For more information, contact headquarters of the Forest of Nisene Marks State Park, P. O. Box P-1, Felton, CA 95018.

Aptos has the distinction of harboring 400 of the last of the earth's **long-toed salamanders.** The main swampy breeding ground of these remnants of the Ice Age was threatened when the highway depart-

ment announced plans to widen the freeway between the Rio del Mar and Rob Roy interchanges. Workmen dug a ditch to start draining the swamp, stranding the salamanders in the middle of the right-of-way. When protests mounted, the highway people hurriedly dug an extension to the ditch (actually a swamp) and planted cattails and other thick weeds in the muck so that the last of the long-toed salamanders can continue to exist. They are also protected on their annual trek to nearby mating grounds. Some of the people who buy houses in this area may not be aware that there are salamander easements across their property.

Aptos is also the site of the World's Shortest Parade, put on by the Aptos Ladies' Tuesday Evening Society and usually scheduled for the July Fourth weekend. Starting at 11 A.M. at the huge Rancho Del Mar Shopping Center, which many local people now consider the center of Aptos, the parade straggles down Soquel Drive into Aptos Village Park. Often antique car drivers take part in the parade. Other thrills include booths, and games like sack races, shoe kicking, and watermelon eating.

Just off Highway 1 at the Rio del Mar turnoff is the smaller Deerpark Shopping Center, a tasteful collection of stucco shops and firms surrounded by landscaping and fountains. The developer who started this center first queried local people as to what shops they would like. He also promised to keep the old orchard and barn, which is now used for local events. The traditional but distinctive Deer Park Tavern (408/688-5800) is in this area; here you can get lunch on weekdays, dinner every day, and breakfast on Sunday.

Seacliff State Beach Park, off Highway 1 at Aptos and five and a half miles south of Santa Cruz, is so popular it's often hard to find a parking place. Twenty-six lucky trailers and campers can be accommodated right on the sand, if winter storms haven't interfered. The eighty-five-acre park also has one night "en route" campsites for over 100 self-contained vehicles, but it's first come, first served. Seacliff Beach is nearly two miles long and is usually gloriously sunny. If you don't sunbathe or swim, you can watch pelicans dive for fish, and there are pleasant hiking trails. As at New Brighton Beach, you can often find ancient sea fossils in the cliff behind the beach. For information on reservations, call (408) 688-3222 or 688-3241.

Another reason Seacliff is so popular is the wheelchair accessible pier that juts out to the huge old concrete ship *Palo Alto*. It's great for fishing; many

Local residents banded together to repair the much-loved pier leading to the old concrete ship at Seacliff State Park.

regulars, some on old-age pensions, fish for their dinners here. Remember, you need no fishing license when you try your luck off a public pier and, since there are nearby restrooms and a snack bar here, you can stay a long time. The cement-hulled ship was started in 1918, but World War I ended before she took to the seas. She was towed to Seacliff, sunk, and turned into an amusement pier and dance floor, but the enterprise folded two years later. From then on, many generations have visited the old stripped-down hull. However, storms almost destroyed the pier, and it was considered unsafe to walk on. The neighboring inhabitants became impatient that nothing was being done to repair this landmark. Spurred on by long-time resident Rose Costa, citizens banded together and donated cement, supplies, work, and services. As a result they and thousands of visitors can once again enjoy this much-loved pier.

The town and beach of **Rio del Mar,** as its name indicates, is where Aptos Creek runs into the bay. Here, as at Seacliff, hunting for driftwood is usually productive after winter storms. This is a free beach, but parking is limited. Amenities include restrooms, hotdog stands, and miles of soft sand for walking.

Manresa Beach State Park (408/688-3241 or 724-1266), the next public beach south, has restrooms and an outdoor shower. Stairways lead down to the beach near the main parking lot at the north end and also off Sand Dollar Drive. If you're a born optimist, try digging for Pismo clams here from September through April. At the tiny town of **La Selva** — don't blink your eyes, or you'll miss it — there's a free bikini-sized beach.

Both the Manresa and La Selva beaches are off the **San Andreas Road,** which continues south to the Sunset Beach turnoff. For a change of pace, why not take this fairly fast route instead of Highway 1? It's real country, with trees and undulating hills to the north and flatter land when you get close to Watsonville. The big KOA campground (408/722-0551) is at 1186 San Andreas Road.

Sunset Beach State Park is more than ten miles south of Seacliff. Watch for the turnoff on Highway 1 or, as suggested, take the San Andreas Road. This 218-acre park has ninety overnight camping sites, but no hookups, and it's generally foggier than Seacliff. Surf fishing, however, is usually good, and you might find a Pismo clam or two if you dig here. Since the beachfront is three and a half miles long, you should find a semisecluded spot. The day-use and camping areas on a high bluff behind the beach are surrounded by meadows where poppies and lupines put on a colorful show in early spring.

Before you leave Sunset State Beach, take a look at one of the most beautiful beaches along this stretch. It's **Palm Beach,** reached between two sections of the fancy **Pajaro Dunes** complex of homes and condominiums. (To rent one of these for a super deluxe family vacation call (408) 722-9201.) Take Beach Street to the parking area when you run out of road. You'll find picnic facilities under groves of trees, a par course for physical fitness, restrooms, and that spectacular dune-dotted beach which is also a good place to find sand dollars. As you stand on a rise watching children romping in the surf, you'll see Sunset Beach to the north and Zmudowski Beach to the south.

At the lengthy **Zmudowski Beach State Park,** about where the Pajaro River reaches the sea, you can try shore fishing along the river. Hiking is good, too, but no camping is allowed.

Take Beach Street inland and you're in an entirely different world: **Watsonville,** in the heart of the fertile Pajaro Valley, calls itself the "Strawberry Capital of the World" and "Apple City of the West." It's easy to believe the latter in the spring when miles of orchards, some planted over 100 years ago, burst into blossoms. More than eighty factories pack and process $100 million worth of produce.

You can get in on this largess for surprisingly low prices at many fresh produce stands and farms. To get a free "Country Crossroads" map showing locations where produce is picked each day, or where you can pick it yourself, write to Santa Cruz County Farm Bureau, 600 Main Street, Suite 2, Watsonville, CA 95076, and enclose a stamped, self-addressed envelope. Or visit the nearby Watsonville Chamber of Commerce (408/724-3849) at 444 Main.

If you've come from Gilroy over Hecker Pass (Highway 152) and have had the willpower to pass

The elegant Tuttle Mansion on East Lake Drive in Watsonville features beautiful hardwood floors and panels and is open to the public.

up the many small wineries with tasting rooms en route or the world's largest garlic farm, once you're down off the summit you're close to several farms that welcome the public. Probably the most famous place to pick your own produce is the Gizdich's Ranch (408/722-1056) at the corner of Lakeview and Carlton Road, about three-fourths of a mile south from Highway 152. You'll find other farms and stands along Freedom Boulevard and many outlying areas. Even at stands closer to town, the produce is usually fresher and the prices lower than where you came from.

Besides fruit, vegetables, and nursery crops, Watsonville has produced dozens of proud old structures dating from the mid-nineteenth century; many have been restored to their former glory. A "Walking and Driving Tour Map of Historic Watsonville" is available from the Watsonville Chamber of Commerce (408/724-3849), 444 Main Street. Maps are also carried at the tiny Pajaro Valley Historical Association, 226 East Beach Street, which is housed in a historic structure; it's open only briefly, usually on Saturday afternoon. Even without a map you can see many beautiful Victorian-style homes northeast from the plaza along East Beach Street. Another mostly older group is strung along East Lake Avenue, which parallels East Beach. The stunning Tuttle Mansion at 723 East Lake Avenue, built in 1899, now contains commercial offices. The rather plain Ford's Department Store at Main and West Beach, founded in 1852, is the oldest operating department store in California.

The relatively flat area around Watsonville is popular with bicyclists. A few minutes' drive from Watsonville on Green Valley Road is small **Pinto Lake** (408/722-8129), surrounded by greenery. You can fish, swim, water ski, boat, and picnic or barbecue. The lake and park are owned by the city but rented to a concessionaire who charges a modest fee for day use and overnight for self-contained RVs, which can park on the lake shore.

The big annual event in Watsonville is the **Antique Fly-In.** On one Saturday and Sunday near the end of May thousands flock to the Watsonville airport to see the antique and experimental airplanes and to watch demonstrations and stunt flying. For more information, phone (408) 724-3849.

Where to eat? Downtown on Main there's everything from a hotdog stand to elegant dining in the prize-winning restored interior of the circa 1871 Mansion House Restaurant (408/724-2495). The Edo Restaurant, 946 Main, has reasonable Japanese or American lunches weekdays and dinners every day except Tuesday. For Mexican food, many locals swear by the Rancho Grande (408/722-1606), at 1934 Freedom Boulevard, a short distance from downtown. The portions are big and the prices small.

Many roads lead out of Watsonville into Monterey County. Number 129 connects with Highway 1 soonest. Or you can continue on G–12 to the old Salinas Road turnoff, which leads into Highway 1. If you have time and an adventurous spirit, turn off at the back country Elkhorn Road that wanders through hill and dale to Castroville. Turn toward the ocean onto Dolan Road or you will miss one of the most delightful villages along the coast—**Moss Landing.** Of course, you probably will stay on Highway 1 all along, which funnels you into Moss Landing anyway.

Fog or sunshine, fishing is popular off the sandy beaches near Moss Landing.

10

Moss Landing, Elkhorn Slough, and Castroville

~~~~~~~~~~~~~~~~~~~~~~~~~

Going south on Highway 1 after you leave Santa Cruz and all the tempting signs directing you to state beaches—soon after the Watsonville turnoff—you see, looming up ahead, the smokestacks and façade of pipes of the huge Pacific Gas and Electric (PG&E) steam-generating plant at **Moss Landing,** population 500. Some proud citizens say that when the plant is lit with a myriad of lights it resembles a battleship; a few fishermen insist that the lights and hum of activity keep them company at night. The next big plant is the Kaiser Refractory Plant, which makes fire bricks.

If you're bound for uncrowded and undeveloped **Zmudowski State Beach,** turn right at Struve Road to Giberson Road and follow it to a parking place. Don't go clear to the end or you may be trapped in sand. You can also join the pelicans and other creatures fishing, including man, on **Moss Landing State Beach,** also known as Jetty Beach. It's almost hidden behind sand dunes; turn right on the signed access road before those two giant PG&E stacks. Fishing is often exciting here, especially surf casting for perch, rockfish, and flounder; there's a jetty if you prefer that type of angling.

Before you arrive in town you can't help seeing Little Baja, which sells a staggering variety of colorful Mexican imports, especially terra-cotta pottery for gardens.

The town of Moss Landing was established about 1864 by Capt. Charles Moss. At one time it was part of Monterey but was auctioned off for nonpayment of taxes. Soon it became a busy harbor for schooners loading produce from the Salinas Valley. At times wagons from Salinas Valley farms were lined up five miles waiting to unload. It was also a whaling station that advertised its presence for miles around when the wind was right (or wrong). As many as five whales a week were towed in until around 1930 when the Board of Health declared whaling a public menace.

Now Moss Landing's T-shaped harbor is filled with pleasure craft, and dozens of fishing boats chug out early each morning in search of salmon, tuna, albacore, and other big fish. Besides all these boats on the water, half-finished boats, boats being repaired, and derelicts are parked, like motor homes, in some streets and yards.

Moss Landing boasts a **Chamber of Commerce** (408/633-5202), located at 345 Moss Landing Road in the tiny Buy-a-Button Co., which specializes in political and other message buttons. One that can be used over and over reads: "Throw the rascal out." Another reads, "Fishermen don't die. They just smell that way"; another, "I'm not deaf. I'm just ignoring you." Clustered nearby and toward the bay are dozens of enterprises, including antique shops, a book shop, fresh produce markets, and ongoing flea markets. As expected, several carry nautical items. One shop, Yesterday's Books, is self-explanatory. It's nearby a huge building, cluttered inside like an attic and with many finds rusting away outside. Right on Highway 1 at the south end of Moss Landing is another string of antique and art emporiums, along with produce stands and one advertising fish.

During the flea market that takes place the last Sunday in July, as many as 300 antique vendors and flea-market entrepreneurs bring their wares. This annual event attracts thousands of visitors, many of whom start arriving before dawn. So come early or you may have to park miles away. Besides vendors of collectibles, there are usually stands selling pancakes, hot dogs, beer, and French-fried artichokes.

Another annual event that draws crowds is the open house at the **Moss Landing Marine Lab,** usually on the first weekend after Easter. The lab is to your left just after you cross the small, one-lane bridge to "the island," which is home to hundreds of boats. During the open house, visitors can tour the newly modernized facilities. There's a "touch tank" arranged so that children can feel anemones, starfish, sea cucumbers, sponges, snails, and other small marine life. Students also put on slide shows and movies and act out stories about marine life in and by the sea.

Because of its location, the marine lab, run by a consortium of six state colleges and universities, can carry on valuable shallow- to deepwater studies. The head of the Monterey Submarine Canyon is a few hundred meters away, making thousand-meter depths available within an hour's steaming time on the lab's seventy-nine-foot boat, the *Cayuse*. Just a few hundred yards away, researchers can also study the geology, tides, and marine life in the shallows of Elkhorn Slough. Some students are presently conducting a mussel watch; these bivalves are a valuable index of pollution, especially by heavy metals like mercury. Most students are enthusiastic about their work, but there are drawbacks. After studying and smelling them for a long time, a few have given up eating fish.

If previously you've just zipped through Moss Landing, you might have thought that, except for the PG&E and Kaiser plants, there was little industry. This is not true, for the island hums with activity, what with its marine industries and fishing boats that unload, and refrigerated trucks that thunder over that one-lane bridge to load up for their trips to the canneries. The fishing industry provides the area with close to $13 million in annual income and employs nearly 1,500 people, many second- and third-generation fishermen. A store on the island, usually open at 10 A.M., sells some of that just-caught fish over the counter.

The person who keeps a finger on the pulse of all this marine action is Lillian Woodward, who has lived in Moss Landing since 1950, helping run a boat brokerage and launching dock. White-haired, tanned, and energetic, Mrs. Woodward likes to sit on an outside bench to keep track of the comings and goings so that she can write it all up for her weekly column in the *Monterey Peninsula Herald*. A collection of her observations, along with ink drawings of the area, is now out in book form. People are constantly stopping to chat with Lillian. It's a friendly, sleepy town, although what will happen when the sewage problem, which has curtailed building, is solved is anyone's guess.

Another big *if* concerns **Elkhorn Slough,** the state's first federal and the country's ninth estuarine sanctuary. Up to and including early 1985, if you entered Moss Landing from the north, you crossed a decrepit low-slung bridge over Elkhorn Slough. Although there was concern that too many motorboats might enter the slough and disturb its fragile ecology, this bridge is being replaced with a higher one, farther inland. Most people hardly glance at the marshy brown inlet surrounded by mud under the bridge. But scientists and others who like nature, wildlife, and fishing have realized that these 2,500 acres of tidal flats, submerged marine areas, and salt marsh (the second largest salt marsh in California) are necessary habitats. And Elkhorn Slough represents only a remnant of California's disappearing wetlands.

What's so valuable about a muddy, sometimes smelly estuarine slough? Estuaries are sometimes called the "cradle of marine life." The mixture of

As cows graze against a hillside at Elkhorn Slough, hundreds of shore birds rest on the mudflats.

diluted seawater with its minerals and waterborne humus, decay, and topsoil doesn't sound delicious, but it creates a rich broth that is nutritious to protozoa which are eaten by plankton which are eaten by young fish and so on up the scale to shrimp, oysters, flounder, lobsters, and humans. Ecologists have found that many of these natural areas provide more food per acre than the best midwestern farmland. Probably more than two-thirds of the fish caught and eaten by Americans today depend on these estuaries; fifty varieties of fish are found in this slough.

Elkhorn Slough is particularly unique because it's close to the deep Monterey Canyon, which provides it with a constant source of upswelling nutrients. Because of this and because Elkhorn Slough is relatively undamaged, many colleges and universities find the area invaluable for study.

Besides its ability to educate and to produce food, the slough has many intangible gifts. Here you can glimpse the primeval chain of life that also accounts for our beginnings. Then there is the environment, which can be beautiful in any weather, even when muted by fog or mist. To fully savor a marsh or estuary you need patience, for the enchantment grows on you slowly, almost imperceptibly. You won't see waves crashing against sand or stone.

Pelicans — Ungainly Diving Wonders of the Seashore

Pelicans may look ungainly, with their big pouched bills, but you'll change your mind when you see their thrilling dive after fish.

Of all the sea birds you'll see along the Central Coast, chances are you'll find the **brown pelican** the most fascinating. This large, web-footed bird may look like a lumpy bulldozer, but when you see a pelican dive, you can't help but catch your breath.

Often you'll see a streamer of pelicans twenty-five to fifty feet above the water, soaring or flapping their wings (they have a six-to-ten-foot wing span). Suddenly one peels off and plunges in a thrilling dive, its wings half folded, its long beak pointed at a hapless fish. A pelican has protective air sacs on its chest, enabling it to crash into the water with a staggering impact. After it gulps the fish and a sizable amount of water, it bobs up, facing windward for takeoff. You may see a lone pelican or a squadron soaring just a few feet above the water. That, too, is thrilling.

For many years, because of the high percentage of DDT in their fish diet, brown pelicans' eggs were so thin-shelled that scarcely any hatched. When DDT was banned, the pelicans recovered, and you now can enjoy these ungainly yet graceful birds. Occasionally you'll see white pelicans along the coast. Instead of diving, like their brown cousins, they hunt in unison, driving the fish into a pocket so they can dine.

Wherever you see pelicans you usually see gulls eager to snatch the fish from the big bird's pouch. They rarely succeed, but it's an interesting show anyway, and you can see it all while you're combing the coast.

Instead, you may see a procession of clouds or a lone white egret reflected in the still, dark water or birds, perched like blossoms, on distant eucalyptus or cypress trees. Because of the earth tones and the dark edging of willows, in early spring sunshine the hills glow with greens, the wildflowers seem brighter, and the old dairy buildings shine a brilliant white. Pickleweed, the most abundant marsh plant, also lends its share of beauty, with its pale green changing to coral and then to crimson red as the seasons progress.

In its present relative isolation (somewhat a question mark because of that new bridge), you can savor peace and quiet and watch an amazing variety of wildlife. Where else can you see thousands of shore birds feeding together at low tide or half a dozen great blue herons on a bank, silhouetted against the sun? This slough is also a vital link in the coastal flyway. Not only do migratory birds feed and rest here six to eight months a year, but many are permanent residents, including the shy, endangered California clapper rail. Almost 100 water-associated birds have been spotted here, including the once-endangered brown pelicans, who fly out in formations early in the morning. Add these to the forty-one species of land birds, including the golden eagle, and you have a bird-watcher's paradise.

Small harbor seals often bask on the mudflats, and four-legged wildlife use the estuary, too. You might glimpse black-tailed deer, muskrats, and the more exotic bobcat and gray fox. Sometimes you can get close to the wildlife because they seem to sense that this area is presently protected and that they won't be harmed.

But there's still that big *if*. So far the Fish and Game Department, which has been given responsibility for the wetlands portion of the slough, has acquired only 1,250 acres, including "fingers" of the slough, with 544 more acres of marshland recently added for a wildlife refuge. Industrialist David Packard purchased the 600-acre Rubis Ranch on the north shore to help protect the slough and wildlife. This property is south of some 500 acres owned by the Nature Conservancy, a national organization that helps save endangered natural areas through private action. If you're interested in nature study or bird-watching, you are welcome to their preserve, which you can reach by a trail on the eastern side of the slough beginning at **Kirby Park,** with its small boat launching area, inland about four miles off Elkhorn Road. Write the Nature Conservancy, 156 Second Street, San Francisco, CA 94105 or phone (415)

777-0541 to obtain maps and information.

Eventually, perhaps, more of the public will be able to enjoy this marine cradle of life, one of the last surviving on the West Coast. Then, from the shore or on walkways where the wildlife won't be disturbed, you and your children will learn why this sanctuary is important, not only for wildlife but also for man.

Since it is difficult to enjoy the entire slough at present, what brings most people to Moss Landing again and again? Most come to try their luck at catching seafood at the end of a fishing line or shovel or net or spear. Or they may bring along a two-man jump net to try surf netting for smelt on the wide sandy beaches on each side of the harbor entrance, usually from 9 P.M. to midnight during spring or summer. Off the jetty they're fishing for jacksmelt, surf perch, and other shore fish or they're catching crabs. Besides striped bass, halibut, and other delectables, many try for shark, which are in such plentiful supply that shark derbies are held every June. Rock fishing is not good, since the ocean shoreline in these parts is delightfully sandy; nevertheless some optimists try it off the rocky jetty.

At very minus tides (more than an hour earlier than at San Francisco's Golden Gate), clam diggers can be seen braving the chill of dawn. The big Pismo clams that used to be plentiful on the ocean side of the harbor are almost gone. You can still find gaper (horseneck) clams or Washington clams in the harbor areas and slough. A warning, though: The area along Elkhorn Slough has been posted as unsafe for clam digging, mainly because of septic tank and chemical fertilizer runoffs. So just dig clams for bait here. If and when the sewer line from Moss Landing to Castroville is connected, you can again go after these slough clams for your table.

Moss Landing is a popular gathering place for birders. Occasionally in the midst of flea market furor, a small covey can be seen peering at the action on the mudflats. Many families come just to enjoy the beaches: Zmudowski, as mentioned, to the north, and **Salinas River State Beach** to the south. Both have primitive restrooms plus plenty of sand and brilliant blue and white surf cascading in. This is good kite-flying country—it's often breezy. A small kite stand opens up along Highway 1 during peak tourist periods. This is near W.A.R. Enterprises, which sells military collectibles and surplus.

If you're hungry and in a hurry, a scattering of small stands and restaurants sells hamburgers, fish and chips, and Mexican food. If you have time for a

Artichokes — The Thistle with a Heart

Castroville calls itself the artichoke center of the world, but you'll see this delicious thistle growing along much of the coast.

Don't let the prickly looks of the divine green globe artichoke put you off. Italians and other converts insist that this member of the thistle family is nutritious, full of vitamins, and delicious. Besides, green globes are grown commercially in the United States in only four counties: San Mateo, Santa Cruz, Monterey, and Santa Barbara. While combing the coast, you'll be in or near one or more.

So you're sure to meet some on a menu — perhaps french fried or in soup. If you're new to California, don't be ashamed if you don't know how to eat a choke if it's just sitting, naked, on a plate. Usually you tear off a leaf, dip the large end in mayonnaise or hot butter, and strip off the tender green portions with your teeth. Under the fuzzy choke, which you throw away, is the even more tender heart.

There are many exotic recipes, but the simplest way to prepare artichokes is to pull off the lower outer leaves, cut the stems to one inch, and snap off the tips of the remaining leaves. Stand the artichokes up in a pot in three inches of water and add one-quarter of a teaspoon of regular or garlic salt for each artichoke. Some cooks top each artichoke with olive oil or butter and lemon juice. Cover and boil the chokes gently for thirty-five minutes or until a fork pierces the base easily. Many growers prefer to eat the tiny artichokes which are usually less expensive and more convenient; they can be cut in two and added to stews, for instance, without the preparation the larger chokes require.

sit-down meal, many locals eat at Skippers (408/ 633-4453), just north of Elkhorn Slough. Nearby, Harbor Inn (408/724-9371) features seafood with an Italian accent—calamari for example. The restaurant overlooks the water, so you can view the boating and fishing. Some evenings there's live entertainment and dancing inside.

Soon after you leave Moss Landing, Highway 1 passes by the edge of **Castroville,** population around 9,500. If you turn off and drive through town, you can't miss the big sign that overhangs the main street proudly proclaiming "Castroville—The Artichoke Center of the World." No matter what season, there's usually a companion sign advertising the **Artichoke Festival** that takes place the first weekend in September.

Castroville, the second oldest town in Monterey County, was started by Don Juan Bautista Castro, a scion of the prominent Castro family. In 1915 when Castro died, almost penniless (he's buried in the small cemetery here that he donated to Castroville),

the town had dwindled from a population of more than 1,000 people, with eleven saloons to service them, to a few hundred. Before the Southern Pacific Railroad switched its main line to Salinas and Highway 1 was enlarged and rerouted to bypass Castroville, whether you wanted to be or not, you often found yourself in Castroville.

Yet the town survives, due to that edible fleshy thistle, the artichoke. Castroville may be the artichoke center but it's not the tourist capital of the world; however, you can visit the Giant Artichoke Wine and Cheese Room, 11221 Merrit. If you're very hungry, look on Main Street for Bing's Diner, which sprouted from an old railroad car decades ago. It's usually surrounded by cars and trucks whose occupants are inside in the early-frontier ambience eating the hearty breakfasts or barbecued viands.

After you leave Castroville you're soon swept onto the new, improved, and widened Highway 1 freeway heading toward the world-famous Monterey Peninsula.

One of the many spectacular golf courses that overlook Monterey Bay in the Pebble Beach area.

Monterey Peninsula Tips

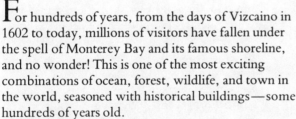

For hundreds of years, from the days of Vizcaino in 1602 to today, millions of visitors have fallen under the spell of Monterey Bay and its famous shoreline, and no wonder! This is one of the most exciting combinations of ocean, forest, wildlife, and town in the world, seasoned with historical buildings—some hundreds of years old.

Robert Louis Stevenson, who visited in 1879, describes Monterey Bay as a bent fishing hook with Santa Cruz at the shank, the mouth of the Salinas River at the middle, and Monterey cozily ensconced beside the barb. In "The Old Pacific Capital" from *Across the Plains,* he continues:

> The ancient capital of California faces across the bay, while the Pacific Ocean, though hidden by low hills and forests, bombards her left flank and rear with never-dying surf. ... Waves which lap quietly about the jetties of Monterey grow louder and larger in the

distance... and from all around, even in quiet weather, the low, distant, thrilling roar of the Pacific hangs over the coast and the adjacent country like smoke after a battle.

Around this bay you can see and hear the ocean in *all* its moods, not only as it hurls waves at rocky cliffs but as it laps quietly on sun-drenched beaches. Here you, too, can photograph cypress trees bleached and sculptured by wind, sand, and spray. Close by, you can often hear the wet, deep barking of seal lions and can watch a sea otter turning somersaults in the water.

Soon after Highway 1 turns seaward it crosses the **Salinas River,** which Gaspar de Portola and his men followed to the ocean when they were attempting to rediscover Monterey Bay. The river you see is wide, but there's an underground Salinas River also. From headwaters in the mountains above San Luis Obispo, this upside-down river flows through the warm, inland lettuce-growing country to its mouth in cooler artichoke country.

You are now officially on the **Monterey Peninsula,** but before you reach its famous quartet— Carmel, Monterey, Pacific Grove, and Pebble Beach —you pass a series of cities and hamlets less well known. Both Marina and Seaside call themselves "The Gateway to the Monterey Peninsula," but you cross Marina's boundary first driving south on Highway 1.

Marina is popular with the hang-glider set, whose headquarters is at Kitty Hawk Kites (408/384-2622) at the end of Reservation Road; their motto is, "Learn to fly on the soft sands of Marina Beach." In late April there's an annual hang-gliding steeplechase to watch or join, but on almost every day you'll see these colorful gliders circling and swooping over the soft dunes.

After the 1906 earthquake and fire, sand from these dunes helped rebuild San Francisco. In 1915 William Paddon acquired 1,500 acres of this sandy desolation. It took years of promotion before he sold a handful of parcels. After an equally long struggle, the few Monterey cypresses that he planted survived. Now the town is crammed with housing, shopping clusters, and mobile home parks.

About 200 acres at the end of Reservation Road are presently in the **Marina State Beach,** for day use only. Bring sunglasses; the sometimes daily fog off the ocean near Carmel and Pacific Grove rolls in here last. Another bonus—there are restrooms and a small parking area and if it's too windy you can stay in your car to watch the surf and the hang-gliding activity. But you'll be missing a lot if you don't get out and explore the sand dunes. In the spring they explode with wildflowers, but all year they are beautiful in their subdued way.

Monterey Peninsula sand dunes are not the barren, arid dunes of the desert. Here, because of fog and winter rains, shrubs, plants, and wildflowers keep the dunes anchored through brisk offshore winds— if the dunes are left undisturbed. However, these fragile plants expend most of their energy just to keep alive in the inhospitable terrain, so don't add to their struggle. Walk between them or look from afar at the golden California poppies, the yellow seaside painted cups, the morning glories, the yellow or pink sand verbenas—all against a background of silver-green sagewort. You may see some exquisite plants and flowers, so rare they're endangered. Look, don't pick!

Going south you next pass **Fort Ord,** a 28,500-acre infantry training center. If you see red flags flying to your right and hear a pop-pop-pop, it's probably not your engine but soldiers lined up shooting at targets. Fort Ord, named after a famous Indian fighter and Civil War officer, was the training and staging area for up to 50,000 men during World War II. Now about 20,000 are stationed here. When you include the thousands of civilian employees, you'll understand why motels are usually full and low-priced housing is almost nonexistent in neighboring towns.

If you're arriving on a bike (or horse) you can use the wide paved trail alongside Highway 1. It starts in Marina, continues to Fort Ord's main gate—where you can view Monterey Bay—and then proceeds south to the edge of Seaside, the next town south, which also calls itself the gateway to the Monterey Peninsula.

Seaside was founded by Dr. John L. D. Roberts. Soon after graduating from medical school, he arrived here with one dollar. He purchased 150 acres from his uncle (with that dollar?) and started the Seaside Post Office where he and his wife acted as postmaster. Dr. Roberts became famous, especially along the Big Sur; day or night he would travel any distance to take care of his patients.

A map-brochure handed out at the modern city hall, 440 Harcourt off Canyon del Rey Boulevard, is honest about Seaside's later history. It confesses:

> During the Depression years of the 1930s, Seaside lots were of little value. (You could buy a lot for as little as $1 then and some lots were given away free to entice people to subscribe to a San Francisco newspaper.) The general area known as "Seaside" was a scattered collection of shacks and open spaces. Lots were unstaked, streets unpaved. Then came World War II. What was worthless began to pick up value. Fort Ord was established and thousands of soldiers and workers descended on the area. Helter skelter, substandard construction was the order of the day, without plans, codes or ordinances. The already blighted area with its narrow lots became frowsy and unkempt. It took courage to incorporate the place in 1954.

The write-up admits that Seaside is striving to become the retail center of the Monterey Peninsula and adds: "Seaside sprang from nowhere, which gives us an immense advantage over our contemporaries as we pursue the future." A big start is the huge, brightly lit Monterey Peninsula Auto Center where it's almost a pleasure to buy a new car as you wander from dealer to dealer on pedestrian malls. Seaside may be a good place to gas up, too; at last reports prices at some pumps, especially along Del Monte Boulevard, were among the peninsula's lowest.

Where else but Seaside would you find a bit of Japan, the tranquil Monterey Peninsula Buddhist Temple at 1155 Noche Buena? You can wander about the complex with its Asian-style gardens and carp-filled ponds any day, but try to time your visit for May, when the temple sponsors a bonsai show. Call (408) 394-0119 for information.

Back to Highway 1, the huge hotel to your right between the highway and the ocean, the Monterey Holiday Inn, is also in Seaside. Whether it's like Waikiki or Miami Beach West, as some contend, this is a change from the way the beach was when the town was founded. The public, after a hard fight, is now allowed access to the shoreline fronting the hotel.

Sand City, a hamlet on each side of Highway 1, next south, is aptly named. It, too, is asking permission to build a wall of hotels.

If you're in the mood for quiet and sunshine, punctuated by the krekk-krekk of frogs, turn inland on the Canyon del Rey Road through Del Rey Oaks. On your right, at the bottom of the canyon, is the Work Memorial Park, with picnic tables, tennis courts, and a golf driving range. Continue on to the seventeen-acre **Frog Pond Natural Area,** geared for naturalists and birders. The hard-to-find entrance is an opening in the willows near the Del Rey Oaks City Hall. You might park and get directions first at city hall. The pond here is actually a seasonal fresh-water marsh, but if you have patience and binoculars you may see the rare Pacifica tree frog, only an inch long. You're sure to see and hear other frogs, toads, and many birds.

After you step out from between the willow trees and drive back toward Highway 1, you're almost painfully aware of the noises of civilization, although you may have already heard airplanes taking off or landing at the Monterey Peninsula Airport nearby.

The two small lakes to your left just before the onramp to Highway 1 are fed by the stream in the canyon you've just left. It's usually a surprise to note the number of birds bobbing about so calmly in the midst of all this convoluted concrete freeway, especially since crowds of miniature-boat buffs often run their craft here.

Once you're back on Highway 1, if you don't watch it and take the turnoff to Monterey, you'll be swept past to Carmel. Many people prefer turning off on the slower-paced Del Monte Avenue.

This road passes the entrance to **Del Monte Beach,** one of the least touristed portions of sandy surf and sun along the bay. There are no facilities, however, and suburbia crowds close. To get to this beach, turn right at a traffic light and drive over the railroad tracks and around and up a sandy hill. The late lamented Del Monte Special train once chuffed its glamorous way into Monterey along these tracks. (Some local citizens are trying to resurrect the railroad, but since most of the tracks were torn up, it probably won't happen.)

Del Monte Avenue also passes the U.S. Naval Postgraduate School, the only naval institution of its kind in the world, where many hundreds of American and allied officers study for undergraduate and advanced degrees. Part of the school is housed in the former **Del Monte Hotel,** once called the "Queen of American Watering Holes." It was established in 1880 by Charles Crocker in a pine forest, with 126 acres of landscaped gardens, a race course, and a pool. Inside, thousands of gaslights and mirrors everywhere reflected its glories. When the turreted and pinnacled Victorian Gothic resort opened, it attracted Vanderbilts, Carnegies, President William McKinley, and hundreds more famous elite, many of whom came in their own Pullman cars.

The huge wooden hotel burned in 1914; only its two wings were saved. Even when it was rebuilt with fewer turrets, the hotel inspired a writer for the W.P.A. Guide to the Monterey Peninsula to say: "Without a rival in the world, they say, its magnificence unequalled even by the fashionable spas of the French and Italian Rivieras, the Del Monte resort engirdles the neck of the Monterey Peninsula with an array of luxurious facilities which invited the elite of international society."

In 1948 it was sold to the U.S. Navy. Although you can't go into the buildings, you can see the outside and the beautiful grounds of the school daily from 8 A.M. to 4:30 P.M.

Del Monte Avenue also passes charming **El Estero Park,** with its tiny lake where you can feed ducks or rent boats to paddle or sail. There is also a par course for physical fitness buffs. The popular and

The Del Monte Hotel, built circa 1880 but burned down in 1914, was called the "Queen of American Watering Holes."

free Dennis the Menace Play Area is across the lake. Go over the bridge at Pearl Street to the parking lot, skirting the San Carlos Catholic Cemetery, where many old Montereños are buried. The play area is closed on Monday and open other days from 10 A.M. to 5 P.M., but scores of children crawl over the fence at other times to enjoy the unusual play equipment that cartoonist Hank Ketcham helped design. Among free-form activities, youngsters can run over a swinging bridge, clamber over a real Southern Pacific Railroad switch engine, wallow in sand, and drink out of a fountain shaped like a lion.

Close by El Estero Park, between Camino el Estero and Webster, is the **Tourist Information Center** (408/372-7568) where you can load up on information, brochures, and maps, including an easy-to-read map you'll need to cope with Monterey's tangled streets. If you need it, pick up the listing of over 100 places to stay; the staff might even help you reserve a motel room. The center, in the Armed Services YMCA, is open every day except December 25 and January 1 between 10 A.M. and 5 P.M. or later. The main Monterey Peninsula Chamber of Commerce is now in an old restored adobe in downtown Monterey at 380 Alvarado. They're open 9 A.M. to 5 P.M. weekdays only, but parking downtown is

sometimes difficult. You can phone them at (408) 649-1770 or write to P. O. Box 1770, Monterey, CA 93942. The **California State Automobile Association** (408/373-3021) is at 53 Soledad. Drive into a cul-de-sac behind a small shopping center across Munras from the big Del Monte Shopping Center; turn off Munras at Soledad. At these and other tourist facilities and also at most motels you'll find the **Monterey Peninsula Review,** a valuable guide to events and attractions, and it's free.

If you have any questions about public transportation, call **Monterey Peninsula Transit** any day from 8 A.M. to 8 P.M. at (408) 899-2555 or 424-7695. Buses cover most peninsula points of interest, but some run rarely. You'll find maps showing local transportation in front of the yellow pages in the Monterey telephone book.

Before you get settled, you might like a capsule look at the various types of recreation the Monterey Peninsula offers.

Golf? Avid golfers can tee off on over sixteen courses, including Carmel Valley and Laguna Seca. Eight are open to the public. Two recognize reciprocal agreements with other country clubs. Many courses are equipped with deer, most have ocean views, and on Cypress Point's 16th hole, the drive to reach the green must carry 277 yards over an inlet of the ocean.

Tennis anyone? Buffs can play at over seventy-four courts on the peninsula — some harboring celebrities like Clint Eastwood — plus two dozen courts on the area's military reservations.

Spectator sports? Every year the area produces at least five sports car races, ten horse shows, seven yacht races, plus polo matches and rugby tournaments. Check the events schedule in this book for the big ones, or the *Monterey Peninsula Review* for the complete list.

Bicyclists are welcome along any public street on the Monterey Peninsula provided they obey regular traffic rules. Joselyn's (408/649-8520), 638 Lighthouse, or Freewheeling Cycles (408/373-3855), 188 Webster Street, are just two Monterey firms that rent bikes where you can also obtain information on the Velo Club Monterey that schedules group rides.

Cyclists can pedal close to postcard-caliber shorelines along the ocean in Pacific Grove and Carmel if they don't mind occasionally sharing the road with slow-moving cars full of tourists. At the Pacific Grove entrance to the Seventeen-Mile Drive, from 8 A.M. to 11 A.M. weekdays, except during major holidays and sporting events, cyclists on their bikes are admitted free after they sign a release absolving Del Monte Properties of all liability. Many cyclists use this scenic route to get from Pacific Grove to Carmel.

The Ventana Chapter of the **Sierra Club**, P. O. Box 5667, Carmel, CA 93921 (408/624-8032) occasionally schedules group bike rides, although they specialize more in hikes. You can buy local trail guides at their small office, staffed by volunteers, above a shoe store on Ocean Avenue near Dolores in Carmel. It's open Tuesday through Saturday from 12:30 P.M. to 4:30 P.M.

As for hikes, the area is replete with **hiking and jogging** trails, many relatively unknown. In busy Monterey, for instance, on Munras Avenue across from wall-to-wall motels with cars whizzing by is an oasis of green called Dan Danvee Park. A hiking-biking trail sprinkled with picnic tables stretches from the end of Abrego to the entrance of the huge Del Monte Shopping Center. So you can get in your exercise by just crossing over from your motel if it's on Munras. You can continue on to the edge of Carmel or, in the other direction, hike along the Don Danvee Canyon Road clear to El Estero Lake and then south to the Fisherman's Wharf area.

To join runners of all ages for a one-mile or longer run on a Sunday morning, get to Lovers Point in Pacific Grove before 8 A.M. Better contact the sponsoring Peninsula YMCA at (408) 373-4166 to be sure they're running on the Sunday you're there.

If you like to hike while breathing sea-fresh air, stick to the many roads, walks, and trails by the bay and ocean. You'll be joining many locals who treat daily walks as almost religious rituals. Eventually the Monterey Peninsula Regional Park District hopes to have an improved recreational trail from downtown Monterey to Asilomar in Pacific Grove and on to Pebble Beach, mainly along the old Southern Pacific Railroad right-of-way. The Pacific Grove section is ready now, but the other areas are still in a state of flux.

If you're willing to pay the admission fee to the Seventeen-Mile Drive, you have a choice of five well-marked trails from three and a half to nine miles. One trail loops through the S. F. B. Morse Botanical Reserve; others lead through forests or to vista points. The Shore Course Trail may be the most beautiful of all, for you're right at the edge of the sea.

Many other hiking trails are described in the following Monterey Peninsula chapters. The trails through the thousands of acres of the Jack's Peak, Toro, and Garland Regional Parks are described in the Salinas chapter. Many hikers consider surf-fringed **Point Lobos State Reserve** the most rewarding, for each path leads to a cove or vista point that has been memorialized by famous photographers, artists, or writers. This exciting area is described on pages 144–151.

As for **fishing,** besides surf fishing, you can fish off the Monterey piers for the little ones or take party boats out for the big ones. You'll find party boats listed in the previous chapter.

Horseback riding? If you'd rather ride a four-footed animal than a bucking boat, you can hire a horse from the Pebble Beach Equestrian Center (by reservation only: 408/624-2756) at Portola Road in Pebble Beach. You must be able to ride English saddle to enjoy the many miles of bridle trails in the Del Monte Forest. You can rent horses or take lessons (Western tack) at the Jack's Peak Stables, 550 Aquajito Road, Monterey, but phone ahead to (408) 375-4232. Off Highway 68, inside the park, is the Toro Regional Park Stables (408/484-9932), open 10 A.M. to dusk.

Skin diving and scuba diving are popular near the Coast Guard Dock in Monterey and from Carmel Beach south. There's also a skindiving practice area at Lovers Point Beach in Pacific Grove. In Monterey you can obtain lessons and equipment at Aquarius (408/375-1933), 2240 Del Monte Avenue, or at Bamboo Reef (408/372-1685), 614 Lighthouse Avenue.

For the most esoteric active sports, the adventurous can rent equipment and take lessons in **wind surfing** at Dilworth's Windsurfing (408/375-1111), 1021 Olmstead, Pacific Grove. **Hang gliding?** "You don't have to be super-macho and twenty years old to learn," promises Kitty Hawk Kites (408/384-2622), at the end of Reservation Road in Marina.

Even if none of these sports appeals to you, there's still plenty to do after you've snapped pictures of the crashing surf and twisted cypresses, the tiny black bobbing dots that you swear are sea otters, and the historic adobes and Victorian homes. That free weekly *Monterey Peninsula Review* lists many other activities, including ballroom dancing, bowling, bridge, chess, fencing, folk dancing, ice skating, polo, racquetball, square dancing, and roller skating.

If your hobby is **wine tasting** you can head for the **Monterey Peninsula Winery** (408/372-4949) about ten minutes away near the airport turnoff on Highway 68. Here in the stone tasting room you can admire the cobwebs and sample wine, from vintage Riesling to jug Big Sur Red.

As for more mundane activities, you'll probably find essentials from clothes to groceries to glasses to pharmacy items in the oak studded **Del Monte Center** on Munras, just off Highway 1. Saks Fifth Avenue and Macy's are among the dozens of shops and restaurants in this big, attractive shopping mall.

Where to stay? Rather than checking along Monterey's motel row on Munras, contact the Carmel **Information Center** (408/624-1711) during weekdays. They'll try to get you accommodations, and the service is free. You can pick up maps and local books of interest at their office on Mission and Ocean Avenue in Carmel.

If you arrive at an odd hour and haven't reserved, on rare occasions Pacific Grove motels may have a late vacancy. Try for modestly priced accommodations at the **Asilomar State Conference Grounds** in Pacific Grove (408/372-8016); read about it on page 134. There's a Motel Six (408/373-3500) at 2124 Fremont in Monterey, but a lot of other people are trying to get a room there, too, so keep your options open.

As for **camping,** if you're desperate, Veterans Memorial Park (408/646-3865), on a hill overlooking Monterey Bay and open all year, may have vacant campsites; it's $8 for RVs and only $1 if you arrive on bike or foot. Obtain a permit to stay from the ranger

These skin divers are preparing to view the exotic undersea life that can be found in Monterey Peninsula waters.

here. Enter off Skyline Drive, Johnson Street, or Via del Rey. A larger, and probably sunnier, campground run by Monterey County Parks (call toll free 800/822-CAMP) is in the Laguna Seca Recreation Area on Highway 68 between Salinas and Monterey. Many other campgrounds that allow tents are along the Big Sur; see pages 153–173.

Seventeen-Mile Drive Village (408/373-2721), at Sinex Avenue and Seventeen-Mile Drive in Pacific Grove, may have a few vacant hook-up sites for RVs, but no tents, please. This is a beautiful location, within walking distance of many tourist highlights. The Marina Dunes RV Park (408/384-6914) is in another prime area at 3330 Dunes Drive, Marina. There are thirty-three full hookups for RVs and ten to fifteen sites for tents. Inland in sunny Carmel Valley you have a choice of two campgrounds, both on Schulte Road. Saddle Mountain Resort (408/624-1617) has spaces for campers or small RVs and tents. The Riverside RV Park (408/624-9329) by the Carmel River has TV connections but does not allow tents.

Are you visiting the peninsula for a special occasion? A honeymoon would qualify; or perhaps you don't like to stint. In that case, why not try one of the **country inns** that have become so popular? In Monterey you can stay in a two-story adobe built in 1830—the Merritt House (408/646-9686), 386 Pacific Street. Or how about the gracious Old Monterey Inn (408/375-8284) at 500 Martin Street near the waterfront? Carmel has several choices, including the Spanish-style Cypress Inn (408/624-3871) with its courtyard garden at Lincoln and Seventh. It's in the hub of Carmel. So is the Normandy Inn (408/624-3825) on Ocean Avenue and Monte Verde and the Western-style Vagabond's House (408/624-7738) at Fourth and Dolores.

Pacific Grove has a plentitude of old-fashioned bed and breakfast inns with a country air. One of the first, Green Gables Inn (408/375-2095) at Fifth Street and Ocean View Boulevard, right on the bay, was built by a judge as a summer home in 1887 and 1888. This unusual Gothic-style building faces in three directions on three levels. The House of Seven Gables Inn (408/372-4341) at 555 Ocean View Boulevard has niceties like private bathrooms and promises an ocean view from each room. The Centrella Hotel (408/372-3372), 612 Central Avenue, is in another olden-days building that begs to be photographed. So is the big yellow Queen Anne–style house at 643 Lighthouse, built in 1886–1887 by J. F. Gosby, a shoemaker. Since his home was always overflowing with guests, Gosby kept adding more rooms. Eventually it became the fourteen-room Gosby House Inn (408/375-1287), a charming place to stay. More country inns and bed and breakfast establishments are arriving, including some along the "new" Can-nery Row, so you'll really have a choice if you can get reservations.

Where to eat? The *Monterey Peninsula Review* lists over 250 restaurants on the Monterey Peninsula or within easy driving distance. It would take almost five years to sample every one. If you prefer French cuisine, you have seventeen choices, and twenty-six for European, some with a French accent. Fast food? You can buy hamburgers or whatever at over fifty places. Like Mexican food? You've a lot to choose from. Oriental—twenty-seven, plus one Filipino restaurant. Pizza lovers have a dozen choices; there's one true vegetarian listing plus several that lean that way; and seafood is stressed in two dozen restaurants. You'll find a sampling of restaurants in the chapters on each location.

You can buy an inexpensive hamburger at one of the most scenic spots on the Monterey Peninsula, the outside stand overlooking the cove at Lovers Point in Pacific Grove. However, if you're short of cash, you don't have to exist on hamburgers. Many restaurants—including some of the fanciest—have modestly priced dinners if you get there before 6 or 6:30 P.M. Check when you call them.

A huge pillar at the Monterey Presidio honors John Sloat, who captured Monterey for the United States in 1846 without firing a shot.

12

Enjoying Monterey Peninsula History

~~~~~~~~~~~~~~~~~~~~~~~~~~~~~~~~

The Monterey Peninsula has a lot of history going for it; you can relive the past by visiting many buildings and sites where it all took place. However, little remains of the era before the Indians were corralled into missions. The Pacific Grove Museum and Pacific House in Monterey have artifacts. In shallow caves at the Carmel River headwaters the persistent may find Indian pictographs on stones; no one knows for sure whether they are mystic symbols, travel routes, hex marks, or doodles. At the Carmel River's mouth, searchers have found beads and other Indian relics. At the presidio in Monterey you can see the ceremonial rain rock the Rumsen Indians used. A large archaeological find containing burial sites, artifacts, and many abalone shells left by pre-Ohlone Indian people was hurriedly excavated before being paved over as a parking lot for the Aquarium and other Cannery Row tourist establishments. That's about it. As with the Esselen who lived at the Big

Sur, many pages of Indian history have been erased by the white settlers' arrival.

According to anthropologist Alfred Kroeber, Indians may have existed undisturbed on this land for up to 5,000 years. In those days dense forests of redwoods, oak, and bay covered hills and canyons, and the water level was high. At the mouths of rivers, including the Carmel and Salinas, and also of lesser creeks and streams, huge estuaries and marshes spread out, thick with cordgrass, pickleweed, and tules. This supported an incredibly rich wildlife. Besides herds of elk, antelope, and deer; flocks of geese, ducks, and other sea birds rose, when frightened, in a "dense cloud with a noise like that of a hurricane," according to a visiting French sea captain. This was in addition to an abundance of fish and shellfish.

The lifestyle of the Indians during the Spanish-Mexican period, is well documented through diaries and travelers' reports. Yet the end came fast, since these native Americans were the first to be felled by broken spirits and imported diseases. Only a handful of coast Indians survive.

The epoch of the white settlers in Monterey started one stormy day in 1542, just fifty years after Columbus discovered the New World, when Juan Rodriguez Cabrillo, a Portuguese sailing for Spain, glimpsed this "bay of pines" with its gleaming sand edged with foam.

The bay was calm on December 17, 1602, when Sebastian Vizcaino, who sailed up from Mexico, came ashore with his crew to erect a cross and celebrate a thanksgiving mass under a great oak close to the mouth of a small stream. Vizcaino was impressed by this noble harbor with its mild temperature, fertile soil, and inhabitants whom he found "soft, gentle, docile and very fit to be reduced to the Holy Church." He named the land Monterey after the then Viceroy of Mexico.

In 1769 Spain became worried that another great power might move in. Franciscan friar Junipero Serra and Capt. Gaspar de Portola were sent out from Mexico City to found a settlement on the shores of Monterey Bay. Portola was one of the few visitors who did not find the Monterey Peninsula delightful. After exploring the bay for a week, he and his men decided this couldn't be the harbor described by Vizcaino. So they continued north and, as described in the Coastside section of this book, discovered San Francisco Bay.

The second time around, in June 1770, Captain Portola and Father Serra did find the site on Monterey Bay where Vizcaino had landed. Here, near the same mighty oak tree, Serra set up a cross and the royal standard of Spain. As was the custom, the men threw stones and pulled up grass to take possession of this new land. They then established a presidio and a mission. Later in 1770, to take advantage of more fertile soil and to create more distance between the presidio soldiers and the neophyte Indian girls, Serra moved the mission to Carmel.

In 1775 the first colonists arrived from Mexico, led by Col. Juan Bautista de Anza. As the century came to a close, four groups lived somewhat uneasily together in this mild land. The rancheros, who resided on huge land grants and occupied themselves with rodeos, gambling, and fiestas, considered themselves the aristocrats. As expected, the mission fathers frowned on these frivolous goings-on. Their regime was stern, their converts virtual prisoners. Female converts were kept busy embroidering or making

pots and handicrafts, some of which were sold to visiting ships. Indian males were taught trades or became hersdmen and butchers, and the hides and tallow they produced were sold to visiting ships. The townspeople, a mixed group, regarded the mission's prosperity with envy. So did the eighty or so soldiers stationed at the presidio, who had to get by on paltry pay, if any.

The beginning of the nineteenth century was known as the Golden Age. You don't have to be a history buff to get a thrill out of visiting some of the wonderfully preserved old adobes and reliving a period that now seems so romantic. You can start at the edge of El Estero Park since you have probably stopped by the Tourist Information Center (408/ 372-7568) on Camino el Estero at Webster by the YMCA. The first French consulate, originally built about 1830, was moved to El Estero Park in 1931 and is now headquarters for the Girl Scouts. It's private, but you can look at its outside, anyway.

While you're at the Tourist Information Center or Chamber of Commerce, pick up a street map. Street signs are considered unsightly on this peninsula and downtown Monterey is a tangle of streets, some of which change names every few blocks. As important is the "Path of History" map that lists dozens of landmarks in this cradle of California history. If you're driving, a somewhat faded red line in the center of streets follows most of this path. Another must is the "Downtown Guide Map of Walking Tours in Historic Old Monterey." The historic sites are grouped into seven walking tours that take about one hour each; walking is the way to really savor this historic and beautiful area.

The **Royal Presidio Chapel,** also known as the San Carlos Cathedral, is close by at 555 Church Street in a quiet cul-de-sac overhanging busy Fremont Street. Church Street curves in toward the north almost immediately after Camino el Estero ends at Fremont. (This sounds more complicated than it is.) Although it lacks the grace and magnificence of Mission San Carlos Borromeo del Rio Carmelo (the Carmel mission), this small L-shaped chapel is older. Junipero Serra founded it as Mission San Carlos in 1770. It burned to the ground, was rebuilt, and has been in continuous use since. Above the façade is the Virgin of Guadalupe, patron saint of Mexico, carved in chalk rock. The inside walls are decorated in the style of Mexican-Indian folk art. The walk was once formed by whalebone, but ladies caught their heels on the edges, so it was removed. Still remaining is a statue of Our Lady of Lourdes guarding a spring.

Behind the church is a portion of the stump of the mammoth oak tree under which Vizcaino held mass in 1602 and Serra services in 1770. More about the unfortunate saga of the oak later.

The marshy area close to where Camino el Estero ends at Fremont used to be known as Washerwoman's Gulch. Here Indian and Mexican women exchanged gossip as they washed clothes and linens in the clear water. Walter Colton, writing in 1847, called it the "washtub mail."

Many historically significant buildings are included in the **Monterey State Historical Park** (408/649-2836), with headquarters at 210 Olivier Street. You can pay one modest admission price that will cover all buildings visited that day. To avoid frayed nerves park in one of the public parking lots and walk the few blocks. The highlight of this tour will be the adobes, probably looking better today than they did when they were built. As Richard Henry Dana noted in 1834 in his book *Two Years Before the Mast*:

> The houses here, as everywhere else in California, are of one story, built of adobes, that is, clay made into large bricks . . . and hardened in the sun. These are joined together by a cement of the same material, and the whole are of a common dirt colour. The floors are generally of earth, the windows grated and without glass; and the doors, which are seldom shut, open directly into the common room, there being no entries. Some of the more wealthy inhabitants have glass to their windows, and board floors; and in Monterey nearly all the houses are whitewashed on the outside. The better houses, too, have red tiles upon the roofs.

Many adobes were built crosswise to the points of the compass, with the patio facing south to catch the winter sun and the veranda north to take advantage of the cool summer winds. The living room, dining room, kitchen, storerooms, veranda, and perhaps a ballroom were on the first floor. Bedrooms on the second floor were entered from outside stairways that led to a balcony. This meant that the inhabitants didn't track mud through the main rooms. It also meant that the adventurous and romantically inclined could come and go inconspicuously. This happy arrangement was later changed, however, and the stairways were enclosed in the house.

Almost all homes had adobe-walled fences, many draped with bougainvillea and enclosing gardens which are pockets of fragrant tranquility today. The Spanish padres imported olives and figs from the Mediterranean to Monterey's similar climate, and other immigrants brought plants from their native lands. Later, Victorian immigrants planted varieties from around the world. As a result, the gardens today are a colorful combination of roses, fuchsias, and other non-native plants blended with occasional native plants. You'll often find wooden or ornate iron benches in some secluded spot, a good place to sit down and imagine yourself back in the romantic era of the Spanish dons.

Larkin House at 510 Calle Principal is one of the first and finest examples of old Monterey architecture. It was built in the 1830s of wood and adobe for Thomas Larkin, California's only American consul. The house, which combines a bit of Spain, New England, and the deep American south, was widely copied by admiring neighbors. It's open daily except Tuesday, but since it's furnished with priceless antiques and furnishings, you must take a tour. On heavy visitor days, tours start at 10 and 11 A.M. and at 1, 2, 3, and 4 P.M. (5 P.M. in the summer) for the first sixteen who sign up. If you miss the tour you can still peek in the windows, rest in the small enclosed garden, and also see the headquarters of Lt. (later Gen.) William Tecumseh Sherman.

Casa Gutierrez, at 580 and 590 Calle Principal, was a typical early Monterey family home. Now it's the Sancho Panza Mexican Restaurant and Coffee House (408/375-0095), a pleasant place to pause, either inside the historic building or outside in the garden patio. Do stop, at least for a beer.

Colton Hall is across Pacific Avenue, looking out across deep lawns and gardens; you'll recognize it by its impressive pillars. It's open 10 A.M. to noon and 1 P.M. to 5 P.M. Tuesday through Sunday. A small museum commemorates some of the events that took place here after it was built, starting in 1847, of local white stone. The first public school in Monterey was on the first floor and the town hall on the second; four dozen delegates from around California met on the top floor in 1849 to write the constitution for this new state.

The old Monterey jail, built in 1854, is next door. Nearby, also on the Pacific Avenue civic center grounds is Friendly Plaza. In 1930 local artists drew up plans for this one-acre square plaza, designing it around an old walnut tree.

Before you leave this area of historic sites, look in at the **Monterey Peninsula Museum of Art** (408/372-7591) at 559 Pacific. It has excellent changing exhibits and is free to the public. The post office and library are close by, too. Also nearby is the Clock Garden Restaurant (408/375-6100) at 564 Abrego Street, where many local professionals eat lunch. If it's a sunny day, you'll probably join them in the patio garden. The restaurant also serves breakfast and dinner.

A few short blocks away is the wonderful **Stevenson House** at 530 Houston. Don't miss it! In 1879 Robert Louis Stevenson followed his American love, Fanny Osbourne, to Monterey and stayed in this home, then a boardinghouse. Three years later Fanny and he were married. Stevenson often wrote in his sunny room here; you can see the small portable desk at which he is said to have written *Treasure Island*. On tours at 10 and 11 A.M. and 2, 3, and 4 P.M. daily, you can see the large collection of Stevensonia, including illustrations of his stories and furnishings and effects of the period. These include a delightful children's room with antique toys and children's clothes.

Ghosts? A previous caretaker reported that after dark she often felt the presence of her beloved Stevenson. Others have reported seeing his shadowy presence and also the ghost of the wife of Jules Simoneau, the owner when Stevenson resided there. The present caretaker and park people reject the idea of having a ghost on their hands.

Casa Abrego, at Webster and Abrego, is now a private women's club. It was started in 1834 by wealthy Don José Abrego and built of adobe and timbers from the shipwrecked five-masted schooner, *Natalie,* after she broke apart on a rocky Monterey beach that year. Abrego was the proud owner of the first full-length mirror and one of the first three pianos to come around the Horn. It is said that Abrego's sixteen-year-old daughter, who had never seen her reflection, commented unknowingly to her husband as she walked down the stairs and saw herself in the mirror: "Who is that lovely girl?"

Probably the best known of the adobes clustered near Fisherman's Wharf is the old **Custom House,** now surrounded by acres of asphalt and concrete urban renewal. The Custom House, started in 1827, is California's oldest government building and has flown the flags of Spain, Mexico, and the United States. Comm. John D. Sloat raised the American flag here in 1846. From 10 A.M. to noon and 1 P.M. to 5 P.M. daily you can see items typical of those that passed through the Custom House before San Francisco became the more important port.

The **Pacific House,** nearby, a two-story adobe with long balconies and a wall that encloses a mem-

ory garden, was a hotel for seafarers. It had its own inside well and was the site of bear and bull fights. It's tamer now, with a museum of early Monterey days on the first floor and an extensive collection of Indian and Eskimo handicrafts and artifacts on the second floor. It's open 9 A.M. to noon and 1 P.M. to 5 P.M. daily.

At **Casa del Oro,** on the corner of Scott and Olivier streets, every day from 10 A.M. to 5 P.M. visitors can look at merchandise from early days when the building was a general store. It may have received its name, which means "house of gold," from reports that returning miners stored gold here—fine gold in condor quills, heavier gold in bags. Another valuable site, a restroom, is just next door.

Continue on Olivier Street and turn left for Monterey's first brick house, worked on by Gallant Dickenson in the mid-1800s. Dickenson built a kiln to fire his own bricks, but before he finished his two-story house, he left for the gold fields. The home and 60,000 bricks were sold at a sheriff's sale in 1851 for $1,091.

The old **Whaling Station** next door was a boardinghouse for Portuguese whalers in the 1850s. A profitable but odoriferous operation was conducted on the nearby beach, where the whales were cut and the oil rendered. A reminder of this era is the whalebone walk in front of the Whaling Station and a chair of whalebone inside. The Junior League has leased the building and has been busy renovating it and furnishing it with artifacts of its era. The whaling station is open only briefly Friday afternoons or by reservation. The garden, enclosed by a chalk rock wall, is open every day. Enter the gate at the left of the house and enjoy a moment of peace away from exhaust fumes and concrete.

California's First Theater, at Scott and Pacific, now doubles as **Jack Swan's Tavern,** where you can enjoy light meals, beer, and wine from 11 A.M. to 10 P.M. (closing earlier when the vintage melodramas are presented). Originally built as a boardinghouse and saloon for sailors, in 1847 Jack Swan, the sailorowner, loaned it to bored soldiers to put on plays. Curtains were run up out of blankets, candles and whale oil lamps became footlights, and the wood benches were rough, yet receipts at $5 a ticket totaled $500 the first night. Also visit the theater's charming walled garden in back.

Within the same general area is **Casa Soberanes,** built in 1830, at 336 Pacific, two blocks south of California's First Theater and almost in the shadow

A reminder of the whaling era of the 1850s is this chair made from whalebone, which can be seen at the old Whaling Station in Monterey.

of the 344-room Sheraton Hotel. This adobe, recently lived in, has furnishings from each era of its ownership, and a portion of the original adobe wall is open to view. Tours are from 10 A.M. to 5 P.M. during summer, but you can peek in at the grounds any time to admire the neat flower plots, some circled by century-old sunken glass bottles.

Not all historic buildings in Monterey are adobe. Walk up Scott Street to see three built of wood. At the corner of Scott and Van Buren is a charming Victorian house built in 1860 by Manuel Perry, a whaling boat captain. A restaurant since 1960, Perry House (408/372-7455) advertises comfortable candle-lit dining overlooking Monterey Bay.

The small New England–style **Doud House,** near the end of Van Buren, now contains antique and gift shops. Francis Doud, who was sergeant-at-arms at the Constitutional Convention in 1849, supplied his own homemade kitchen table for the signing of the California constitution. Doud prospered through the years and in the 1860s was able to build this home on a hill so he could enjoy a view from every room.

Next door is the oldest Protestant church built in Monterey, the former St. James Episcopal Church and now a library of Californiana. The tiny building, which once stood in the way of urban renewal, was rescued by the Monterey History and Art Association and moved to this location.

Close by, on the 402-acre **Monterey Presidio,** more than a dozen interesting historic sites are clustered around the tiny U.S. Army Museum off Corporal Ewing Road. As a bonus, you'll have a sweeping vista of Monterey Harbor, probably the best panorama around. (Unfortunately views of the bay are becoming rarer as more and more tourist attractions are erected.) Artillery Drive leads into the presidio off Lighthouse Avenue. Street widening and urban renewal have made the approach difficult, as the portion of Lighthouse Avenue that connects it is a one-way street leading south toward downtown Monterey. You have to continue north and make a U-turn, then cling to the right going south or you may be catapulted through the Lighthouse Avenue tunnel into downtown Monterey.

This mass of concrete and traffic also makes it difficult to visit one of California's most important historic sites, where Vizcaino landed in 1602 and Serra in 1770 and where they each celebrated mass under a great oak tree. A fenced-in granite cross bears a medallion of Serra and a relief of the Carmel mission, his final resting place. A few feet away is a smaller monument to Serra's traveling companion, Gaspar de Portola. The monuments have been moved three times to escape renewal bulldozers, and new developments may have pushed them somewhere else by the time you arrive.

The famous old oak tree where centuries of visitors sought shade is long gone; the controversy about it is still alive. Was the tree chopped down by a utility company in 1905? Or was it axed in 1906? The latter version contends that when the present stone cross honoring Serra was erected, the workmen took their orders too literally. In order to place the monument on the exact location of the oak, they cut down the tree. Both versions have the perturbed chaplain sending fishermen to bring the oak back from where it had drifted twelve miles out to sea. Both versions have the chaplain placing the oak's remains behind the Royal Presidio Chapel, where you can see it today. Soon after the tree's demise, Hattie Sargent Gregg planted a seedling that grew from an acorn dropped by the historic tree. That tree—now huge—stands in the front yard of her home, the Stokes Adobe on Hartnell Street, and it, too, is on its way to becoming venerable.

There are many more points of interest on the presidio, which is one of the oldest military posts in the United States. The **U.S. Army Museum,** formerly a tack house, is open Thursday through Monday 9:30 A.M. to 12:30 P.M. and 1:30 P.M. to 4 P.M. Military buffs will enjoy its army memorabilia, and a librarian will answer questions. Pick up a folder here describing a nearby "Walk Through History." This takes you to the long-gone site of Fort Mervine, with its toy-size cannons pointing toward the bay. The huge pillar, topped by an asthmatic eagle, was erected in honor of Commodore Sloat, who captured Monterey for the United States in 1846 without firing a shot.

Many remains of a 2,000-year-old Rumsen Indian village were destroyed when Lighthouse Avenue was widened and the tunnel bored. About all that's left is the ceremonial rain stone, bedrock mortar used to grind oak flour, and an ancient burial ground marked by a tall wooden cross. The smaller wooden cross nearby commemorates Father Serra's burial mass for Alexo Nino, the only casualty of the march north. At that time Nino, a black freeman, was the only non-Indian buried in Monterey. Close by, a granite Father Serra stands on a granite boat, gazing at the magnificent harbor below.

Also on the presidio grounds is the world's largest language training school, the Defense Language Institute. Instructors usually teach in their native tongue, and students are often required to use the language they're learning during their working, eating, and leisure hours.

Down below you'll see Cannery Row stretched along the bay, and Fisherman's Wharf surrounded by boats. They, too, had their moments of history, but that's another story.

13

Fisherman's Wharf, Cannery Row, and Other Tourist Lures

"Funky and enjoyable" or "too touristy"—opinions differ about Monterey's **Fisherman's Wharf.** Certainly it is picturesque: the hundreds of boats bobbing at anchor, some with rusting sides; the crying gulls and terns wheeling overhead. The brown pelicans not only fly by in formation but the bolder ones have moved in to battle the sea lions for fish handouts from tourists. To say nothing about the shops and fish markets, each painted a different color, and everything reflected in the water.

The original Fisherman's Wharf was built of stone in 1846 by military deserters, convicts, and Indians who became enmeshed in the white man's tentacles. Then it was used mainly by trading schooners to unload cargo from around the Horn. Eight years later whaling vessels took over. That gave way to a commercial fishing wharf run mainly by Italian-Americans for unloading daily catches of salmon, albacore, mackerel, rock cod, and sardines.

Since the commercial fishing fleet moved over to the Municipal Wharf, multicolored enterprises have lined up on the now wooden pier. Besides around ten restaurants—some contend the pier should be called "Trencherman's Wharf"—there's a bookstore; art gallery; restrooms near the end; and a Wharf Theater that helped train many a famous actor, including Richard Boone. Yes, there are gift shops galore. The first, the Harbor House at 1 Fisherman's Wharf (the one with the make-believe lighthouse), carries a typical mix of souvenirs and nautical knickknacks which are sold, according to a sign, by "meek and timid" salespeople.

Many visitors, especially families with children, like to stroll along the crowded wharf past the trucks that continue to come and go. They buy seashells and postcards, treat themselves to crab or shrimp or octopus walkaway cocktails, and buy fish to toss to those barking sea lions that swim right up to the

Fishing boats, marine hoists, and storage sheds testify to the authenticity of Monterey's popular Fisherman's Wharf.

wharf to beg. If it's a sunny weekend or summer day, the crowds pause at the entrance to watch the nattily dressed monkey with his organ grinder. On days like this it is touristy, but you can avoid much of the crush by arriving before 10 A.M. or during the off-season. No matter how mobbed, you can usually find a place to eat lunch or dinner and sample the sand dabs, cod, calamari, crab, jumbo prawns, or the prized salmon in season. Prices are similar along the wharf, so you might try for the restaurant with the best view. Rappa's, at the end, fills the bill with a panoramic view from every table; most restaurants have tables with adequate views.

Several firms on the wharf offer deep-sea fishing on party boats; take your pick of Randy's, Monterey Sport Fishing, Sam's, and Chris's, to name a few. You have to be an early riser to connect with the fishing trips; most leave the dock at 7:30 A.M. Some outfits offer frequent short sightseeing trips that chug around the marina and along Cannery Row. You don't have to get up so early to take them.

You can walk or drive out on to the neighboring **Municipal Wharf** to pier fish or watch and smell the day's commercial catch being processed. The

number of pilfering sea gulls and begging sea lions is an indication of the size of the catch. You can rent a sailboat or a yacht on this wharf (sorry, no skiffs), dine, or quaff cocktails at restaurants that overlook the water. You can also sunbathe and swim at the small municipal beach near the pier's entrance.

After Fisherman's Wharf and Carmel, the locale that attracts the most tourists per square foot is **Cannery Row,** especially after dark. Follow Lighthouse Avenue away from downtown Monterey, and you're speeded through a tunnel that surfaces beyond the presidio entrance and the Vizcaino-Portola memorial site. Stay in the right lane, watch for the Cannery Row sign, and turn right. You'll be at the Coast Guard buildings and dock.

If you like to scuba dive or watch sea lions, otters, and pelicans close up, drive on to the big parking lot (with restrooms). Walk to the end of the pier, keeping an eye out for big, colorful jellyfish that look like parachutes. You'll hear and see dozens of barking sea lions draped on rocks or swimming or all tangled up together in rafts, except during July when they're off breeding. Pelicans now share the rocks with the noisy mammals, so close to where you can stand that you should get amusing photographs. You'll probably also spot playful sea otters; one old scarred male has taken to the area to your right just as you start out on the dock.

If your goal is Cannery Row, turn left at the Coast Guard buildings and continue on, always hugging the water. This was once a continuation of Ocean View Avenue, but John Steinbeck changed all that when his lusty book, *Cannery Row,* came out in 1944, followed by *Sweet Thursday.* Steinbeck, who later won a Nobel prize, was not too popular when he was writing about the Row and his ribald pals. Now a theater is named after him; the Chamber of Commerce quotes him; and a bronze bust of him, near Prescott, greets visitors with this quote from his famous book:

> Cannery Row in Monterey in California is a poem, a stink, a grating noise, a quality of light, a tone, a habit, a nostalgia, a dream. Cannery Row is the gathered and scattered, tin and iron and rust and splintered wood, chipped pavement and weedy lots and junk heaps, sardine canneries of corrugated iron, honky tonks, restaurants and whorehouses, and little crowded groceries and flophouses.

At this writing, you can still see weedy lots and chipped concrete at the beginning of the Row, but the sardine canneries that actually can are almost gone. In the summer of 1981 the mackerel catch was so bountiful that the lone cannery was unable to handle it all. One young fisherman complained about the ever-present smell. "Don't complain," an old-timer told him. "When the sardines were running we used to call it the sweet smell of prosperity."

Those years when the Row was going (and smelling) strong, thirty canneries and plants handled the sardines. When the whistles for each plant blew, the women, wearing rubber boots and aprons, hurried down the hill to the waterfront, chattering in Italian. According to one report, the record catch was processed in 1941–42: one quarter of a million tons. Just before Steinbeck made Cannery Row famous, the sardines vanished. They probably were overfished or left for a warmer clime—no one knows for sure. "Doc" Ricketts, Steinbeck's crony, contended the sardines all disappeared into cans.

The new, ever-changing Cannery Row swings with boutiques, a theater, art galleries, antique emporiums, and a long row of restaurants. There's now Cannery Row Square complex and, at the far north end, the American Tin Cannery with shops and whatnot, including Sewers of Paris, Inc. Antiques, more boutiques, shops, and restaurants. The bulldozers and cement mixers are still busy. The 291-room Monterey Plaza Hotel will cover an eight-block area on or near Cannery Row, ranging from 82- to 400-unit hotels, garages, a Victorian-style hotel, a Scuba Inn with scuba facilities (perhaps), another plaza with more restaurants, and more.

Perhaps it's just as well the late Steinbeck can't visit his beloved Row. In *Travels with Charlie,* published in 1962, he noted: "The canneries which once put up a sickening stench are gone, their places filled with restaurants, antique shops, and the like. They fish for tourists now."

What's left of Steinbeck's Cannery Row? Flora's Bar, not the original, near the Warehouse, is self-consciously nostalgic, with stained-glass saloon doors; a red velvet, early-whorehouse decor; and Flora, the former heart-of-gold madam of the Bear Flag, staring voluptuously from the ceiling. Except for the prices, Kalisa's Cosmopolitan Gourmet Place, once known as the La Ida Cafe, still retains that old Row atmosphere of the days when you could buy dago red for thirty cents and a cheap blended whiskey known as "old tennis shoes." The Wing Chong Market, next door, known in the book as Lee Chong's Store, is now the General Store. Instead of edibles and bottled goods for the former sardine workers, loafers, soldiers, and dedicated drunks, it now sells collectibles to tourists.

In 1984 "Doc" Ricketts' old biological lab at 800 Cannery Row was still the original building, brown and dusty, with frayed curtains at the windows, looking a bit forlorn amid all the antique emporiums. For twenty years before he died in 1948 when his car was struck by an express train at a railroad crossing, Edward F. ("Doc") Ricketts collected sponges, anemones, barnacles, and octopi, and entertained droppers-in at 800 Cannery Row. The memory of this man who loved women, tipped his hat to dogs, and bandaged the wounds of derelicts lives on—both in Steinbeck's eternally popular books and in commercial establishments that have borrowed his name. The reason his old lab has not been improved or renewed or turned into a high-rise concrete hotel is that it was bought by twenty men—artists, writers, and businessmen—who use it as a private club to get together to talk and drink. "Doc" would probably approve.

A must for small children on Cannery Row is Hossenfelder's Gay Nineties Carousel at Prescott. Nostalgic music pulses out as the merry-go-round, the fastest in the West, revolves. The carousel, built around 1905, has thirty-four handcarved horses, two handcarved zebras, two handcarved chariots, and 940 lights. A restaurant adjoins (try the milkshakes), and space-age electronic games await your coins.

Awaiting your folding money are the many shops and malls that have taken over the abandoned and burned-down canneries (there have been twenty-one major fires in twenty-eight years). At the Pearls of the Forest, 408 Cannery Row, you can watch young men making furniture out of redwood burls and tree roots. A historical Wax Museum at 700 Cannery Row shows figures and vignettes from 1550 to the Steinbeck period. It's open from 11 A.M. to 11 P.M.

The big attraction along Cannery Row is the huge, recently opened **Monterey Bay Aquarium** (408/375-3333) at the far end, near "Doc's" old lab. Exhibits include a kelp forest with marine life; a slice of Monterey Bay showing ocean fish, sharks, rays, flatfish, and jellyfish; a walk-in aviary; and exhibits of shorelines and sand dunes. To keep the fish and marine life happy, water is pumped into the tanks at a rate of 2,000 gallons per minute. Even before it was finished, the indoor/outdoor tidal basin attracted an otter who seemed to prefer resting here among the artificial rocks to outside in the bay. The aquarium, one of the world's largest, is expected to attract half a million visitors a year, and will be self-supporting. In addition to the many exhibits, including replicas of whales and other sea mammals, there's a giftshop and bookstore, restaurant, and small cannery museum

showing how it was "without the smell." Rather than wait in long lines for your tickets, obtain them early from Ticketron

Many of the numerous restaurants along the Row open after 5 P.M. Bring a fat wallet or valid credit card, although several establishments offer modestly priced early-bird specials, usually before 6:30 P.M. The Steinbeck Lobster Grotto (408/373-1884), 720 Cannery Row, overlooks a portion of Monterey Bay that otters visit and, as a bonus, has a glass window in the floor through which you can see these fellow mammals. Several restaurants nearby have marine views, including the Captain's Galley (408/649-8676), 711 Cannery Row, where children are charged proportionally for each year of age.

If you're on a tight budget or have a large, hungry family, Lighthouse Avenue, the next thoroughfare up the hill, caters mainly to workers and modest-income types living in "new" Monterey. You'll find markets, fast-food chains, hamburger stands, and cheaper gas stations up here.

One of the swingingest spots on Cannery Row, without a view but with a Roaring Twenties atmosphere, is the Warehouse (408/375-1921—an appropriate number). Weekdays from 4:30 P.M. to 11 P.M. and Saturday and Sunday from noon to midnight, it serves pizza, spaghetti, and ravioli, along with booze. After you enter through a phone booth and your eyes adjust to the dusk, you have a wide choice of speakeasy-type entertainment from old-time movies to dart throwing.

The new Monterey Aquarium at the end of Cannery Row, one of the world's largest, is expected to attract half a million visitors a year.

14

Carmel-by-the-Sea

~~~~~~~~~~~~~~~~~~~~~~~~~~~~~~~

The population of the mile-square "real" **Carmel** is under 5,000. You won't believe it during summer or on a weekend if you're trying to park or if you're among the hundreds of fellow tourists milling up and down crowded Ocean Avenue, peering into shop windows. There must be a reason why Carmel is so popular (some say too popular). There is—in fact, there are many reasons.

There's no getting around it; almost every portion of Carmel is scenically attractive. It all goes to show the lure of keeping things quaint and woodsy, of not bulldozing away trees and other natural assets. There *is* beauty in a town that blends into its oak- and pine-covered sand dunes that slope to the sea. As for Carmel's beach, that famous crescent of dazzling white sand rimmed by Monterey cypresses, it *is* glorious (except for swimming—a sign on the beach warns: "Surf Unsafe"; and the water is too icy even for Eskimos). The beach is perfect for strolling, as are secluded parks and paths all over town, and there's not a hotdog stand in sight. The galleries and shops are almost all unusual and artistic. A brochure once put out by the Carmel Business Association (408/624-2522) at San Carlos and Seventh, P. O. Box 444, Carmel, CA 93921, summed up Carmel's pros and cons:

Welcome to Carmel-by-the-Sea. We have some most unusual shops, galleries displaying some of the finest contemporary art, and one of the most beautiful settings in the whole world. On the other hand, we lack sufficient parking and we probably always will. Parking garages and acres of blacktop could spoil the very thing you come here to see and enjoy, so we hope you will enjoy the walk from your parking space.

Carmel Mission was founded in 1770 by Junipero Serra, who is buried inside beneath a beautiful sarcophagus.

Why does Carmel still retain most of its quaint charm when the natural waterfront in Monterey has been smothered in concrete? In the 1960s the city council passed stringent ordinances to help preserve the town's distinctive ambience; one of the first was to protect trees: molesting a tree is absolutely illegal. In conflicts between a tree and a homeowner, the tree almost always wins; even cutting a branch is forbidden without permission. As a result, some buildings are partly wrapped around a neighboring pine or oak; streets wind around trees, sometimes splitting to circle a stately pine or redwood.

Businesses, too, are regulated. A 1925 ordinance forbade "obnoxious industries like stables, soap factories, match factories, chemical works, and other industries of similar character." Outside signs, even street addresses, are frowned on. The care, feeding, and charming of tourists, however, is encouraged. But there is much soul searching in the weekly *Carmel Pine Cone*: Are almost 500 businesses catering mainly to tourists too many in a mile-square "village"? Is there overkill in having over 70 galleries and 90 or so gift and souvenir shops?

Yet Carmel's olden-time quaintness has not been crowded out. The garbage cans wear wooden overcoats with drawings of squirrels and cypress trees. The town still has a Cinderella Lane, and some of its gas stations look straight out of a Grimms' fairy tale. The Tuck Box English Tea Room on Dolores off Ocean is typical of the once pervasive dollhouse architecture started in the 1920s. These structures—a typical house is at Sixth and Torres—were patterned after an actual dollhouse built by Hugh Comstock for his wife, who made and sold Otsy Totsy dolls.

Carmel has been quaint and even eccentric from its start. Property here looks, and is, expensive, but back at the end of the nineteenth century, lots sold for as little as $20. Even after developers like James Devendorf and Frank Powers arrived, lots could be had for around $100. The town was kept purposely primitive, with no gas or electricity. The latter didn't arrive until 1914; plumbing was also a low priority. Citizens usually transacted their business with local food purveyors by way of wooden boxes on posts in front of their cottages. The village did, however, have one necessity of necessities: an Arts and Crafts Club started in 1905.

That same year, poet George Sterling and his wife bought a small home in the Carmel woods at Tenth and Torres, and writer Mary Austin built her smaller cottage near the Carmel mission. The two—mainly Sterling—invited artistic friends to visit. A trickle came; after the 1906 San Francisco earthquake, the trickle became a flood. This informal group, which became known as the **Seacoast Bohemians,** included at one time or another Jack London, Sinclair Lewis, Upton Sinclair, William Rose Benet, and others of their ilk. One member defined a true Bohemian as one who would give you his shirt any time—or take yours. The Seacoast Bohemians blossomed for only a decade or so, but they set the tone for the Carmel that remains to this day.

Sterling looked and acted the part of a poet and was probably the most arresting figure in Carmel then. He resembled Dante, with his curly, tightly cropped hair and large, luminous eyes. Little of Sterling's poetry has lasted. He is remembered for his charisma, hijinks, and for the doggerel he originated. When the Seacoast Bohemians gathered to pound abalone for chowder around the open-air grill at his cabin, or at picnics along the ocean, jingles were created. Spurred on by Sterling, some lasted for 100 or more verses. Although his façade was joyous, Sterling was often despondent. In 1926 he committed suicide by swallowing cyanide, as his wife and an early great love, Nora May French, had done.

Mary Austin was an admirer of American Indians and author of the sensitive *Land of Little Rain.* She wrote many articles while living in Carmel, after first climbing into her wickiup, or tree platform, to await inspiration. Mary Austin said of her adopted Seacoast Bohemia:

Beauty is cheap here . . . it may be had in superlative quality for the mere labour of looking out of the window. It is the absolute setting for romance. No shipping ever puts in at the singing beaches. The freighting teams from the Sur, with their bells a-jangle, go by on the country road, but great dreams have visited the inhabitants thereof.

Robinson Jeffers, whose poems, as well as the man himself, symbolized this country and "the wild, free hawk and the rock," stayed aloof from the Seacoast Bohemians, although he knew and liked his fellow poet, George Sterling. Jeffers preferred planting trees, writing, or working on his stone **Tor House** and Hawk Tower, which still stand on Ocean View Avenue overlooking the end of Scenic Drive in Carmel. Jeffers and his wife, Una, first glimpsed this land of "unbridled and unbelievable beauty" in 1914. Prevented by the war from traveling to Europe, they and their infant twin sons, Donnan and Garth, came to Carmel. Jeffers wrote, "When the stagecoach topped the hill from Monterey and we looked down through pines and sea fogs on Carmel Bay, it was evident that we had come without knowing it to our inevitable place."

On January 20, 1961, Jeffers died in his sleep, by the sea window at Tor House. Nature appeared to take notice of the poet's passing, for it snowed on that day, an event so rare along this seacoast it made newspaper headlines.

His son Donnan and his family continue to live in part of Tor House, which is presently hemmed in by well-groomed Carmel houses. On the outside, the gray stone home looks bleak and solitary, as if it had been built in an earlier age. Inside it is mellow with dark redwood walls and beams and the worn glow of Oriental rugs. You can now visit Tor House and the Hawk Tower Jeffers built for his Una. You can walk through the pleasant gardens to the fence and admire the "great sea wall of coast." You can try to spot the 100 or more unicorns the Jeffers collected—some stone statues, others pictures, and carvings embedded in stone. Docents who know and admire the poet's work lead tours of six persons for a moderate donation. Because this is a residential area, tours are limited to twelve hours a week on Friday and Saturday, and reservations are a must. Phone (408) 624-1813 from 9:30 A.M. to 12:30 P.M. weekdays, or write to the Robinson Jeffers Tor House Foundation, P. O. Box 1887, Carmel, CA 93921. The foundation has also developed a "packaged" program for eligible groups. The group meets at Sunset Center for a showing of the Tor House film, narrated by Burgess Meredith, followed by a talk on Jeffers's work, and then visits Tor House in groups of six.

By the 1920s Carmel was beginning to lose its privacy. More and more sightseers arrived to savor its undisturbed beauty. Prices inevitably rose, and many working writers and artists were forced to move to other locations—even to Salinas. As late as the middle thirties, however, you could still find workers or storekeepers who considered themselves artists and who would halt bagging your groceries or sawing to give an impassioned critique on art. The big reason residents decided to forgo home mail deliveries, rumor has it, was that many artists did not want to make it easy for bill collectors to find them.

There are still working artists around. The Business Association (typically, Carmel has no Chamber of Commerce) reports that Carmel's central district is "the heart of a cultural community that exhibits the work of hundreds of local painters, sculptors, and craftsmen." Some critics insist, however, that much of the art leans toward the surf-crashing-against-the-seashore-with-bent-cypress school of painting.

The cashmere-sweatered townspeople you now see chatting as they pick up their mail at the Carmel post office are a mix that includes mostly professional people, retirees, shop owners, and a sprinkling of descendants of early-timers who had the acumen to buy or build homes before prices went into orbit. The automobiles many Carmel citizens drive are a clue to their solvency. Besides a scattering of restored collector's cars and Rolls Royces, the VW of the village appears to be the Mercedes Benz.

If you drive or, preferably, walk a mere two or three blocks away from the congested shopping area, you'll understand why some people are willing to pay astronomical prices for cottages here and why two dozen realtors are listed in the Carmel Business Directory. There may be few streetlights and side-walks, no public school within the boundaries of "real" Carmel, and—of course—no home mail delivery, but there are trees: towering, gnarled, bent, straight, shadowing deep canyons, reaching out over homes and winding roads, sometimes dappled with sunshine, often festooned with mist or fog.

Carmel is still quaint enough to have several **footbridges** in the residential area. One is near the Mountain View entrance to Mission Trail Park, one is near Lincoln and Fourth, and another is in Forest Hill Park. Nearby, the Pipe Bridge parallels big pipes that cross a ravine; at one time the pipes were the only way to cross over.

Considering its small size, Carmel has a bounty of walking trails and parks, many tucked away amid discreetly designed and landscaped homes. The biggest, **Mission Trail Park,** has thirty-five acres of unspoiled native vegetation (weeds?) and five miles of trails. Walking these trails you'll see groves of toyons; redwoods; wild poppies; a willow trail tunnel; and, especially in the spring, wildflowers.

The brochure at each entrance states that "each new season announces the coming of subtle alterations in the character of the park's vegetation and provides new color displays for the avid or occasonal hiker."

The four entrances to Mission Trail Park are all easy to miss. If you start at the one off Rio Road near the Carmel mission, you'll have to walk uphill. The entrance at Eleventh Street and Junipero is near the middle of the park. The entrance off Hatton Road at Flanders Drive is cleverly hidden, with no indication that the **Lester Rowntree Memorial Arboretum** is just inside. It's a challenge if you're not an "in" Carmelite, but do try to locate it on a curve on Hatton Road; there's a wood sign, "outland 25800" on Flanders Drive. Parking, too, is a challenge.

When you solve the problems and enter, you'll be rewarded. Inside are dozens of native California plants neatly labeled, a painless and refreshing way to take an outdoor botany course. Soft cinder paths wander up and down the hillside, and there are benches to sit on while you admire the many birds flitting about. You might also see a raccoon or deer or perhaps a golden Monarch butterfly on its way to Pacific Grove. From one bench you can see Point Lobos, the Carmel mission, and the ocean between. The brochures describe the arboretum as a "quiet retreat where we can all enjoy the beauties of nature." To help keep it quiet, there are hitching posts outside for dogs.

The arboretum was named for Lester Rowntree, a lively and dedicated self-taught botanist who died in 1971, five days after reaching 100. Mrs. Rowntree, who had her first garden when she was two, became interested in native plants while married and living in New Jersey. With practically no information or in-structions, growing them was difficult. So she set about to learn. After her divorce from Rowntree ("I didn't want to be owned"), she would leave her Carmel Highlands home for six-month stays in the wild, sleeping out under the stars and living on dried fruits, grains, and chocolate. She collected samples and seeds. She later incorporated her copious notes into books like the *Hardy Californians* and *Flowering Shrubs of California.* She was also instrumental in starting the California Native Plant Society and get-ting the highway department to put native plants along freeways.

With all Carmel's bucolic and piney areas, to say nothing of the seashore, it's no wonder that walking is a way of life for many residents. Besides the hiking trails mentioned, take a stroll to the **Forest Theater** at Mountain View and Santa Rita streets. This is

This entry in Carmel's annual Sandcastle Building Contest has bucket-formed towers and carefully sculpted stairs.

California's first outdoor theater, built in 1910 with walls of pine "whose roof is the sky." There you can attend Shakespearean plays and concerts. Performances on summer Sundays are free. On foggy evenings (dress warmly), huge bonfires are lit on each side of the stage.

No nightclubs are allowed in Carmel, but there's a plethora of Cultural events (culture comes with a capital *C* in Carmel). A major reason is that the city can afford it. All those tourists are bringing in dollars; 60 percent of Carmel's funds come from hostelry and sales taxes. The result? The little city is more than self-supporting.

Besides earmarking $10,000 for its own playwriting contest, a big slice of funds for Culture goes to the famous two-week-long **Bach Festival** in July, held at the Sunset Center at San Carlos and Fourth streets. This is perhaps the highlight of Carmel's cultural events, but there are other musical affairs, plays, and meetings at this big center. The Friends of Photography have their office here. Besides a long list of writers, artists, and sculptors, the area has attracted more than its share of world-famous photographers from the late Edward Weston, Wynn Bullock, and Ansel Adams on. For information on the musical events, dance festivals, film showings, and other activities, phone (408) 624-3996.

On weekday afternoons at the Cherry Foundation (408/624-7491), Guadalupe and Fourth, you can check on what is being performed or what art is hung. If you're in Carmel in March when it's usually windy, check out the **Kite Festival** at Carmel High School on the east side of Highway 1. The kites, which must be handcrafted, are a pleasure to watch as they swoop, glide, and spiral in the sky.

In December, Christmas-oriented activities include a Renaissance Faire at the Sunset Center, crafts and Christmas doings at Carmel's La Playa Hotel, and the moving **"Music for Christmas"** show at the Carmel mission. Twelve days after Christmas, the biggest beach bonfire of the year officially blazes. Residents contribute their old Christmas trees at the foot of Thirteenth Avenue, and then watch as the flames leap high to celebrate the beginning of Epiphany. And that's just a sampling of what goes on in this tiny town. You'll find current dates in the information-packed **Monterey Peninsula Review,** free at motels and tourist centers.

One typically Carmelish event that is not usually mentioned is that exercise in human fantasy, the **Great Sandcastle Building Contest.** Once each fall, usually on a crisp Indian summer Sunday, thousands of people lucky enough to find a parking place flock to the Carmel beach, almost driving away the resident sea gulls. Their mission is to ogle at or participate in this contest. Solitary grubbers, couples, families, clubs, or groups loosely joined for the day compete in various categories, including Novice Sandpile, Advanced Sandbox theme, and Grand Sand. There's also a Sour Grapes Award for the loser who is ascertained to be the poorest sport. Prizes are modest—usually plaques or seashell-encrusted objects or statuary resembling mermaids; there's a gold-colored shovel for the Grand Sand Winner. Win or lose, everyone appears to enjoy the affair, including the judges, who are mainly architects and civic luminaries.

Paper cups of adequate California wine in hand, the judges begin their official wanderings about 2 P.M. They compare hundreds of entries, ranging from witty to fairy-tale fanciful to political satire. This all transpires against a background of sounds: the music of the surf and plucked guitars, the popping of champagne corks. Inevitably, inexorably, the late afternoon tide wipes away the masterpieces. It's worth lingering on the beach for the sunset. Real or imaginary, the Carmel sun seems larger and more golden as it sinks into the sea.

Local residents, unhappy about the crowds this event attracts, are shy about announcing the date. Usually, however, it takes place in late September or early October and the Monterey Peninsula Chamber

Leathery fronds of ice plant erupt into bright blossoms of iridescent yellows and reds on Pacific Grove beaches.

of Commerce (408/649-1770) or the Carmel Business Association (408/624-2522) have been known to divulge the date. So next fall, bring shovels and sunburn lotion and join the fun.

A scenic drive starts at the foot of Ocean Avenue, hugs the beach, then turns into a narrow hair-raiser as it rounds the southern headland. (When former movie queen Jean Arthur lived in the home at the point, she had to erect a big fence to protect her privacy.) The drive continues to the **Carmel River State Beach** at the end. The bonus here: It's often uncrowded when the main Carmel Beach is packed

with dogs and with sunbathers slowly turning red—remember, you can get a bad burn in fog, too. Nearby among the reedy marshes, there's also a bird sanctuary. A story goes that unnamed citizens wanted the cattails cut so they could see the birds better. This, of course, would have destroyed one of the main reasons the birds gather in this spot. Luckily, this small, accessible marsh was left for birds, birders, and other nature lovers.

Just a whistling distance from the small parking area, especially in winter, you can see shore birds, woodland birds, and marsh birds gathered together. You may glimpse kingfishers and hawks hunting, pelicans diving, and cormorants fishing. You'll see busy sandpipers, herons, and egrets pondering life as they stand on one leg, and you'll hear ducks and geese making noisy comments as they migrate.

A secret beach in Carmel? Not usually publicized is the small beach with a wide jogging path even more secluded than the Carmel River State Beach (although it's actually part of it). This curving arc of sand and surf, called **Middle Beach** by the State Park people, is tucked between the mouth of the Carmel River to the north and San Jose or Monastery Beach to the south. Most years in the summer and fall you can reach this beach by walking over the dry Carmel riverbed. Any day of the year you can take the Ribera Road turnoff off Highway 1, drive to the end, park, and walk down the steep staircase. Unless it has been ripped down again, there is a sign announcing Public Access and another warning about the hazards of freak high waves. For information on these beaches, call (408) 649-2836.

Next to its beaches, probably the most interesting noncommercial attraction in Carmel is the **Mission San Carlos Borromeo del Carmelo,** founded in 1770 by Father Junipero Serra. This artfully restored Carmel mission with its backdrop of green mountains is flanked by peaceful gardens and a cemetery where 3,000 mission Indians are buried. Most of the graves are unmarked, but one headstone reads: "Old Gabriel—died at age 151 years." (Local historians think old Gabriel more likely died at the tender age of 119.) Father Serra is buried under the church floor just in front of the chancel, and many relics and mementos date from his time. The original silver altarpieces Serra brought from Baja California to Monterey are in the museum; some rooms, including Father Serra's simple cell, depict how they were almost two centuries ago when the mission was flourishing. A magic time to relive those days is during a mass when music, candlelight, and ritual blend with the ageless beauty of the mission itself.

Whether you've come to Carmel for a festival or a romantic weekend or to treat your family to some of its scenic highlights, you're sure to look into at least a few Carmel shops, that is—if you find a parking spot. Try to browse during an off-season weekday if you can, so that the storekeepers have time to chat with you. You'll discover that many of Carmel's shops have charm to spare. Even local food stores have an artistic flair, like the Mediterranean Market on Ocean Avenue and Mission that displays exotic cheeses, sausages, and other temptations.

You could spend hours in the **Carmel Plaza** nearby on upper Ocean Avenue, with its three stories of shops, restrooms, outside plaza with fountain, bridge, and—perhaps optimistic in this town where summer fog is a way of life—the Harbinger Restaurant and cocktail lounge (408/625-1483) with outside fireplace. There are nautical shops and a store that specializes in wooden decoy ducks. The sculpture gallery run by identical twins Bob and Tom Bennett shows bronze figures and abstract forms. Previous to working full-time at metal sculpture, Bob was an iron worker and Tom a railroad brakeman. The two then owned a gas station where they started their artistic endeavors by bending coat hangers in a back room of the gas station. Discovering that wire welding was hard on their eyes and back, they switched to bronze.

An enormous bookstore in the Plaza, Books, Inc., always has from four to seven sale tables. Many shops have self-explanatory names like Everyday is Christmas and Come Fly a Kite, which sells small paper kites and dragon kites that are 350 feet long. Byron & Schiller, in the back of Carmel Plaza, carries a wide selection of gifts for the kitchen or any room.

From there you can walk into a miniplaza with more shops.

Looking for fun and games? Try the Game Gallery in Vendervort Court, between Seventh and Ocean avenues on San Carlos (near where the Carmel Business Association has its office). The two owners gave up careers as a dental hygienist and a computer systems designer to run this shop where you can test your skills against an electronic game or try out games before you buy. The Music Box & Doll Shop on Ocean between San Carlos and Dolores displays music boxes and dolls from around the world.

There are shops specializing in steins, candles, straw baskets, brass rubbings, apparel of every type, and, of course, art. Courts and malls and shopping nooks are everywhere you wander in the inner Carmel area. Almost all tourist literature, free for the asking, has lists and maps.

If the desire to feed the inner person has brought you here, you'll find that Carmel and environs contain dozens of restaurants, some the best bargains on the peninsula. Here's a sampling. Even on foggy nights, the Clam Box (408/624-8597) at Mission and Fifth is full of locals. For breakfast or lunch, the Little Swiss Cafe (408/624-5007) at Sixth between Dolores and Lincoln is hard to beat, with its homemade breads and pastries and especially the split pea soup. For a change of pace, the Hog's Breath Inn (408/625-1044), in a rustic courtyard at San Carlos near Fifth in Carmel, serves up steaks to vegetable plates to "Chicken 'n Whiskey" to occasional wild pig. Chopped sirloin is called Dirty Harry, after a Clint Eastwood movie; he's an owner.

So happy hunting—first for a parking space, then for whatever it was that brought you to Carmel-by-the-Sea.

The famous bleached, sculptured lone cypress tree along Seventeen-Mile Drive in Pebble Beach.

15

Seventeen-Mile Drive and Pebble Beach

Highly advertised scenic attractions sometimes disappoint, but the **Seventeen-Mile Drive** at Pebble Beach is worth every glowing adjective. Many celebrities and socialites who have chosen to live or vacation here agree.

The late Samuel F. B. Morse, nephew of the inventor of Morse code, started developing this huge private park and playground in the vast Del Monte Forest in 1915. "It was my good fortune," he is quoted as saying, "to find this region in almost entirely a primitive condition. I have had a most pleasant time preserving the beauty . . . while doing the development work which was obviously dictated."

Seventeen-Mile Drive skirts most of the tastefully developed areas. The original drive was twice that long, circling the entire Monterey Peninsula from the old Del Monte Hotel in Monterey and back. The present Seventeen-Mile Drive is worth the healthy admission fee, which includes a map. (The fee is refunded if you register or dine at The Lodge at

Pebble Beach. If you're expected by a resident you also get in free.) Visitors on bikes are not charged at the Pacific Grove gate at certain times; biking is a great way to take the tour. (See the previous chapter for biking and hiking information.)

Gazing at the more visible of the over 1,000 exclusive residences is a big reason for taking the drive. Movie and television stars and the old and new rich have their estates here. Architectural styles vary from the early Spanish Colonial preferred by Morse to Cape Cod to Old Southern Mansion to Mineshaft Modern. Some mansions are in the woods behind gates; others overlook the ocean behind gates, like the marble Byzantine castle you see soon after entering the Carmel gate. Started in 1926 and finished in 1930 for one of the railroad and banking Crockers, the castle contains many rooms; they, the baths, and numerous arches both inside and in the garden are mainly of Italian marble. Besides the decor, another extravagance is the beach in front, which is heated by underground pipes. Prices for many of these mansions run to so many millions they can now only be afforded by the Very Rich or by big corporations to be used by their brass.

To keep residents and select but solvent vacationers happy, there are seven **golf courses,** most of championship caliber, many used during the Annual Bing Crosby National Pro-Am Tournament in January. Robert Louis Stevenson, who loved the Del Monte woods and shoreline, was the inspiration for the Spyglass Hill Golf Course, open to the public. All the holes are named after characters in his books. The exclusive Cypress Point Golf Course has that renowned 16th hole that goes out over an inlet of the ocean. Part of the Pebble Beach Golf Links, open to the public, is on the ocean in front of the Lodge. It, like the other courses, has sweeping views.

Most of the yacht clubs, country clubs, tennis courts, swimming pools, and other niceties are on private turf, but the Pebble Beach Equestrian Center (408/624-2756) on Portola Road is open to those who reserve early and ride English saddle. You can get a map of the more than thirty miles of riding and hiking trails there or at The Lodge. The map shows jogging courses, also, and a one-and-a-half-mile par course that starts at the 9-hole Peter Hays Golf Course, also open to the public. If you get lost, which is possible, just head downhill. You're sure to arrive at the shore.

If you drive in at the Highway 1 gate and turn right—as your map suggests—you'll pass an acre called Shepherd's Knoll, where sheep often graze and where wildflowers grow. You'll then proceed up to Huckleberry Hill, one of the highest points in the Del Monte Forest. Here you'll see native plants and trees, including Bishop or Monterey pines and the rare Gowen Cypress. Driving downhill, you pass the prestigious Monterey Peninsula Country Club with its two private golf courses and manicured links. At the Pacific Grove gates to the ocean, the crashing surf steals the show.

At **Spanish Bay** picnic tables overlook the surf, but at **Point Joe,** next south, the ocean really puts on a wild show. The sea directly off Point Joe is one of the few places in the world where several conflicting ocean currents meet. This unusual turbulence, resulting from the configuration of the ocean floor, is present even on the calmest of days. At night or in heavy fog the currents have sent many coastal ships to their graves, including the 889-ton iron-hulled steamer *St. Paul* and the 172-ton lumber ship *Celia.*

Near midnight on December 14, 1923, south ot Point Joe at Cypress Point, the 967-ton *Flavel,* piled high with lumber, grounded on the rocks. A local man returning home from a dance heard the captain's distress signal. Soon police and nearby residents were gathered on the shore. The crew and captain made it to safety during the night, but the drama was not over. Although lumber was strewn on beaches for miles around, the battle for the remaining salvage became so heated it was headlined in the local newspaper. Thousands of people stood on the shore watching the ship being stripped. At the end of two days the *Flavel* sank and the show was over.

Seal and Bird Rocks are both aptly named, for you're sure to see and hear barking sea lions and harbor seals. Besides the many gulls, cormorants, and sandpipers, rare birds like the black-footed albatross have been sighted here. Before leaving, look for a small round building near the picnic area. It's a camera obscura whose lens rotates, giving a close-up panoramic view—more than your eye can take in outside—of Seal and Bird Rocks and the surrounding area, while a recorded voice describes the highlights.

Farther on, you'll discover a secluded picnic spot at lovely, crescent-shaped **Fanshell Beach.** Fishing is allowed from this point south. Swimming is allowed also, but, although there is white sand and blue water, swimming in the rough seas anywhere along the Seventeen-Mile Drive may be hazardous to your life.

You're sure to recognize **Midway Point,** next, with its lone Monterey cypress; it's the one on all those postcards. No one knows how many years the twisted tree has survived, whipped about by winter storms and shrouded by summer fog. Now it is propped up by guy wires, watered during the summer, and given an annual feeding. Actually, the tree is no longer lone; a small Monterey cypress, probably a descendant, juts out by its side. Although Monterey cypresses have been planted elsewhere, the few miles along this particular coast are the only place they grow indigenously. Here the wind has sculptured them into shapes that have kept photographers and artists busy for years snapping and painting them. Farther on, near **Pescadero Point,** you'll see the Ghost Tree cypresses, bleached white by wind and spray. Robert Louis Stevenson called these trees "ghosts fleeing before the wind."

The drive now leads you by the 159-unit Lodge at Pebble Beach (408/624-3811), which has played host to a long list of celebrities. Golfing presidents have included Kennedy, Ford, and Reagan during his years as governor of California. Movie celebrities from W. C. Fields and Clark Gable to Elizabeth

Taylor and local resident, Clint Eastwood, have played here. Two of the Beatles checked in. A bell captain at The Lodge, interviewed in the *Monterey Review,* commented, "You don't stay at The Lodge if you're poor, and probably not very often if you're middle class . . . The amount of wealth here is incredible." He went on to add up the room rent and golf costs. "By the time you eat three meals, it's nothing for a couple to spend $400 a night here."

The public is allowed in to shop and dine at the three dining rooms or coffee shop. The public is also invited in—for an admission fee—to Pebble Beach horse shows, soccer matches, the Bing Crosby Invi-tational Golf Tourney in January, and the somewhat esoteric **Concours d'Elegance** in late August. This display of antique and classic cars, each polished to a blinding finish, takes place on the lawn in front of The Lodge "where the surf meets the turf."

If you leave by the Carmel gate you can revisit that quaint village or take Ocean Avenue back to Highway 1. One final warning: Before you start the Seventeen-Mile Drive, especially if it's one of those sparkling clear days in fall or spring, be sure you have enough film for your camera. You'll never forgive yourself if you run out.

Harbor seals find perches on rocks just a few yards offshore along Pacific Grove's Ocean View Boulevard.

16

Pacific Grove: The Last Hometown

Many peninsula visitors who have sampled the crowded charms of Monterey's waterfront or Carmel prefer sedate **Pacific Grove,** population around 18,000. Its two and a half square miles sit on the peninsula's tip where bay and ocean meet. Here the sea and the sea mammals always put on a show. You can often watch sea lions and otters in the water just offshore; within camera range, harbor seals perch on small rocks, overhanging on each side. Deer graze in open parkland and woods. You're sure to interrupt them browsing along almost any road near the ocean at dusk or glimpse them nibbling flowers placed in front of headstones in the El Carmelo Cemetery.

Pacific Grove is also known as Butterfly Town, U.S.A., because of the hundreds of thousands of **Monarch butterflies** that visit between October and April. It's easy to follow the signs to their favorite trees; these are well marked, especially the grove at 1973 Lighthouse Avenue and the trees nearby. You'll also meet Monarchs in Washington Park between Sinex, Short, Alder, and Melrose streets. As at Natural Bridges State Park, the thousand or so that may cluster together on a three-foot branch look like dead leaves when it's foggy or rainy. When the sun comes out, they fly about—a colorful sight. (Read more about them on page 66.) These may be the only butterflies in the world protected by city ordinance. There's a $500 fine and up to six months in jail for anyone who molests them. Pacific Grove celebrates the return of these velvety gold-and-black-winged insects in early October. Then thousands of schoolchildren march in a parade, and later there's a carnival and bazaar.

In 1879 Robert Louis Stevenson, while wandering about, discovered a dreamlike tent village where people "come to enjoy a life of teetotalism, religion, and flirtation." He had found the Pacific Camp Grounds, run as a Methodist retreat. When the summer retreat ended, the tents were stored in Chautaqua Hall at Seventh and Central avenues, which is still used for many community meetings. Pacific Grove *is* still sedate; about the only thing that's lit up is Christmas Tree Lane during the holiday season. (Another yuletide custom is the Singing Christmas Tree, put on by the Assembly of God every evening the week before Christmas at the corner of Pine and Fountain streets.) Until recently no liquor could be sold within city limits, a heritage of Pacific Grove's religious past.

In the early days a curfew bell was rung and all lights had to be extinguished by 10 P.M. Forbidden fruits included waltzing, playing the zither, reading the great Sunday dailies, selling popcorn on the beach, or playing tenpins. The main irritant to many, however, was the fence that circled the retreat area. The gate was locked after curfew and most vehicular traffic was forbidden. (When Pacific Grove fathers finally faced the fact that automobiles were here to stay, they passed a ten-mile-per-hour speed limit.) The fenced town and the locked gates amused nearby towns. An early neighboring newsman commented: "Fog in Monterey today. Last night the Pacific Grove gate must have accidentally been left open."

In 1880 Judge Langford, who had forgotten his key, became enraged and axed the gate to tinder. Half a century later, Dr. Julia Platt, the town mayor, also known as "Lady Watchdog," took an axe to another gate at a barricade to the bath house and beach at Lovers of Jesus Point. She did this to protect the public's right of access to this beautiful area, which she had spent so many years weeding, planting, watering, and raking.

Judge Langford's home, with its square tower and ornate Gothic fretwork, is at 225 Central at Evans. A particularly imposing mansion at Lighthouse and Seventeen-Mile Drive, formerly called Pinehurst Manor, was built in the 1880s by an Englishman. Dozens of other pre-turn-of-the-century houses remain in Pacific Grove. Ask their location at the **Chamber of Commerce** (408/373-3304) at Forest and Central. On most weekday afternoons, from noon to 4 P.M., the friendly staff will supply you with information. Many of the historic structures have gone public, especially along Central, Ocean View Boulevard, and Lighthouse Avenue. (See bed and breakfast inns on page 107.)

The Right Stuff (camping wear and gear) at 231 Seventeenth Street, occupies one of the small older cottages that has been converted into a store or professional office. Many cottages were built right over the drafty tents of the retreat days; some owners, when remodeling, have found shreds of the ancient canvas. In the 1880s a steamboat was wrecked on rocks near the lighthouse; her cargo of paneled wooden doors was promptly rescued from nearby beaches and nailed over many of the tents. A cluster of these gemlike cottages is on Eighteenth Street between Pine and Lighthouse and extends to nearby Nineteenth Street. An attractive transitional home surrounded by a white picket fence, the Sea Star, is at 720 Grove Street just off Lighthouse at the end of Central. When the house was built in 1883, small lots in Pacific Grove could be had for $50.

Over a dozen **churches** presently operate in Pacific Grove, with more to come. The town's first church, built around 1887, was St. Mary's-by-the-Sea Episcopal Church at Twelfth and Central. When the congregation outgrew the original tiny chapel, it was sliced in two and three bays were added in the middle. The dainty seventy-five-foot spire was there originally. Don't miss the small but exquisite Tiffany glass windows showing white lilies and pink foxgloves. Across Central near Carmel Street in the same block as the Christian Church is a miniscule white chapel with vivid turquoise trim, complete with a tiny tower and bell. This was erected by a Portuguese immigrant as thanksgiving for his safe arrival.

You can spend many happy nostalgic hours on these quiet streets by yourself. If you want to learn more, the Chamber of Commerce and Art Center sponsor a **Victorian House Tour** each year, usually in March, when you can admire the beautifully restored interiors as well as exteriors.

Soon after you arrive, visit the **Pacific Grove Museum of Natural History,** downtown at Forest and Central streets across from the Chamber of Commerce. No wonder it was named by the American Association of Museums as the "best of its size in the United States." You'll learn about the natural history of Monterey County from the displays of Monarch butterflies, sea otters, and birds; there is a relief map of the ocean's Monterey Canyon which drops— steeper than the Grand Canyon—from 300 to 8,400 feet and is a big reason marine life is so abundant in the area. The museum also has changing exhibits, often from their collection of Indian artifacts. Outside you can walk through a small garden of native plants. Try to attend one of the peninsula's most popular events, the **Annual Wildflower Show,** held at the museum on the third weekend in April. In September there's a Watercolor Show. For information, call (408) 372-4212.

As for fine art, Carmel may have over seventy-five galleries, but Pacific Grove has several in or near the museum. The faintly arty downtown seems to revolve around big, square **Holmans,** built in 1891, once the largest department store in the West and still

At Lovers Point in Pacific Grove you can swim, sunbathe, and picnic on a grassy headland.

going strong. Holmans faces on Lighthouse Avenue, between Grand and Forest. (No, this isn't the same Lighthouse Avenue you took above Cannery Row in "New" Monterey. That turns into Central Avenue the minute it crosses the city limits. This is Pacific Grove's very own Lighthouse Avenue, inland a block or two.)

Oh, yes—the galleries. The Pacific Grove Art Center (408/375-2208) at 568 Lighthouse Avenue (just look for the green awning) is open Tuesday to Saturday form 11 A.M. to 5 P.M. Also, from Tuesday to Friday 1 P.M. to 5 P.M. and on Saturday from 10 A.M. to 5 P.M. or by appointment (408/373-3811), you can view historical photographs from the extensive Pat Hathaway collection dating from 1880. Farther away, but worth the trip if you like fine pottery, is the Peninsula Potters Gallery (408/372-8867) at 2078 Sunset Drive, open 10 A.M. to 4 P.M. Monday through Saturday.

If you can't spend much time exploring this old-fashioned little town, at least drive along Ocean View Boulevard; it's worth every drop of gas. Starting at David Street at the end of Cannery Row, you pass the much painted Monterey Boat Works, which built or repaired many of the old sardine boats. The restored building is now the library for the **Hopkins Marine Station** of Stanford University, the second oldest facility in the country geared to biological research and teaching. When it first started, nearby Chinese fishermen supplied the station with marine animals. Because the water is unusually clear offshore and the marine life abundant, scientists from all over the world come here to study. The station is off-limits to casual visitors. Some nonscientists have been students, including John Steinbeck, who took classes here in 1923. Although never officially con-

nected with the station, Steinbeck's pal, "Doc" Ricketts, befriended many of the students.

The marine station is on Point Cabrillo, which is also known as China Point. In 1906 a suspicious fire swept through the shanties, mainly built on piers, of a fifty-year-old Chinese fishing village clinging to this same point. All that is left are a few yellowing photographs and Pacific Grove's week-long **Feast of Lanterns,** held every year during the last week in July. The parade of boats with lanterns reenacts the ancient Chinese fable of villagers searching with lanterns for the mandarin's daughter who runs away to kill herself after being forbidden to marry her peasant sweetheart. The festival includes a procession, the crowning of a queen, and colorful fireworks at Lovers Point.

Just off China Point on September 27, 1905, the coastal freighter *Gipsy* went aground. A relief skipper who captained the *Gipsy* when she left Moss Landing sighted the buoy at China Point and steered the ship toward Monterey. Next, in the dense fog, he spotted the red light at the end of the Monterey pier. Too late, the *Gipsy* crashed into rocky shoals. The red light? It was a red lantern by a sewer project near the end of Hoffman Street. The *Gipsy*'s crew was saved, but the ship was a total loss. The only ones to profit were nearby Chinese and soldiers who helped themselves to the bottled beer the ship carried.

From this point for about three miles you'll see some of the most postcard-perfect scenery on the peninsula. You can enjoy it as you drive slowly along Ocean View Boulevard, but to really savor it all, get out of your car. For a starter, why not take off your shoes and run barefoot through grassy **Berwick Park** overlooking the shore? If you're not up to that, at least walk along the walking and biking trail that replaced the old Southern Pacific Railroad tracks that parallel the shore.

At **Lovers Point** you can picnic on the grassy headland, use the restrooms, and admire sculptor Gordon Newell's Monarch butterfly statue, one of the few in the world celebrating an insect. You can clamber over rocks at the end to watch the sea and the marine mammals usually offshore. You can sunbathe if the sun cooperates and swim (brrr) at the small protected beach which you will share with scuba divers and other bipeds in wetsuits. Rock fishing is also popular here.

From April through July and sometimes into August, the ice plants and flowers along this rockbound boulevard are a riot of unbelievable color. This vivid shoreline swath was almost singlehandedly the work of Hayes Perkins, who—while in his seventies—transformed the weed-covered shore. A seafaring man who had traveled over much of the world, Perkins retired at sixty-five to a small one-room cabin across the boulevard. He noticed that the poison oak that grew thick along the shore brought itching misery to the children who played there. Because he was immune, he started to pull out the poison oak clumps, replacing them with exotic plants from around the world. Most of the yuccas, palm trees, and century plants died, but the geraniums, pelargoniums, scarlet aloe, and daisies flourished in the wind and sea spray. The crowning glory of his garden, now called **Perkins' Park,** were the succulents he planted as ground cover: the lavender-pink mesembryanthemum, so bright in early spring it almost hurts the eyes. Through his seventies and into his eighties, Perkins kept his garden alive by toting water in buckets from his cabin. Finally the city put in water pipes and assigned gardeners to help. Only when he was ninety did Perkins retire for the second time. He died at the age of ninety-six.

Paths, popular with joggers, wend through many areas of this seaside park and there are benches at intervals. Even if you miss the springtime showing, any time of the year is spectacular, especially when surf crashes over the rocks. Do get there for at least one sunset.

The 18-hole city-owned **Pacific Grove Golf Links** (408/375-3456) sprawls its greenery along the route, slightly inland from the bay. It's an easy course, often visited by browsing deer. With so much open space, parkland, and woods around, you'll probably glimpse California quail marching along. You'll also see many squirrels and chipmunks, raccoons, and perhaps a kit fox or two. In the 1890s elk wandered through Pacific Grove; so did bison

abandoned by a Wild West show. Finally the bison were donated to the Golden Gate Park in San Francisco, where onlookers can now see their (the bison's) descendants.

Pacific Grove is popular with birds: as a hometown and as a stopping-off place for those migrating. Old-timers remember many more birds, perhaps because of the wild blueberry and huckleberry bushes that once grew thick in untamed areas. Now among the woodland and garden birds are blackbirds, crows, and the more unusual yellow-billed magpies with their long flowing tails. You may see or hear the acorn woodpecker, with his bright red cap, boring holes into a tree or wooden house in order to deposit an acorn. In springtime cedar waxwings and swallows visit, and all year you see hummingbirds, goldfinches, juncos, chickadees, and sparrows wearing different hues.

Sea birds are somewhat scarce because of so many homo sapiens, but you will see many varieties of gulls. A good place to watch them take baths is at the tiny freshwater **Crespi Pond** (Father Crespi notes it in his annals) at the edge of the golf course right by Ocean View Boulevard and the start of Asilomar Boulevard. You'll also see ducks and coots and, especially in the early morning before golfers start hitting balls into the pond, more exotic migrating sea birds. Offshore in spring and fall you'll see shearwaters doing just that.

Your rockbound tour continues along the beach and loops around **Point Pinos,** which was named in 1542 by the Portuguese adventurer, Juan Cabrillo, for the dark green Monterey pines indigenous to the area. By now you'll see the squat **Point Pinos Lighthouse** on a slight hill, surrounded by the golf course, and perhaps hear the air-diaphragm horn blasting its mournful warning to fogbound travelers. The oldest still in operation on the California coast, the lighthouse's main building was completed in 1859 of eighteen-inch gray granite walls quarried on the site. The tower had to be rebuilt after being damaged by the 1906 earthquake, but the building looks like it will stand a few centuries more. The first light was a simple sperm oil lamp; then came kerosene; then electricity. Now its 1,000-watt lamp is visible 115 miles at sea, thanks to the help of its original French Fresnel lenses and prisms. You can visit the lighthouse Saturday and Sunday from 1 P.M. to 4 P.M. Enter at the parking lot on Asilomar Boulevard across from the **El Carmelo Cemetery,** where many of the headstones are over a century old.

At the edge of Pacific Grove, after Ocean View Boulevard turns into Sunset Drive, is **Asilomar**

The oldest still-operating lighthouse along the California coast is the charming Point Pinos Lighthouse in Pacific Grove.

State Beach and Conference Grounds (408/372-8016), referred to by a perceptive reporter as the "Thinking Man's Park." Along the blue-green water is a lovely wild beach and, just inland, huge snowy white sand dunes that get their appearance and soft texture from the high percentage of silica in the sand. Generations of painters and photographers have tried to capture the beauty of these dunes with their stark trees—now leafless and bleached white by sun and spray, and the green of living Monterey cypresses and pines inland. There are interesting tidepools to explore (look—don't take!) and if you hunt in the rocks and sand at a very minus tide you may see the remains of the wrecked lumber barge, *Roderick Dhu,* which went aground in 1909. On the horizon you'll see passing ships and sailboats. Closer in you'll often watch sea lions hunting fish; one surprised swimmer surfaced in the center of three friendly but curious sea lions. Sea otters like the isolated coves and harbor seals often haul out on the nearby rocks.

The Asilomar grounds are restful and beautiful; the structures blend into the sand dunes and woods. The early buildings were all designed by Julia Morgan, the architect who also designed the Hearst Castle (a far cry from the prize-winning architecture here). The landscaping is nature's own, relying heavily on native ice plant, sand verbena, and live oak. Deer and squirrels wander about inside the grounds or outside the entrance on Asilomar Boulevard at Sinex. The sixty-acre grounds also contain a training center for state rangers; park employees will answer your questions about the plants and the wildlife, which includes a rare tailless lizard.

This is a place to beachcomb, picnic, stroll, or try to settle the problems of the world at one of the many conferences held here. Even if you're not attending a conference, you can stay at Asilomar if there's spare room, and there often is. The cost? You can pay a moderate price for a room with bath down the hall to several times that for luxury accommodations in buildings with views of the sea. You can eat here, also, in a special room for nonconference people, where you're likely to get into conversation with interesting fellow guests. You'll have no trouble finding this attractive spot. Pacific Grove believes in putting up signs to guide people.

Asilomar is a coined word meaning "haven by the sea." It is that—a prime location for a conference, often a refuge if you haven't found a vacancy elsewhere, and (almost) always serenely beautiful. But nothing is perfect; fog often shrouds this end of Pacific Grove.

Continue on Ocean View Boulevard, now Sunset Boulevard, and you'll arrive at the Pacific Grove gate of Seventeen-Mile Drive, where you'll be charged a fee to view the Pebble Beach portion of this coastline. If you drive inland instead, then south on Asilomar Boulevard, you'll find yourself on Highway 68 and you can go up over the wooded hill to connect with Highway 1.

Where to eat in Pacific Grove? If you want to go all out dining on gourmet French food and can get reservations, Maison Bergerac (408/373-6996), in the ornate and beautiful old Hart Mansion, 649 Lighthouse Avenue, has seatings at 6 P.M. and 8 P.M. Decidedly less pretentious but popular with locals, including the late Ansel Adams, is Pablo's (408/646-8888), 1184 Forest Avenue. If you're looking for atmosphere and don't like to dress up, two Pacific Grove restaurants fit the bill: Tillie Gort's Coffee House and Art Gallery (408/373-0335) at 111 Central Avenue features sandwiches, soup, vegetarian dishes, and cheesecake in a relaxed atmosphere. Margot's Cafe Balthazar (408/373-1474), 170 Forest Avenue, also has a gallery and serves soup and salads, burgers, and Mexican dishes. If you're more interested in a scenic view outside, try the Old Bathhouse (408/375-5195) at 620 Ocean View Boulevard near Lovers Point.

If it's getting toward sunset, do take one last drive or walk along Ocean View Boulevard. It may turn out to be your most memorable experience on the Monterey Peninsula.

John Steinbeck was born in this handsome Salinas Victorian; you can lunch here by reservation and buy books in the basement.

17

Monterey Peninsula Satellite Cities and Parks

SALINAS, THE BIG REGIONAL PARKS, AND SAN JUAN BAUTISTA

In early rancho days when the wild oats and mustard grew so tall that a horseman had to stand in his saddle to see his way, the **Salinas** area provided pasturage for stock belonging to the Carmel mission and the Monterey presidio. In 1858 Deacon Elias Howe built a combination inn, store, and meeting hall, and the town of Salinas—meaning "salty ponds" for some obscure reason—was established.

What is there to see in Salinas? Until recently, about the only people who traveled to Salinas, unless they were headed for the rodeo, were Monterey County citizens who had business in this county seat. For dining, entertainment, or showing visitors around, they stuck to the Monterey Peninsula. It was as if Monterey County had a split personality.

True, Salinas—"the salad bowl of the nation"—is flat and surrounded by fields instead of crashing surf. However, this is **Steinbeck country,** and a surprising number of tourists have discovered Salinas, population around 75,000. The Chamber of Commerce

(408/424–7611), 119 East Alisal Street, off Soledad, points out that its town does have amenities. There's the Salinas Golf and Country Club at 474 San Juan Grade; it's private, however. A Buddhist temple is at 14 California. And there's the start of a mall downtown near the civic center.

As for historic sites, a short distance out of town on Boronda Lane off West Market is the well-preserved **José Eusebio Boronda Adobe.** It's furnished partially as it was in Boronda's day, and the fremontia trees add color in late summer when they're in bloom. Old farm equipment is scattered about; you could find a square nail or other old artifact on the paths. For information on when the adobe is open, call the Monterey County Historical Society at (408) 757-8085. On the adjacent property is an old Japanese water tank. At Boronda Lane and Central Avenue, surrounded by lettuce fields, is an old cemetery with headstones dating back to the last decades of the 1800s.

The **Salinas Rodeo** in early July has been roping in fans since 1911. It puts on a big week with cowboy action in the arena and simultaneous entertainment on the track, including parades, a carnival, and a cow-chip throwing contest. For information, write California Rodeo Salinas, P. O. Box 1648, Salinas, CA 93902, or phone (408) 757-2951 until June 1, then (408) 424-7355.

Besides the rodeo, the **Steinbeck House** and **Steinbeck Library** draw the most visitors. It's easy to drive by the stately Victorian at 132 Central Avenue, close to downtown, where Steinbeck was born and raised. To get inside you must visit Monday through Friday from 1 P.M. to 3 P.M. That's when you can buy Steinbeck books, antiques, and gifts at the Best Cellar, run by the up to 200 volunteers in the Valley Guild. Volunteers also serve two weekday gourmet luncheons, using fresh produce from nearby fields and local wines. Reservations are needed for lunch or for group tours of the house (408/424-2735). The guild, which rescued the Steinbeck House when the Diocese of Monterey put it up for sale in 1972, now makes enough profit to keep everything in sparkling shape here and contribute to other valley charities.

The **John Steinbeck Library** (408/758-7311), 110 West San Luis Street, contains over 30,000 items: autographed first editions; manuscripts; galley proofs; scripts; posters; photographs of Steinbeck; and biographical material, including letters, dissertations, and other memorabilia. Come here if you want to learn more about the only novelist to win both a Nobel and Pulitzer prize. The library is also the main locale for the annual **Steinbeck Festival,** usually held the last two weeks in June. His plays and films are presented, and lectures are given about the late author. Participants come from Japan and all over the world.

Besides that special Steinbeck House luncheon, where in Salinas can you eat? Since the area has a large Spanish-speaking population, Mexican restaurants abound; most locals recommend Rosita's Armory Cafe (408/424-7039) on 231 Salinas Street near the Greyhound Bus Depot. Decor is simple, with a touch of chrome, but seven days a week if you come in wearing shoes and shirt you can fill up on mammoth helpings of delicious south-of-the-border food at modest prices. Much fancier is "east of eden" (408/424-0819) in the old Salinas Presbyterian Church at 327 Pajaro Street. In the mood for Chinese food? The Republic Restaurant (408/424-3366), 37 Soledad Street, has been in business since 1937, which speaks for itself.

The quickest and most scenic route from Salinas to the Monterey Peninsula and vice versa is **Highway 68** through hills dotted with oaks, passing near three big regional parks: Jack's Peak, Laguna Seca, and Toro.

Soon after the turnoff to Highway 68 from Highway 1 is the sign for 525-acre **Jack's Peak,** two miles inland. The park, open for day use only, has scenery to suit almost any mood, picnic areas, flower-carpeted meadows, pine groves, views of Monterey Bay and Carmel Valley, and miles of developed and marked hiking and riding trails. You'll also find plenty of colorful poison oak, so stay in the developed areas and don't touch this attractive plant with its shiny three-lobed leaflets. As for wildlife, if you stroll or sit peacefully, looking out over the panoramic views, you should get a glimpse of many winged or four-legged creatures; almost every land bird, animal, and butterfly known on the Monterey Peninsula comes to Jack's Peak on occasion.

The **Laguna Seca Recreation Area,** which calls itself the "Gateway to the Monterey Peninsula," is about five miles farther on Highway 68. Laguna Seca was once famous only for its sport car races, which have featured names such as Mario Andretti, Jim Hall, and Al Unser; at present, movie star Paul Newman leases facilities here for his racing team. Now, however, there's a much wider choice of recreation. As you enter from Highway 68 you can turn left on a dirt road and visit a small wildlife refuge. Continue past the entrance after you've paid the fee for day use or for parking your tent or RV in the 180-site campground. There are picnic grounds for small to large groups, a shooting and archery range, and many restrooms.

To get to the day-use area, you cross a bridge that goes over the beginning of the race track. On weekends when the races are on, it's inclined to be noisy, but there is a big bonus. Since Laguna Seca is inland, at least you'll probably have sunshine even when fog drips along the coast. For overnight reservations here, as at all Monterey County parks, phone (800) 822-CAMP, or write to Monterey County Parks, P. O. Box 367 (Courthouse), Salinas, CA 93902.

The entrance to **Toro Regional Park** is thirteen miles from Monterey and six miles from Salinas. In its 4,756 acres are many hiking and riding trails plus a camping complex to be used by organized nonprofit youth groups. The names of picnic areas hint at the terrain in this huge park—Sycamore, Oak Grove, Badger Flats, Buckeye, and Creekside.

Enjoy the tranquility of these county parks while you can before returning to Highway 68. Official

The premier historic highlight in charming San Juan Bautista is its restored mission, dedicated in 1797.

The premier historic highlight is the mission itself, dedicated in 1797, the fifteenth Franciscan mission in Spain's new California. As the 1700s drew to a close, the chapel and quarters became too cramped, so the present mission was started in 1803. By the time it was finished, in 1812, it was already too large for the congregation, so the two big arches leading to the nave were bricked up.

Be sure to note the bell tower of the mission church, the scene of Kim Novak's plummet to the roof below in Alfred Hitchcock's *Vertigo,* filmed here in the late fifties.

At the side of the mission overlooking the valley is mute evidence as to why the church population dwindled so drastically. A sign there reads:

> Mission Cemetery. Buried in this sacred ground in unmarked graves are 4,300 Mission Indians. Their names can still be read in the old records of the Mission. This Mission's first offering to God, marked with the sign of the Holy Trinity, is Maria Trinidad, a child buried April 23, 1798.

The mission is forty feet away from the infamous **San Andreas earthquake fault.** Although it has never totally collapsed, the building has gone through two major restorations, one shortly after the 1906 quake. Among other improvements made then was the removal of an ugly bell tower built by a priest in 1867 so he could ring the bells from his bedroom. The second restoration returned the mission to its original plans. New tiles for the roof were fired to match the old, and clay bricks for the walls and arches were made by hand in the old way. The original "intended" tower was built and the three aisles, the only such among mission churches, were opened up. The result is a magical vignette, especially when the bells are ringing, music and chanting are pouring out of the church, and the cactus on the grounds are in flower. Landscape architects are studying the original garden plans to help return the grounds to the way they were.

Across the way is the Plaza Hotel, built in 1814 and 1815. Originally an adobe barracks for soldiers, it became a famous stagecoach stop. One authentic feature revived is the two-story outhouse (that's correct—*two* stories) in back of the hotel. Also built in 1815 the nearby Zenetta House was a dormitory for Indian girls

The stables, housing a fascinating collection of horse-drawn carriages, saw much action during the Gold Rush days of the 1850s and 1860s, when this

scenic route or not, some locals use the highway as a race track, much as they do with the Carmel Valley Road.

Charming is an overworked word, but it applies to **San Juan Bautista** (population 1,200), which grew up around its venerable mission. It's three miles off Highway 101, thirty-three miles from the Monterey Peninsula, and ninety-seven from San Francisco. One of its charms is its invariably sunny, although breezy, afternoons. The local Chamber of Commerce calls the weather salubrious.

Its main charm, however, is that when you drive or cycle into San Juan, you're back in the leisurely days of the Spanish grandees. No wonder almost half a million tourists visit each year. The grassy plaza in front of the mission is much the same as it was when Mexican soldiers drilled there, and the grounds that overlook the San Benito River Valley are still almost as pastoral. The buildings fronting the plaza's other two sides have been restored, as other historic structures through the town have been. Much of this community is now included in a state historic park. You can get walking-tour guides at most stores and at the Chamber of Commerce (408/623-2454), 201 Third Street.

little town boomed. At one entrance a plaque gives instructions for stagecoach passengers. A few are:

> Spit to the leeward.
> Don't shout, as it might frighten the horses.
> If you have anything to drink in a bottle pass it around.
> Don't point out where murders have been committed, especially if there are women passengers.
> Don't grease your hair, because travel is dusty.

Across from the Plaza Hotel on Mariposa, beside an old-fashioned mixed garden, is an old rough-hewn wooden settler's cabin, moved here because it was so typical of mid-nineteenth-century living quarters. Much more elegant is the two-story **Breen-Castro Adobe** on Second Street, built in 1825 by José Castro and used as headquarters for his successful military excursions. For a small fee you can see the rooms, some furnished in the Spanish style and some in later Victorian styles. (As a reminder of the town's past, on the first Saturday of each month many inhabitants don costumes of the 1860s.)

Probably the most famous of the many restaurants and delis in town is La Casa Rosa (408/623-4563), 107 Third Street. It's open for lunch and frequently for dinner, with reservations. Here you can expect the same menu they've served since the early 1930s: butter lettuce salads dressed with fresh herbs; fresh, locally baked rolls; and a choice of Peruvian-inspired Old or New California casseroles, with melted sharp cheese and meat sauce or a hearty soufflé with butter-bread topping. Early birds can enjoy this outside in the small herb garden in back. While you're there, notice the size of the ivy trunks. Another gourmet find in town is the Mariposa House (408/623-4666), which serves a different menu for lunch and dinner each day; this includes the "chef's whim of the day." People from around the world bring recipes to the chef-owner. You can eat outside here, too. It's at 37 Mariposa. If you prefer to picnic, you have a choice of many attractive areas, including a huge picnic area near the mission.

As for entertainment, El Teatro Campesino (408/623-2444), a resident and touring Chicano theater group has a permanent theater in a renovated packing shed at 705 Fourth Street. Besides their Spanish-language plays, they are now presenting old-time plays in English.

Two big annual events draw crowds to San Juan Bautista. The **Fiesta-Rodeo,** held in early July, started in 1907 and 1908 to raise funds to help repair the 1906 earthquake damage to the mission. The annual **Flea Market** in early August is a gargantuan affair. The hundred or more booths vending crafts, antiques, and whatnots are almost strangled by blocks of milling tourists. However, even on the most crowded weekends, you can escape to the peace of the mission and its plaza.

Where to stay? If you're in a camper or RV, you have few choices. The KOA Campground (408/623-4263), 900 Anzar Road, has a swimming pool and recreation area. Close by town on the Alameda is the Mission Farm RV Campground (408/623-4456).

A motel is scheduled to open soon and may have by the time you read this. Bed and Breakfast San Juan (408/623-4101) at 315 The Alameda is a delightfully "fun" place to stay. The only objection seems to be that the proprietor and other guests make your stay so entertaining you don't spend enough time sightseeing in this town, one of the most attractive and historic in all of California.

18

Carmel to the Edge of Big Sur

~~~~~~~~~~~~~~~~~~~~~~

At Carmel's Ocean Avenue, going south, Highway 1 funnels into two lanes. Soon after is the left-turn lane for **Carmel Valley** that goes fourteen miles inland between the peninsula mountains and the Santa Lucias. The Carmel Valley Road follows the Carmel River, which originates thirty miles southeast in the rugged coast ranges. Carmel Valley itself is often called the golden ghetto. Here the elite meet at "ranches" to play tennis or golf or indulge in other sports, under usually tranquil sunshine. Most literature about this valley describes it as pastoral or bucolic, but by the time you visit, it may be wall-to-wall condominiums, resorts, and shopping centers.

Just inland off Highway 1 are two huge collections of shops, restaurants, and bakeries. The newer arrival is **The Crossroads** with over fifty establishments, including a supermarket, a bagel bakery, a boutique for car buffs, a wood carver's gallery, an Arctic Bay Trading Company, and an odd-looking concrete post office. You can spot **The Barnyard** complex by its wooden windmill. Here you'll discover fifty-five shops and galleries plus eleven restaurants, nine with outdoor seating, all in a garden setting. Even if you're an anti–shopping center person, wander around for a while. The barns and walkways, liberally decorated with flowers, are attractive. Perhaps the hub is the **Thunderbird Bookstore** (408/ 624-1803), with over 100,000 volumes *and* a restaurant. Most other establishments are also hard to resist, especially Country-Wide Crafts in the Valley Barn or the Scotch House with its sweaters or the art galleries or—find your own favorites. You'll also come upon a tiny office for **Friends of the Sea Otter,** whose volunteers are dedicated to preserving this captivating little sea mammal.

The **Carmel River,** which runs near the Carmel Valley Road for miles inland, is one of the few rivers where steelhead trout still spawn. To give them a chance to accomplish this, fishing is prohibited in the portion of the Carmel River upstream from Robles del Rio Bridge in the Carmel Valley Village. Downstream from there, when the fish are running—from November through February, usually after a heavy rain—fishermen stand elbow to elbow in the water trying to hook the legal limit of two each. Property owners along the way are not happy, to put it mildly, with these trampling hordes who often climb over their fences and stalk across their gardens to reach the river.

One mile inland from Highway 1 is the Rancho Canada Golf Club (408/624-0111), open to the public, with two championship courses that cross over five bridges. Three and one half miles from Highway 1 is a discreet sign for the award-winning **Quail Lodge,** which adjoins the private Carmel Valley Golf and Country Club. Turn in at Valley Greens Drive. Park among the Rolls and Mercedes Benz (you can even hire a Rolls taxi here) and take a look at the lodge, where each room or cottage looks out on greenery or water and where even the ducks have homes designed by architects. You can dine in the appropriately named Covey Restaurant (408/624-1581), but jackets and reservations are required.

If your budget is geared more for camping, turn right at Schulte Road, a short distance farther for the Saddle Mountain Recreation Park (408/624-1617) or Riverside Park (408/624-9329). Both have overnight facilities, picnic grounds, and hiking trails. At Saddle Mountain, for an additional fee, you can use the swimming pool. You can also take the three-and-one-half-mile hiking trail up, up 1,000 feet for a view of mountains and bay.

A historic area—including the remainder of the Berwick homestead, orchard, and the old barn—much painted by artists, is on Berwick Drive. One house, started in the 1840s, still has hand-hewn beams tied with rawhide. Robert Louis Stevenson slept in the barn and also in a weathered shack way back off the semiwild Robinson Canyon Road where owls hoot at night and some wildlife still roams. The Korean Buddhist Sambosa, who have a temple at the beginning of the canyon, find this area secluded enough for the students' long retreats and meditation. The public is invited to attend 11 A.M. Sunday services (408/624-3686).

Six miles in, on your right, are the Carmel Valley Begonia Gardens (408/624-7231). Because of the combination of fertile soil and sunshine, the begonias, fuchsias, hydrangeas, and other flowers and plants seem to be bigger and more showy than in many other gardens. Open 9 A.M. to 5 P.M. except Wednesday.

Garland Ranch Regional Park is eight and a half miles in. Look for the sign on your right just before the Laureles Grade Road and park your car or bike. As you walk over the bridge to the park entrance, pause. You may glimpse egrets, great blue herons, belted kingfishers, and other birds on or by the Carmel River. When you pay the small entrance fee at the visitors center you can pick up folders describing other birds and wildlife found here. There's also a small map showing the many hiking trails. Besides the area by the river, this 2,000-acre park includes gentle oak-covered slopes, beautiful high grassy mesas with vista points, and wildflowers all year. One trail leads to an old Indian grinding stone, another to a waterfall—if the winter and spring rains have cooperated. If you're eager for a stiff hike, go to the top of Sniveley's Ridge, where you have a dramatic view across the valley and bay. There's also a short, easy, self-guided nature trail. For more information, phone the Garland Park Visitors Center at (408) 659-4488.

The **Los Laureles Road,** next, climbs north over the mountains and connects with State Highway 68, which goes between Salinas and Monterey. As you return after further explorations into the eastern Carmel Valley, for a change of pace, why not take this road back?

One of the oldest dwellings in the Carmel Valley, the Boronda Adobe, circa 1840, is now in private hands, but it's worth a look anyway. Turn right on Boronda Lane by a big real estate office and drive a short distance between huge eucalyptus trees. The adobe is behind a fence to your right. At least you will be able to glimpse its red-tiled roof.

Carmel Valley Village, two miles inland from the Los Laureles Road, is where many valley people socialize and shop. Although there are restaurants, gift shops, and a book shop, camera-toting tourists are rare in the daytime. At night, however, many drive in to dine at the restaurants in the village or nearby, such as the Los Laureles Lodge or the Fox Hill Restaurant at the Carmel Valley Inn. Unless you're bound for the COMSAT (Communications Satellite Earth Station) ten miles farther or intend to go into the Los Padres National Forest, bid goodbye to the madonna who stands benignly in a grove of oaks in the center of Carmel Village and turn back.

If you have arranged to go to the **Zen Center** at the **Tassajara Hot Springs Resort,** continue past the satellite station, turn right at the Cachagua Road, then left onto Jamesburg Road or Tassajara Road and drive a slow, jolting ninety minutes to the isolated

Point Lobos has fascinated more photographers, artists, and writers than almost any other scenic spot.

forty-eight-acre Zen Center at the end. This was once a fashionable resort, but the hotel burned in 1949. The Zen Center of San Francisco bought the property for a Japanese-style monastery where students can study Zen. Visitors are allowed from May 1 to September 6, although overnight reservations must be made far in advance. For day use, picnicking, and using the hot baths, reserve at least one week ahead (408/659-2229). For those without cars or drivers who hesitate subjecting their cars to the punishment of this road, a bus for the Zen Center leaves the headquarters in Jamesburg at 11 A.M. and another bus leaves the center for the return at 3 P.M.

The 2,000-acre **Hastings Natural History Reservation,** owned by the University of California, is off the Jamesburg–Arroyo Seco Road. However, it is open only to students and researchers who come to study plants and wildlife in a natural environment. To keep the area natural, no cutting, grazing, or burning is allowed. The wild animals, too, are left alone except for the wild boar; they are shot on sight because they can ruin a whole acre overnight.

As you head west toward the foggy ocean on the Carmel Valley Road, you still have thrills in store. If you're driving the legal speed limit, you're sure to have lines of angry drivers piled up behind you. Unless you want to outrun or out-macho them, you'll be pulling over frequently to catch your breath. As Robert Jones, a writer for the *Monterey Peninsula Herald* commented, "The Carmel Valley Road seems to serve for Peninsulans year round the same purpose as the running of the bulls does for the young manhood of Pamplona every summer."

Just after you reach Highway 1 and turn left, take a look at the Santa Lucia Mountains looming up behind a shopping center (your last chance to stock up on food and necessities before hitting expensive Big Sur prices). If you see a white slash in the flank of the mountain, it may be where Father Serra removed chalk rock to use around the adobe missions he helped build.

The Cabrillo Highway (1) continues over the Carmel River Bridge past a sea of artichokes on land that developers tried to cover, a battle that went on for over a decade. The artichoke fields toward the ocean were finally bought by Carmel to keep them open. The fields on the inland side are still in limbo.

One reminder of early Spanish explorations is the replica of a cross that Portola planted while attempting to find Monterey Bay. It's off the highway but worth a visit. Follow Ribera Road to the right through a housing development, turn right at Calle la Cruz, and park near the chained dirt road. The road and path lead to a simple wood cross on a weed-choked knoll with a 360-degree view of the mountains and sea.

Back on Highway 1 soon after the turnoff, you glimpse a little red wooden schoolhouse, overlooking the sea, that makes even city folk nostalgic. The school, now a cooperative nursery run by parents, was built over a century ago. In 1889 it was sold by a Carmel rancher to school trustees. The price? Four gold dollars for the land, one for the school building. Since then it has been in continuous use, although on occasion, when the Carmel bridge was flooded over, some students could not attend. At one time, all eight grades were in one room and the student population ranged from six to forty-five students. In 1955 when it was decided the children would be bused to the Carmel school, the nursery school moved in. It turned out to be a great place for youngsters to learn about nature; river and ocean were nearby and wildlife was all around—from coveys of quail to excited sea birds. Throughout the years since, parents, teachers, and neighbors—including singer Joan Baez—have worked together to raise money, clean, paint, add play equipment, and repair it to make the perfect little red schoolhouse it is today.

Next, you arrive at the south end of the **Carmel River State Beach,** although this photogenic section with inviting sand and wheeling gulls is usually known as **San Jose Creek Beach** or **Monastery Beach.** (Those black oily monsters you see lurking in the water usually turn out to be skin divers.) The beach is a lovely stretch for strolling and picnicking while you listen to the sea. If you see nuns frolicking about in tennis shoes, they are probably from the small rest home for Dominican nuns across the highway. The nuns, who live in seclusion amid the lush scenery, have taken a vow of silence, broken only for emergencies, prayer, and short periods of recreation. The chapel of the large white **Carmelite Monastery** that dramatically overlooks the area is open to the public. From below it looks as though you could see all over from the monastery, but dark cypresses in front choke off the view.

Get out your camera and binoculars and prepare to spend several hours at the next stop south. **Point Lobos State Reserve** was named Lobos, or "sea wolves," by the early Spanish for the many sea lions that congregate there. This reserve—a reserve is property held in trust as nature intended it for the enjoyment, education, and inspiration of the public —is often called the crown jewel of all California's

Sculptured sandstones at Point Lobos State Reserve evoke the moon's surface and are 60-million-year-old survivors of the Paleocene period.

parks. Its 1,250 acres of headland, underwater reserve, and upland area include some of the world's most spectacular meeting places of pounding sea and wind. Sometimes you'll see surf crash fifty feet up the side of a cliff. The wind (you usually need a sweater) is responsible for twisting many once-green cypresses into bleached, gnarled shapes. Yet for all its wild beauty, gentle, unobtrusive trails lead to little known and secluded beaches or inland into quiet woods where trees are festooned with lichen and where owls nest.

Point Lobos, many say, has fascinated more photographers, artists, and writers than almost any other scenic spot. Robert Louis Stevenson probably used it as a model for Spyglass Hill in *Treasure Island* and Robinson Jeffers set his poem "Tamar" here.

It was off this same rocky headland in July 1845 that the English *Star of the West* went down. When word got out that her cargo consisted mainly of liquor and bolts of cloth, nearby citizens congregated on the shore with empty wagons; three men lost their lives trying to salvage some of the valuable cargo. As a postscript to this disaster, in 1900 the *Star of the West* ship's bell was found on a nearby field. Who knows what other mementos will be uncovered in future years when the sea and sands cooperate?

Park authorities call Point Lobos a living museum of land and sea life, and it is much the same as when Sebastian Vizcaino camped nearby in 1542, after he was sent out by Spain to locate a good port. Any Indians Vizcaino may have encountered were visiting, too: Since there was no reliable fresh water on

Sea Otters—
Captivating Stars
of the Coast

A baby sea otter snoozes on his mother's stomach, as they bob in the water.

Of the sea mammals you see along this California Coast, watching the antics of the sea otter (*Enhydra lutris*) comes the closest to sheer pleasure. (One bridegroom even reported that seeing an otter on his back, cracking shellfish open on his stomach, was the highlight of his honeymoon.) From Monterey south, with any luck, you should be able to enjoy watching these playful mammals frolicking, then rolling over on their backs in the kelp to rest or eat, using their chests like a table and their paws to crack open a shell with a rock.

Otters are much smaller than seals and sea lions; males grow to only four and half feet and females are shorter. They are kin to river otters, weasels, and minks. Besides those dexterous paws they have small ears, alert faces, paddle-

like rear feet, and bright eyes that regard humans like you curiously. A baby otter nurses and rests on its mother's stomach as she paddles away on her back.

It's often hard to spot these little creatures. They like to stay in kelp beds for protection and to rest (waterbeds are nothing new to sea otters); wrapped in kelp, their heads look much like the bobbing kelp bulbs and probably two-thirds of the "otters" spotted by excited on-lookers *are* actually kelp bulbs.

Sea otters' fur is a rich, lustrous brown. Other marine animals rely on a layer of fat for protection against the cold sea; sea otters depend on the insulating capacity of this fine dense fur. To keep it fluffy, they often ruffle their fur with their paws. The slightest contamination by oil or any substance that produces matting causes the fur to lose its insulating capacity immediately. With a loss of body heat, the otter faces lower resistance to disease and death.

Their thick, beautiful fur was almost their downfall. In the 1700s there were probably over half a million sea otters in the waters stretching from the northern islands of Japan along the Siberian coast to the Aleutian Islands, then south along the entire North American coast from Alaska to Mexico. Russian, American, and Japanese hunters killed off almost the entire population. Of the southern subspecies, only a handful of the more wary remained. There was great excitement when a large group (called a *raft*) was spotted at Bixby Creek in the Big Sur. The survivors had learned their lesson well. To this day otters stay offshore in isolated areas, mainly in kelp beds, for almost all their activities, including breeding.

In 1911 the first international treaty was signed prohibiting taking sea otters or selling their fur. California laws provide stringent penalties for taking or possessing sea otters or their skins. Sea otters are now protected within the 140 miles of California coastline that is their home.

This southern subspecies, numbering anywhere from 700 to 1,000 at present, now finds itself in the middle of a violent controversy. It's hard to imagine anyone who isn't captivated by these mischievous sea animals; there's even a group called Friends of the Sea Otter, spearheaded by Mrs. Nathaniel Owings of Big Sur, who is dedicated to protecting them. Commercial abalone fishermen, especially around Morro Bay, are not as entranced. They insist the otters are gobbling up most of their take of abalone and other seafood delicacies that the public has grown to like.

Otters also consume sea urchins, a major kelp predator, which may help in the reestablishment of commercial kelp beds. Abalone, in turn, need kelp for food and may ultimately benefit from the sea otter's presence. The end result would be a good example of ecological balance. You decide who is the real predator in this controversy, sea otters or man?

the headland, for centuries Indians came out here only to fish and gather abalone, mussels, and other mollusks.

It is a miracle that the headland survived unscathed until, with the help of the Save-the-Redwood League, it was made a state reserve in 1933. In the more relaxed days of the Mexican regime, it may have once changed hands in a card game. It was used by smugglers, and between 1861 and 1864 it was the site of a whaling station. At **Whaler's Cove** you can still see the rustic cabin and the iron pot Portuguese whalers used to boil chunks of odoriferous, up-to-forty-ton catches. Later Japanese fishermen operated an abalone cannery.

More recently Point Lobos barely escaped the bulldozers of developers. In the early eighteen-nineties the then owners, the Carmelo Land and Coal Company, subdivided the headland into a grid of nearly 1,000 lots, some only twenty-five feet wide. Luckily, in 1898 A. H. Allen bought 640 acres for a live-in ranch and acquired many of the lots. So the headland remained essentially intact and was available for purchase after Allen's death in 1930. Luckily, also, it survived frequent fires and other hazards.

Although millions of people have visited Point Lobos since it has been protected, the natural environment has actually improved. According to the book *Point Lobos: Interpretation of a Primitive Landscape* published jointly by the University of California and the State of California, "the cypress groves are flourishing, the woods and meadows are alive with birds and other wildlife, and the shoreline teems with life, some rarely seen elsewhere."

More than 300 varieties of plants and over 250 different birds and animals have been located here. The land animals include squirrels; these little beggars greet you at almost every parking spot; when alarmed they emit a whistling bark, then dive into their burrow or a nearby crevice. There are bats, moles, numerous gophers, mice of many varieties, the wood rat, rabbits, opossums, raccoons, long-tailed weasels, striped skunks, and the gray fox. Wildcats show up especially when the black-tail deer population is high. If you time your visit for the early morning, you'll probably glimpse some of these wild animals in the flower-carpeted meadows.

You can admire that floral celebration from early spring into fall; California golden poppies, which the Spaniards called "cups of gold," contrast with blue lupine or purple-lavender ceanothus. You may see yellow johnny jump-ups and buttercups, vivid red Indian paintbrushes, rose mallow, filigree, and acres more. Then, of course, there is poison oak, a beau-

Whales — Migration of the Gentle Giants

If you're fortunate, you will witness the annual migration of one of the world's largest sea mammals, the **gray whale,** on the 14,000-mile round trip from rich feeding grounds in the Arctic to lagoons in Baja California to birth and mate. The migration starts in late November, with the main feature in January. The whales return in the early spring, with mothers and calves lagging behind, sometimes late into March.

The sight of these up to forty-five ton mammals spouting ten to fifteen feet, flapping their flukes (their butterfly-shaped tails) before diving, and perhaps gyrating (breeching) out of the water is unforgettable and deeply moving.

At many exposed headlands all along the coast you have loge seats to this spectacle, especially at the old whaling village of Davenport, at Año Nuevo, Point Lobos, along the Big Sur, and points overlooking the ocean to the south. In Pacifica whales occasionally swim right under the long fishing pier. This is probably as close as you will ever get to these fellow warm-blooded animals who also breathe air and have their babies live.

It is to have their calves and mate in the warm, shallow lagoons in Mexico that the whales are out there migrating. You'll need binoculars to spot their spume, usually past the surf line or kelp line about a half-mile to three miles out. California gray whales usually blow three times at twenty-second intervals; you can actually hear the sound 1,000 feet away. The whale will then usually dive and reappear in three to four minutes. When frightened, however, they may speed up or dive without showing their flukes, exhaling so quietly you see little or no spume.

You may see a whale spyhopping — thrusting out of the water and gazing around. It is even more exciting to see a whale breach, gyrate high in the water, then crash back in a gigantic fountain of spray. No one is sure why they do this. Perhaps it is to shake off the clinging barnacles that have turned their original slate gray to mottled gray. Whales have been seen scratching against rocks off Pedro Point in Pacifica and along the Big Sur to rid themselves of these freeloading pests. Others have been seen showering under freshwater waterfalls along the coast.

Whales were and still are the world's largest creatures. Gray whales, the seventh largest, are impressive enough, but blue whales are the biggest. They may grow to over 110 feet and top the scales at 200 tons, far heavier than two dozen elephants. At the Long Marine Lab, just north of Santa Cruz, you can see the skeleton of a "small" eighty-five-foot female that washed ashore several years ago at Pescadero. It is hard to comprehend this animal whose heart is larger than a small car, with arteries so large you could stand upright in them.

Grays belong to the order *Cetacea,* like all other whales. Instead of having teeth like killer whales, who like to dine on fish and warm

This replica of a gray whale as it was being installed at the Monterey Aquarium shows the mammal's mammoth size.

meat, they and blue whales have a series of sievelike strainers (called *baleen*) so they can filter out small plants and animals from the water. Paradoxically, for such giants, their preferred menu is krill, a tiny shrimplike creature. They eat their fill in the Arctic so they can get on with their migration, the longest undertaken by any mammal.

Some experts consider whales more intelligent than dolphins, who are also in the whale family. Whales are able to communicate and can locate their calves or fellow whales three miles away. Blue and finback whales may communicate their singing/squeaking messages as far as 35 to 100 miles away under extremely favorable conditions.

Once, at the height of the grays' migration, you could see 1,000 whales a day passing by. Now, if you watch from dawn to dusk, you might see 50 to 100. This is a decided improvement over the mid-thirties when only 100 or so of the peaceful gray whales remained, their compatriots hunted to near extinction for their thick blubber and meat, which was often turned into cat food.

"Thar she blows!"

Is it the size of the animals? Whatever the reason, there is an almost primitive thrill each time you see a whale spout. Even if you have stood shivering for an hour on a windy headland or have clung to a pitching boat, the sight of just one gray whale is worth it all. Since whale-watching is now big business, more than fifty commercial whale-watching excursions leave from the Bay Area and ports along the way. During the height of the season, environmental organizations such as Greenpeace, the Oceanic Society, and the Oakland Whale Center offer educational whale boat trips. To help you achieve the thrill, you'll find premium whale-watching spots listed all through this book. The chances are excellent that you, too, will share in this spectacle that has been going on for over 100 million years, the migration of the great gray whales.

tiful red in summer or fall and bright green in spring. Remember, leaflets three—let this plant be!

As for trees, Point Lobos is most famous for its groves of dark green or bleached white Monterey cypresses; it's one of the only two small areas where these grow indigenously. On the northeast side of Cypress Point, an orange-red algae that clings to their dead trunks and limbs turns them to gold-red, especially at sunset.

Besides photogenic sculptured sandstone, even less artistic rocks and pebbles are interesting; some are survivors of the Paleocene period and probably 60 million years old.

If you sit quietly, binoculars at the ready, you're sure to be treated to close-ups of winged wildlife. Because of the numerous small rodents and other prey, you'll spot many hawks and perhaps golden eagles and falcons. The owl is heard at dusk or dawn. You'll see sea birds by the hundreds, often clustered on Bird Island: brown pelicans, pigeon guillemots, gulls, and more. (See page 192 for descriptions of common sea birds.) Inland, just a short distance from the shore, you may see chickadees, sparrows, house finches with their red heads, and busy Allen hummingbirds.

But attracting the most interest here, as all along the coast, are the sea mammals, with the stars of the show the frisky sea otters; you'll often see them just offshore or in coves. It's easy to find the spots the sea lions haul out; just follow the sound of their barking. During the migration of the great gray whales in late November into February and March through April, the trail and rocks at South and North Points are often lined with excited spectators peering through binoculars. Occasionally the whales come right into the coves here. Usually the best lighting conditions for viewing them are in the early morning or late afternoon.

To learn more about the fascinating mixture of land and sea plants and animals, try to get in on the guided tours that are offered twice daily during the summer and less frequently during the off-season. These tours, many led by enthusiastic volunteer docents ranging in age from sixteen to over seventy, may take you to the cypress grove, the pine woods, Bird Island, the North Shore Trail, Whaler's Cove, or the sea lion area. There is also a tidepool walk held early on summer mornings when the weather and tides permit. Because so many foreign visitors come to Point Lobos, a ranger and volunteers produced an

The shy harbor seal is sometimes seen along beaches, but more frequently in harbors, coves, and sloughs.

information pamphlet in five languages. This, however, did not help the contingent of Japanese tourists who were found collecting colorful bouquets of poison oak.

You can swim in chilly **China Cove,** but you can't fish off Point Lobos except along the south shore and offshore at Whaler's Cove, where skiffs can be carried over a gravelly ramp. All waters adjoining Point Lobos are now in a **Marine Ecological Reserve.** Skin divers can observe but not take abalone or other seafood. Spear fishing used to be allowed with a permit, but no longer. Kelp companies are also prohibited from harvesting kelp, which protects sea otters and acts as a nursery for the young of many rockfish.

Making this 775 acres the first underwater reserve was done mainly to protect plants and shoreline creatures. But, in addition to offering protection to central California's richest area of undersea life, this underwater park has its own beauty. In addition to anemones and lush seaweeds, including kelp that can reach seventy feet to the surface, more animals survive here than along the shore. Divers can see brilliant hydrocoral and many varieties of starfish and rockfish, to mention a few. They also find themselves sharing this teeming world with curious otters and sea lions.

For more information on activities in this natural preserve, write Point Lobos State Reserve, Route 1, Box 62, Carmel, CA 93921 or phone (408) 624-4909. Even if you just come to look, Point Lobos is well worth the admission charge, and the maps the rangers hand out are excellent. You are allowed to picnic, but not camp. Hikers and bicyclists are admitted for a lesser fee, but it takes a dedicated walker to cover all the self-guided tours and then hobble back to the gate.

In order to guard the reserve against overuse and so that people can have a more secluded experience, visitors are now asked to wait at the Point Lobos gate when a limit of 450 has been met. This usually occurs on Sunday in the early afternoon, although it has happened as early as 11 A.M. during the heavy tourist season, so be forewarned. Eventually all autos will be banned and visitors will either enter on foot or on shuttle buses that go into the reserve from parking areas near the entrance. In this way the intimate nature of this primitive sanctuary will be retained and even heightened for you and future generations. Where else so close to civilization can you find an area of such dramatic beauty where wildlife outnumbers man?

Carmel Highlands is next, with its lush, succulent gardens and luxury homes, some perched on rocky cliffs overhanging the roiling surf. Watch closely on the left for the turnoff to **Highlands Inn,** a swanky year round resort which, since its recent renovation, is called Highlands Inn Ocean Front Hotel (408/624-3801). (Yes, they bulldozed away that tiny wedding chapel among the scented pines.) Even if you're on a strict budget, stop for a cocktail and enjoy the panoramic view as the sun sets over that incredible stretch of ocean below. This is also a comfortable spot for watching the migration of the gray whales (if you can afford it). Another well-known place to stay, the shocking hued Tickle Pink Motor Inn (408/624-1244), is just south. It, too, has a spectacular view.

On the ocean side of the road below Highlands Inn is an excellent small turnoff for stopping to look back at Point Lobos, especially at the rocks where thousands of cormorants and other sea birds find sanctuary.

Spindrift Road, soon after Wildcat Creek Bridge, twists down toward the ocean, where you'll get a glimpse of secluded mansions and homes.

At **Yankee Point** you'll glimpse rugged coastline where the mountains plunge directly into the ocean, with rarely a rim of sand to soften the blow. Ridges fold into each other into the distance like mountains on a Japanese print. This is the beginning of the **Big Sur,** but that story is still to come.

The Santa Lucia mountains and the raw Pacific meet in a clash of color and sound that is disturbing yet deeply peaceful.

19

Big Sur:
The Northern Edge

T he **Big Sur** is a state of mind, not a place," novelist Lillian Bos Ross wrote decades ago. It is still as true today as when she and her husband, sculptor Harry Dick Ross, lived high on Partington Ridge in a rambling house spawned from a construction shed. The late author Henry Miller called the Big Sur "the face of the earth as the creator intended it to look." He, too, lived at the Big Sur for many years, singing the praises of his adopted Eden, but he later defected to Southern California.

Almost every person who visits or drives along Highway 1 through the Big Sur falls under the spell of this violent yet healing mixture of mountain and sea. Again and again artists, writers, photographers, and filmmakers have tried to capture its wild moods, until it has become one of the most famous areas in the world.

Today it is hard to realize as you drive along the Big Sur coastline that this narrow strip of land was considered virtually inaccessible almost into this century. As late as 1911 Van Wyck Brooks wrote:

> There was down by the Sur and beyond on the coastal trail, a no-man's land, a wilderness, sinister and dark . . . Even the lonely upland ranches overhanging the sea that straggled up from the Big Sur seemed forlorn.

Since it was so cut off from the rest of the continent by the Santa Lucia Mountains, mariners made the first reports. Juan Rodríguez Cabrillo, a Portuguese under orders from Spain, sailed close to the Big Sur coastline in 1542 and noted:

> All the coast passed this day is very bold; there is a great swell and the land is very high. There are mountains which seem to reach the heavens, and the sea beats on them;

sailing close to land, it appears as though they would fall on the ships.

What does Big Sur mean? Sur is Spanish for south, so early Spaniards, with headquarters in old Monterey, naturally called this huge primitive area south of them Sur.

Where is the Big Sur? Unofficially, it's probably the route of the mailman who drives this narrow stretch of coast. He starts delivering Big Sur mail just south of the Carmel Highlands and turns around at Gorda, sixty-five miles farther south. Ed Culver drove this route for the Post Office every Monday through Saturday for "twenty beautiful years." Even after he retired he insisted that the Big Sur is America's last paradise for scenery, natural life, and fascinating inhabitants. The "new" mailman agrees with Ed. Whatever its boundaries, each day when he rounds that first curve south of the Carmel Highlands he finds the sight of this enchanted coastline dramatic and awesome.

To his left as he drives south on this twisting highway are the wild, steep Santa Lucia Mountains; to his right the raw Pacific. The two meet in a clash of color and sound that is disturbing yet deeply peaceful. And the Big Sur is different each hour. Some days when the sun is out, he sees ships on the curve of the horizon; sometimes fog muffles even nearby sounds. Some days he drives through storms as violent as the scenery. At many a turn the ocean changes from deep indigo to turquoise to slate blue. Nearby, so close he can feel the spray, waves hurl against that granite shore as they have for millions of years. Through the car's open windows he can often smell the salt tang mixed with the scent of sage and wild grasses.

Along this coast redwoods, crowded into canyons, reach for the sky. Especially in spring he sees mountainsides of flowers: wild lilac, golden poppies, primroses, lupine; there are rumors of a rare white orchid that grows in high isolated canyons. This edge of the continent, too, is the meeting place of animals migrating north or south. In the hills are coyotes, wildcats, mountain lions, wild boars, and rattlesnakes. In the ocean are seals, barking sea lions, and playful otters. Further out, there's the passage of whales. At several spots along his route at times in the fall the trees are golden with Monarch butterflies that migrate from the south to cluster in certain trees on Monterey Bay. Overhead, beside the usual sea birds and small land birds, the hawk, the buzzard, and the golden eagle soar; once the rare condor with its nine-foot wingspread visited.

Fewer than 1,000 permanent residents live along the Big Sur; most of their ranches, houses, and cabins are hidden in deep canyons shadowed by redwoods and sycamores or are perched high on that tilting mountain. For many of these, the mailman's coming is the event of the day. They walk up from the ocean's edge or drive down dirt roads and meet each other at the mailboxes. This group, a surprisingly mixed bag, includes a few old-time ranchers, artists, nonconformists without a hint of genius, motel and restaurant owners, musicians, millionaires, therapists, architects, monks and nuns, disc jockeys, and alternative types of many varieties. They all prefer contending with the rugged elements here to living in the concrete city jungle with its restrictions on private behavior.

Chances are slim that the average person driving through the Big Sur will meet any of these fascinating inhabitants, except for brief encounters with those who earn their living from tourists. Most Big Sur residents remain hidden away behind locked gates festooned with no trespassing signs.

The Big Sur may also disappoint people who like their entertainment and sports spoon-fed. Many of the more active games people play are out. There are no golf courses, bowling alleys, or tennis courts; the ocean is usually too turbulent for swimming and is often hard to get to.

Still, if visitors don't drive this scenic highway as if it were a freeway at commute time (hard to do anyway, with the often heavy traffic); if they pause to savor the sights, sounds, and color at the frequent ocean overlooks or get out and walk back into forested canyons—these visitors will find the Big Sur worth every hairpin turn

Starting from Carmel Highlands, the first creek you cross is **Mal Paso,** meaning bad crossing, and the canyon with its perpendicular sides must have been so for the Spanish and their mules. (Remember, there were no concrete bridges then.) The name was later used as the title of a love poem by Robinson Jeffers.

At **Soberanes Point,** next, you get your first look south along the Big Sur, your first sight of the Santa Lucias knifed by canyons that plummet into the sea, and your first glimpse of the magical Point Sur light station. Since Soberanes has become part of **Garrapata State Park,** you can now park by the side of the road (you'll see the sign) and take an easy trail along the bluffs out to the rocky promontory. There's also a small sandy beach below, but it's from the point you may glimpse the gray whale migrating and meet sea otters. From this point south along the entire Big

This scene at Point Lobos is common all along the Central Coast.

Sur coast, from the highway to the sea, all guns are prohibited, for this is now a California Sea Otter Game Refuge.

Near **Granite Canyon** are tanks and other equipment used by the Department of Fish and Game to study, among other things, how to grow more sea crops. This facility, however, is off-limits to the public except for an open house in late spring. The bridge that crosses Granite Canyon is one of the rarest in the world because it goes over a portion of the ocean. Park off the road on either side of the bridge and walk down the path to see the caves, grottos, and arches that the sea has sculptured. There's also a small waterfall and a dramatic view, great also from the bridge. But from now on you'll have miles of other spectacular views.

The next creek and beach, named **Garrapata,** which is Spanish for wood tick, is much more beautiful than its name. This curving expanse of white sand cut by creeks, with caves on the south end, has always been popular. Be sure to turn out and stop at nearby **Vista Point.** Besides the vista, you can often enjoy the antics of sea otters from here. Just beyond Vista Point, directly in front of a fenced-in home, is a blowhole where a huge spout of water erupts when

the seas and tide are high enough. Walk farther south along the highway for a view of **Rocky Point** and more of the magnificent coastline that is beginning to unfold.

You're treated to almost the same view from Rocky Point Lodge (408/624-2933), a restaurant on the point that advertises "excellent food on the edge of forever." Lunch is from 11:30 A.M. to 3 P.M., dinner from 5:30 on. Legend whispers that this point was once used by pirates and later by bootleggers. You will not see them, but you will see a natural arch on the shoreline if you walk down the hill from this point. You next cross the Rocky Point Bridge (no, this is not the Bixby Creek Bridge, the one in all those photographs).

About twelve miles south of Carmel a narrow road turns inland to **Palo Colorado Canyon,** which, roughly translated from the Spanish, means tall redwood. At the south side is an old weathered three-story house built around 1890 of redwood logs, cut and notched and fitted together without a single nail and chinked with clay or mud and straw. There are nine rooms, two in the third story; sleeping in one during a storm, when the house rocks with the south wind, has been described as an eerie experience.

Palo Colorado Canyon was aptly named; here the redwoods grow close and tall. A surprising number of homes and cabins are half hidden among these trees. Even in summer, the lower portion of the narrow—very narrow—road is often dark and dank; you can even see moss on some telephone wires. This canyon has been hard hit many years and sometimes cut off by raging winter storms. Living here, as in many Big Sur locations, can be hazardous.

As you drive higher, the road widens and you again see the sun. Eight miles from Highway 1 you reach **Bottchers Gap,** run by the U.S. Forest Service. At this dusty end of the road are views, campgrounds (run on the honor system), picnic tables, and restrooms. Many trails lead from here back into the Los Padres National Forest and Ventana Wilderness. Ventana means window in Spanish. Legend has it that a natural bridge crossed over the gap between two mountains at this overlook, making it a natural window. However, the bridge collapsed in the 1906 quake.

Less than two decades ago a couple lived here with only wild animals for neighbors. The husband earned much of their livelihood by shooting mountain lions for the $50 bounty ($60 for females). Now, with the awareness of the need for ecological balance, the bounties have been removed, and the mountain lion is an accepted, although still rare, Big Sur resident.

Although it appears on some maps, **Notley's Landing** is no more. At the turn of the century, when more people lived at the Big Sur than do now, there was a small village here at the ocean's edge just south of the Palo Colorado road. Tanbark and timber were loaded onto ships at this makeshift port, but the business gave out when timber became scarce; the buildings—including a cliffside dance hall—disappeared.

Start slowing down soon after you cross the bridge over **Rocky Creek,** for you're about to arrive at one of the most famous locations along the Big Sur, **Bixby Creek Bridge,** named after early settler Charlie Bixby. Originally known as the Rainbow Bridge, it is one of the world's highest single-span concrete arch bridges—over 260 feet high and over 700 feet long. You can see its soaring beauty for miles in each direction along the highway. If you walk out to the observation alcoves on the bridge (it's safe if there isn't much traffic), besides a fantastic view, you can see the ruins of Bixby Landing, the setting for Robinson Jeffers' poem "Thurso's Landing." In the early part of the century, lime was carried in buckets on a long aerial tramway from inland quarries deep in Bixby canyon to a pier.

A tiny waterfall cascades through ferns and redwoods at the north end of the Old Coast Road at the Big Sur.

You'll probably also see otters far below at the mouth of Bixby Creek. The survival of sea otters, thought to have been hunted to extinction, was first noticed here by an excited onlooker.

Two restaurants erected on this point disappeared. The first fell into the ocean; the second, called the Crocodile's Tail, was also doomed by the eroding cliffside. It was also here in 1966 that Lady Bird Johnson dedicated this portion of Highway 1 as California's first scenic highway.

The building of this tortured highway has often been called an engineering marvel. The sum of $50,000 was set aside when construction started in 1920. Hundreds of men—free men and convicts—dug, scraped, and labored eighteen years. Ten million dollars later the highway was finished. A plan to turn it into a freeway was defeated when the iconoclastic inhabitants banded together to fight the proposal. The result? This beautiful stretch was saved.

However, maintaining this slender lifeline to the outside is a year round project; slides may block the road for months at a time. The worst within memory occurred during and after the winter storms of 1982–1983. By April 5 there were forty-two slides along this sixty miles of highway, including two so enormous they almost defied comprehension. The Sycamore Draw slide, where a worker was killed, was opened at the end of July. The other monster, north of Julia Pfeiffer Burns State Park, which destroyed 1,400 feet of highway, took over a year to clear, with nineteen bulldozers working in waves to push a mountainside toward the devastated highway 1,000 feet below.

For a change of pace, turn inland on the dirt road just north of the Bixby Creek Bridge and drive down the narrow **Old Coast Road,** which rejoins Highway 1 near Andrew Molera State Park to the south. On this wild and dusty fourteen miles (impassable in rain) you'll have a capsule look at the Big Sur in all its moods: first shadowed by redwoods alongside Bixby Creek, then twisting and turning up to share overlooks of mountains and sea with hawks. You'll also feel admiration for early settlers who built and traveled this corkscrew wagon trail when there were no concrete bridges.

For a real feel of how it was in early days, and possibly to meet some wildlife, take enough time for a hike here. The trailhead for one beautiful two-mile hike starts near the Little Sur River seven-tenths of a mile in after you've crossed two bridges. Park to the left at the only spot that's wide enough and head up toward Pico Blanco camp. Be sure to stay on the trail. As in many areas along the Big Sur, private property owners don't want trespassers. One popular sign that used to be posted on many gates and fences read: "Stay Out! Trespassers will be violated."

The old coast highway also passes through a portion of the original Rancho El Sur, originally owned by Capt. John Rogers Cooper. Cooper, an English mariner in his thirties, landed in Monterey in 1823. A short, stocky man with a withered arm, he wooed and won the charming sister of Gen. Mariano Vallejo and was then baptized in the Catholic Church, adopting the name Juan Bautista Rogers Cooper. Eventually Cooper ended up with his own ship and two mammoth land grants, one of them the then 8,946-acre Rancho El Sur. Although he did not live permanently on his holding, Cooper visited often, and his name is still linked with the Big Sur.

Just south of Bixby Creek on Highway 1 is an excellent spot to unlimber your binoculars in spring to view rocks covered with sea birds—murres—during nesting season. Next comes **Hurricane Point.** When you reach it you'll know why it got its name. This is probably the windiest spot on the high-way, so hang onto your hat and onto the steering wheel. Eight hundred feet below are the remains of several cars that didn't make it. Unless you want to join them, pull off at one of the many turnoffs to do your scenery gazing.

Next you'll see one of the most beautiful beaches along the coast, complete with a lagoon that changes its design every day until the rains come. Then the **Little Sur River** flows directly into the ocean. The river and lagoon are a stopping place for herons, cranes, and egrets. Although signs on the barbed wire fence warn you that all this property is private, negotiations are going on to make this a state park and, hopefully, it will be when you next see it. The beach stretches in a sweeping curve south toward the lighthouse. On a calm day (definitely not a windy day), walking it can be sheer pleasure. Don't even wade here, however; the undertow can be dangerous. From the south end of the low-lying bridge over this "little river to the south," you can see 3,700-foot-high Pico Blanco, with its huge deposits of lime. How the mining company blasting out lime in this watershed of the Little Sur River can get it to market is a matter of much discussion among Big Sur people, who are also concerned about the noise and confusion disturbing the peregrine falcons in the area.

Highway 1 next swings past sand dunes and you get a closer look at the **Big Sur Lighthouse** jutting up far out on a windswept spit. This steep mound of rock and earth, with granite houses barely visible on the top and a road wrapped around it, is like half-remembered fairy-tales, especially when partly veiled by fog. If you ever drive past in a heavy fog, you'll understand why so many ships were wrecked here before Big Sur residents banded together to help erect the lighthouse. The S.S. *Los Angeles* went aground in 1873 and the young doctor who rode the thirty miles from Monterey on horseback found some dead and others alive, clinging to the rocks or washed ashore. In 1879 the *Ventura* was wrecked with its cargo of linens and wagons, and Big Sur inhabitants were well supplied with these items for years. In 1935 the Navy's dirigible *Macon* crashed off Point Sur. Luckily, the lighthouse-keeper saved most of the crew.

Building the lighthouse was a formidable task, even for the hardy Big Sur ranchers. Stone, quarried nearby, had to be hoisted up by ropes and pulleys. Finally in 1889 the lighthouse was opened, and its multilensed lamp, fueled by kerosene, started beaming its light out to sea. According to the book, *California: A Guide to the Golden State,* a W.P.A. project, everyone rejoiced about the lighthouse

Thirty-four acres of windswept sand spit and coast at Point Sur, including the lighthouse, are now a brand new California state park.

except old Choppy Casuse, who commented: "Good light, but she no work. Go all the time sad, 'Boo-Boo,' but the fog, she creep in just the same."

Until that road up the 350-root rock was built, supplies had to be lugged up almost 400 wooden steps to the windswept top. Like so many others, the Big Sur light station is now automated. The present light is visible for 25 miles, and when the lighthouse seems to disappear in the creeping mist, the automatic foghorn sounds its mournful warning. Sunshine or fog, radio signals are sent out to ships more than 150 miles at sea, to guide their course and to warn them off this rocky point. Presently, thirty-four acres at and near Point Sur have been declared a state park. A lighthouse-hostel like those farther north is envisioned for the future.

If you've been impatient with slow, gawking drivers and slow-moving campers you are now arriving at Lighthouse Flats, where you can pass without danger to life and limb. The barrackslike buildings to your right are in the Point Sur Naval Facility, which does oceanographic research but discourages visitors.

Your route south now swings inland by the lacy white buildings of the pioneer Molera Ranch. The Old Coast Road rejoins Highway 1 inland at this point. To your right is the relatively new **Andrew Molera State Park** (408/667-2315); many Big Sur enthusiasts prefer it to all others along this coast. It is here the Big Sur River, flanked by sycamores and maples for a time, finally reaches the sea, and where there's a lagoon often crowded with ducks and other birds. In its 4,786 acres are four miles of ocean front and over sixteen miles of hiking trails. If you walk all these you can try the one to the north of the river's mouth, up and over a steep promontory to Garnet Beach, named for its garnet-colored pebbles. At Andrew Molera you can also enjoy sun-filled meadows with spring wildflowers and views of the mountains all year. Most important, perhaps because you have to walk in from the parking lot, here you can find glorious solitude and perhaps see the golden eagle or mountain lion. The walk-in campground is primitive—chemical toilets and water are dispensed from a tank-truck—but the fee is tiny.

Back in the 1850s the Molera Ranch was part of the Rancho El Sur. Andrew Molera, the grandson of Juan Bautista Rogers Cooper, who originally settled here, was a huge man; a special casket had to be made when he died. In honor of her brother, Frances Molera donated much of the Molera ranch so that the public could enjoy this land. If you like horseback riding, an excellent way to see this area is to join the couple who run Big Sur Trail Rides; for information, write Big Sur Trail Rides, Box 111, Big Sur, CA 93920 or call (408) 667-2666. He's a former ranch hand, she's a former psychologist. Either or both will take you out for a few hours around the park or for a pack trip of several days into this wild country they have chosen as their home.

Youngsters enjoy the sun-dappled Big Sur River, which winds through Pfeiffer Big Sur State Park.

20

Big Sur: Inland Resort Area

Soon after you leave Andrew Molera State Park, going south, Highway 1 curves further inland by the clear Big Sur River, through sun-dappled redwoods, aspen, and sycamores. Most of the accommodations for tourists are here. This area, often called the **Big Sur Valley,** does have the advantage of balmier weather than you find directly on the ocean, but it's certainly not the entire *real* Big Sur, as some tourists think. Also, as visitors and vagabonds discover, prices for everything from gas to wine to food are not cheap.

River Inn (408/667-2237), the first settlement, has a service station, tiny store, motel, and bar-restaurant with windows that frame the crystal clear Big Sur River and its background of incredible greens. At last report this was a popular gathering spot for many locals. Presently the restaurant—which serves breakfast all day, lunch, and dinner inside or outdoors—requires shirts and shoes. In the cocktail lounge you can warm up at a crackling fire in the big stone fire-place—notice the mountain lion skin on the wall. You can also get in on live entertainment most weekends. River Inn possesses a swimming pool, but if you're a hardier type you can sit on a chair in the river and dangle your feet in the icy water. The motel has eleven rooms on the highway and four fancier suites with balconies overlooking the river.

The **Big Sur Campground** (408/667-2322), next south on the river, has rented to generations of families. Presently they have full hookups for RVs and sites for tents. They also rent cabins, trailers, and tents by the day or week. **Riverside Campground** (408/667-2414), also right on the river, has full hookups and rents cabins. A swinging footbridge goes over the river here.

Most of the redwood cabins at the **Ripplewood Resort** (408/667-2242) are by the river, out of sight of the highway. Some have fireplaces; most have kitchens. You can buy gas and there's a store with deli. Often burlwood furniture is on display near the service station. At the south edge of this group of businesses is the well-groomed Glen Oaks Motel (408/667-2105). Across the highway the Glen Oaks Restaurant (408/667-2623) serves breakfast, lunch, and dinner and often lists German dishes on the menu. Civilization, in the form of a beauty shop called The Beauty Bar (408/667-2101), also in this area, is open Wednesday, Thursday, and Friday.

Just past **Juan Higuera Creek Bridge,** a dirt road on your right goes to the **Big Sur Grange Hall** where movies might be shown on Saturday night. The grange is the unofficial social headquarters for permanent Big Sur residents, including remaining pioneers and their descendants. Talented Big Sur inhabitants often put on a big revue here every year, usually in the spring, but chances of getting tickets are slim.

The next road to your right leads to the charming **St. Francis of the Redwoods** where a Catholic mass is usually conducted Saturday afternoon at four. It's a serene experience. The back wall of the chapel, mostly glass, opens up so you can sit inside or outside among the redwoods. Music comes from speakers hidden in the trees.

Fernwood (408/667-2422), half a mile farther south, has a gas station; tiny store; motel; and a restaurant that serves breakfast, lunch, and dinner. The campgrounds are along the river and offer full RV hookups.

About half a mile farther on your left, you'll see the signs for **Pfeiffer Big Sur State Park.** It was named for John Pfeiffer, the youngest son of the Michael Pfeiffer family that arrived in this area in 1869 after a long arduous trek from the north. They decided to winter at Sycamore Canyon, then the end of the trail, and liked the country so well they stayed on. John homesteaded 160 acres nearby and moved into the Homestead Cabin, which still stands in the park. This cabin, built in 1850 or so by George Davis, the first known white man to settle here, was later sold to former mission Indian Emanuel Innocenti (for whom Mount Manuel is named). Innocenti was a vaquero for Cooper, the owner of Rancho El Sur. In 1934 the state park commission started to acquire the nucleus of this 821-acre park from John Pfeiffer, who donated a sizable portion of his holdings.

The park has over 200 sites for RVs and tents, with picnic tables and fire grills. Most are on or near the Big Sur River, which is one of many reasons this park is so popular. Besides wading in the river and fishing in the upland portion (although the practice of stocking the river with trout has been temporarily discontinued), there are guided nature walks and campfire programs put on by rangers. Reserve early, especially for holiday weekends and during summer, through your local Ticketron outlet or write the Department of Parks and Recreation, 1416 Ninth Street, Sacramento, CA 95814. Fees for day use and overnight camping are collected at the park entrance, although there's no charge for just driving through to look. The park number is (408) 667-2315.

Along the river are western sycamores, black cottonwoods, big leaf maples, alders, willows, and redwoods. The forest floor is a carpet of ferns and other shade-loving plants. On south-facing slopes you'll find coast live oaks, chaparral, and other plants that prefer the warmer, drier conditions. The rare Santa Lucia bristlecone fir is native to this area. You'll also find quantities of poison oak. As for wildlife, black-tailed deer often wander through the park after dusk. Upstream, you may see water ouzels, those chunky little birds that walk under water. Close up, you're sure to see jays; they're particularly aggressive around campsites and will steal food right off the picnic tables. Another hazard are those black-masked bandits, the raccoons; they find this area profitable, what with its garbage cans, careless campers, and a river where they can wash their food. Since they have learned to open up almost every variety of ice chest, unless you want to donate your food keep your supplies locked in your car with the windows up.

The Big Sur Lodge (408/667-2171), a private concession, is fenced in from the highway; you drive in through the park entrance nearby. A store sells groceries and camping supplies; a gift store sells gifts; a restaurant serves breakfast and lunch; and there's a swimming pool and sauna. Lodge units vary from small to large. Many face on a large meadow, often so quiet at night you can hear owls calling to each other.

Back on Highway 1, about half a mile farther south on your left is a collection of buildings and trailers shown on maps as **Big Sur,** where much behind-the-scene activity is carried on; the maintenance station crews that work at keeping the highway open are located here. You may also glimpse the gate that is closed across the highway when traveling is considered too dangerous. The Big Sur Post Office was moved here temporarily in 1972. The U.S. Forest Service office (408/667-2423) is here, also, and you can obtain the mandatory permits for campfires or hiking in the Ventana Wilderness and Los Padres National Forest. If you plan to camp at one of the

A long stretch of white sand and caves carved out of rock make Pfeiffer Beach a soothing, if windy, spot.

many primitive campgrounds in this wilderness, after you obtain maps and that necessary permit, there's space nearby to leave your car for several days.

Soon after you leave this Big Sur settlement, Highway 1 going south starts to climb steeply and you may see wisps of fog ahead. Keep a constant lookout on your right on the north side of Pfeiffer Canyon Bridge for the sharp turnoff downhill (the second right turnoff about a mile after you've left the park, and probably unmarked) to the narrow road that winds two miles down **Sycamore Canyon** to **Pfeiffer Beach.** Park near the public restrooms and walk down through an arch of cypresses to this spectacular beach with its long stretch of fine white sand, caves carved out of rocky cliffs, waves that thunder through arched rocks, driftwood, a lagoon, and— almost always—wind that sandpapers your face and lunch. Swimming is not recommended because of the wind, tricky currents, treacherous surf, and icy water. But if you know how, you may succeed at surf fishing. The beach is open from 6 A.M. to sundown.

As the highway starts to turn toward the ocean, to your right is the **Big Sur Bazaar** (408/667-2197), which shows art, artifacts, and pottery by local artists and craftspeople. The Bazaar carries artichoke servers and a special kit so that you can adopt a redwood.

They also sell T-shirts with the motto: "Big Sur by a Landslide." The Loma Vista Inn next door, open sporadically, features begonias, succulents, and cacti, but also sells gas and beer if the management is in the mood.

Farther up the hill, to your left, is the mellow old Post homestead where stages once stopped after an eleven- ot thirteen-hour trip along the old wagon road from Monterey. William Brainard Post homesteaded land here in the late 1860s and Post descendants still live at the Big Sur. The old Post store, restaurant, and campground plus much surrounding land were sold to the Ventana Corporation in the 1970s. If plans go through, the Post homestead will be renovated to contain a store and other facilities at this location.

The Ventana Campground, down below to your left on forty acres of redwood forest, has 100 campsites including RV spaces with hookups, many near a stream. Up above, over 1,000 feet above sea level, is the **Ventana Big Sur Inn** (408/667-2331) whose forty rooms are not inexpensive. Luxury touches include a ninety-foot heated pool, saunas, hand-painted headboards, a chauffered Mercedes-Benz bus called Hazel, and the possibility of meeting a movie star or other celebrity. The restaurant has two levels, and you can dine outside with a view over

To the south of Nepenthe is the mix of sea and mountain that is the Big Sur.

the ocean when the weather cooperates. You can also browse through the "country store," with everything from imported gifts to local porcelain, quilts, and weaving—a tempting display.

Your next stop, **Nepenthe** (408/667-2345), thirty miles south of Carmel, is probably the most famous restaurant along the Big Sur. It's derived from the Greek word meaning *no-sorrow* and was a mythical Egyptian drug given to induce forgetfulness. Now all year from noon to about midnight, tourists by the thousands puff up the steep path from the parking lots to seek "surcease from their sorrows." They sit in the open-beamed restaurant, which is more than 800 feet above the sea, or outside in tiers sipping cocktails or quaffing beer (the pitcher is still the best buy) or munching hamburgers, called ambrosia-burgers. Dinner menus usually include steak and seafood.

Before World War II, Orson Welles had the good taste to buy a small redwood cabin here that had been used by a Trails Club. The woman occupying it planned to move out so that Welles could move in. He never did, and in spite of wishful legends that he and Rita Hayworth honeymooned here, they didn't.

In 1947 Billy and Lolly Fassett bought the place. With the help of a student of Frank Lloyd Wright, they erected a restaurant that seems to float along the treetops. Inside, as you look out, it's as though you were still outside.

Nepenthe is presently open all year. When it used to close for three months during winter, the Fassetts and their five children would throw a gala party on Halloween night for selected guests. Costumes were expected; at the 1954 closing a couple came attired only in fig leaves. But picturesqueness was kept within bonds; berets and beards were welcome, but no rowdiness, please. It is quieter now than when music used to pour out of an outside hi-fi and folk dancers (including Kim Novak), many in bare feet, danced by the light of the open fireplace, creating a picture of a pagan rite under the stars.

Buzz Brown's statue of Jesus is still starkly silhouetted against the sky, but there have been changes. Nepenthe has since added layers of parking lots; sprouted a health food deli; and enlarged the Phoenix gift shop, which features original jewelry, books, handcrafted and woven articles, and a boutique. Though it has grown more elegant, Nepenthe still retains an out-of-this-troubled-world atmosphere. On the flagstone terrace a graceful sculptured wood bird overlooks a new generation of tourists who talk in hushed tones as they contemplate the miles of mountains unfolding into the sea.

Half a mile farther south, keep a sharp lookout to your left for the **Henry Miller Memorial Library** in a rustic house almost hidden in a grove of redwoods. Inside, among piles of Miller's once-banned books, photographs, and other memorabilia, Emil White—long-time radical, Bohemian, primitive painter, lover of women, and follower of Henry Miller—holds court. Miller called him "one of the few friends who has never failed me."

After you leave Nepenthe and the Miller library, the highway dips down by a small canyon near a bridge. On the landward side at a small, dangerous turnoff is **Deetjen's Big Sur Inn** (408/667-2377). To many this rambling flower-covered collection of buildings most typifies Big Sur. Here the ambience has remained much the same as when it was spawned from driftwood and old wharf timbers by the late Norwegian carpenter, Helmut, and bulky Helen "Ma" Deetjen. The Inn and grounds are now a county park and the "new" overseers have done much cleaning up and renovating.

Dinner at the inn is by reservation for the two sittings. Guests are served by candlelight on Royal Staffordshire china to a background of classical recorded music. (Helmut used to inform guests that music, nature, and art were the only important things in life.) The inn rents rooms and cabins at inexpensive to moderate rates. Some rooms have fireplaces, some are back in Castro Canyon near the cool stream that runs through the property, some share baths. If you insist on superscrubbed chrome, the Big Sur Inn isn't for you. But many guests who stop here by chance linger on and come back, again and again.

If you're eager for another look at the ocean, you can park nearby at **Castro Canyon Bridge,** walk over, and gaze down a perpendicular cliff at a sandy beach. Just look—don't ever try to scramble down. At **Grimes Point** is another sheer drop. Far below you'll usually see elephant seals and sea lions, and you can watch the turbulent sea where waves from the north and south smash together.

The **Coast Gallery** (408/667-2301) at Lafler Canyon is next left. Its parking area and garden fronting the highway slid into the ocean several stormy seasons ago. The gallery, housed in two round redwood tanks, happily survived to show Gary's candles as well as sculpture and art by local people, including some original watercolors by Henry Miller. The canyon is named for Harry Lafler, a former editor and friend of Jack London and other Seacoast Bohemians. One legend has Lafler sleeping in the hollowed-out trunk of a redwood before moving to a stone house high on the mountainside above Nepenthe.

Slow down if you want to make the next tight curves on four wheels, especially at **Torre Canyon.** But you're probably in practice by now, and there's more to come.

About a mile farther you'll see a wide turnoff to your right and across the highway a steep road marked "Dangerous and Private," headed up the mountainside. You're now at **Partington Ridge.** In the 1940s and 1950s, the colorful mailboxes at the turnoff carried the names of an interesting mix of residents, including the nephew of President Roosevelt, a scion of railroad millions, a lovable no-good, working artists and writers, and on and on. The most famous resident was Henry Miller, who had the distinction of having an outside bathtub at his home on Partington Ridge. Miller's sojourn here was greatly responsible for the Big Sur's reputation for attracting wild, free-wheeling types.

Then, as now, long-time inhabitants know that it takes a special temperament to live in this secluded grandeur. One anthropologist explained that a person becomes microscopic against this backdrop. Poet Bill Everson (Brother Antoninus) believes that this rugged land searches out the flaw in a person's nature and may destroy him. Doug Madsen, a painter and mosaicist who lived on squirrel and deer while building his home here, once insisted that the only people who can be happy at the Big Sur were born under the signs of Taurus, Virgo, or Capricorn.

Surviving in the Big Sur *is* rigorous, as successive tides of drifters have discovered, and this lesson is continually being relearned by residents. Many old-timers have a hard enough time surviving by themselves without sharing.

There are other hazards. The fog is often chilly, and the rains descend in torrents during the winter. There's no corner grocery store, and growing even simple crops on the mountainside is limited by the thin rocky soil and lack of water. Who gets what share of water from the few streams is a constant source of friction. If water is available and a few vegetables survive, the crop may be shared by gophers, raccoons, wild pigs, deer, and other four-footed thieves, to say nothing about hungry birds.

Even before Miller, this land attracted noncon-formists, some bigger than life. The late Jaime de Angulo, a brilliant enigma, was one of these. In 1914 when he built his ruggedly different home on Partington Ridge, 2,000 feet above the ocean, a neighbor reported seeing him outside plowing, garbed only in

a red handkerchief which was wrapped around his head. This, like most Big Sur legends, may or may not be true. Jaime, who had received an M.D., later became an amateur anthropologist, studying Indians. He eventually spoke thirty languages and Indian dialects, and his collection, *Indian Tales,* is still a cult favorite. In later years Jaime poked a smokehole in the roof of his living room so he could cook on the floor, Indian style.

At one time Jaime put up a sign reading "Trespassers Welcome" on the de Angulo trail, on the east side of the highway a mile south of Torre Canyon. This trail leads to the top of the ridge in the Los Padres National Forest. From here the intrepid hiker can see miles of rugged coast and ocean—on some days a brilliant blue, on others hidden by a quilt of fog. The entrance to this trail is hard to find. Look for the sign reading "Cold Springs Camp" about fifty feet up the hill; take the smaller trail to the left. If you forgo this somewhat chancy adventure, at least sit for a while on the wooden bench on the ocean side of the Partington Ridge mailboxes. This is a great spot to ocean- and whale-watch.

Partington Cove, almost a mile south of Partington Ridge, is now part of Julia Pfeiffer Burns State Park. Park on the east side of the highway and walk over to a black mailbox by a fence. The steep

Looking north along the coast from high up on the Big Sur's Partington Ridge.

At a wide turnoff off Highway 1 just north of Julia Pfeiffer Burns State Park you can see the 1,300-foot scar of the biggest slide in the history of Big Sur.

path leads down to a choice of three experiences. Halfway down you can loop back into the redwoods and by a primitive restroom. Way down at the mouth of the stream is a small beach where you can picnic and watch waves and creek meet in a clash of bright water. The third choice is to the south across a wooden footbridge and through a tunnel, hewn out of rock by pioneer John Partington in the 1880s, that leads to the remains of a dock where tanbark was loaded in those days. The beauty of this cove can be intoxicating. At times the water is the clear, translucent blue of Capri and waves, with their burden of golden seaweed, rise, glitter for an instant in the sun, and crash with a rhythmic hollow sound against the rocky cliffs that are pitted with caverns. Hope for a visit when you can sit immersed in solitude as you listen and look.

Before you reach the entrance to the next portion of beautiful Julia Pfeiffer Burns State Park, pull off at the wide turnoff to your right and join the people gazing at what was one of the biggest slides in the history of Big Sur. Perhaps by the time you see it, the mammoth 1,300-foot-high scar will be partially healed by a cover of grass, plants, and flowers.

Many visitors pick **Julia Pfeiffer Burns State Park** as their favorite along this spectacular coast. Its 3,543 acres extend for miles on both sides of Highway 1. Near the entrance up the canyon by a rushing creek, shadowed by redwoods, are picnic tables and trails leading through redwood groves up to the drier chaparral community. Perhaps even more awe-inspiring is the view of Waterfall Cove and Saddle Rock that you reach by a short, easy five-minute walk toward the ocean through a tunnel under Highway 1. There McWay Creek plummets some fifty feet from granite cliffs directly into the ocean. The path used to continue on out to a terrace where you could see miles in either direction, including a view of rocks to the north popular with seals and sea lions. A slide severed the last portion of the trail, but it may be fixed by the time you arrive. A two-and-a-half-mile underwater reserve lies just offshore; you can get permission to scuba dive from the ranger. The park also contains two secluded environmental campgrounds. Oh, yes, there are restrooms by the entrance. For park information, call (408) 667-2315.

Lucia, perched 500 feet above the ocean, is an outpost of civilization along the essentially lonely Big Sur south coast.

21

Big Sur:
The South Coast

For a time in the mid 1940s, the small collection of shacks on your right at **Anderson Creek** housed an art colony which included Henry Miller and Emil White. Before that, convicts who helped built the highway lived in the cabins. In this isolated region, there were no prison bars, only a $200 reward for anyone who caught an escapee. Many of the convicts, however, preferred life at the Big Sur to inside prison walls, especially since, by California law, they had to be paid. Tales are still told about the convicts' feats of daring. Once when a woman desperately needed a doctor to help with the birth of her child, the convicts volunteered to work during the black, rainy night to blast open the road that slides had blocked.

After you cross **Burns Creek** and **Buck Creek,** you'll see the South Coast Center to your left, open to participants in seminars and other events at **Esalen Institute,** next south. Only a few shell mounds and rumors of a hidden city called Excelen remain of the

Esselen Indians (or Esalon or Esalen—no one is sure of the spelling) for whom Esalen was named. Their history is shrouded in centuries of fog. Perhaps— and this has haunted many: Did the Big Sur itself reclaim its own emptiness? Poet Robinson Jeffers, who knew this land, wrote: "Does this place [the Sur] care? Not faintly. It has all the time. It knows that people are a tide that swells and in time will ebb, and all their works dissolve."

The sign by the road leading down to Esalen Institute says "By Reservation Only." That means the public can no longer drop in for meals and drinks, as when it was called the Big Sur Hot Springs. More important, now only from 1 P.M. to 5:30 P.M. Sunday through Thursday can just anyone pay the fee and soak away the tensions in the sulphur hot baths almost hanging out over the ocean.

This exclusive policy is a far cry from the way it was after being bought in the 1860s by Thomas Benton Slate, who had been told by Indians of these hot, healing waters. Slate was so crippled by arthritis he had to be carried here by friends. Because he was cured, the grateful Slate allowed anyone with the fortitude to find a way here to use the one tub he had brought in by ship and derricked up the cliff. If the tub was occupied a flag was raised and the supplicant waited.

Dr. Henry Murphy, a prosperous Salinas physician (who delivered John Steinbeck), bought the hot springs from Slate in 1910, hoping to start a European-style health spa. It was never built. World War I started, with its blackouts, and almost no visitors ventured along the coast. The Murphy grandsons, Dennis and Michael, who were supposedly used as models in Steinbeck's *East of Eden,* eventually inherited this property. In 1965 Michael Murphy started a center to "expand human potential," exploring philosophy, psychology, and social anthropology. Over the years expensive brochures have gone out describing seminars by renowned people like Aldous Huxley, Paul Tillich, Carlos Castaneda, Alan Watts, Fritz Perls, and dozens more. For information, write Esalen Institute, Big Sur, CA 93920 or phone (408) 667-2335.

At Lime Creek, the frequently foggy twenty-one-acre **John Little State Reserve** is open to the public for daytime use. When the fog clears, you can see forever (almost).

The highway next crosses **Dolan Creek Bridge** and the more dramatic **Big Creek Bridge.** The 4,000-acre Big Creek Ranch, which stretches four miles along the coast and up into the Santa Lucias, was purchased by the Nature Conservancy in 1977 to be used by the University of California at Santa Cruz as an outdoor laboratory for teaching and research in ecological and biological studies. This preserve teems with wildlife and more than 100 varieties of birds. Steelhead spawn in the creek and otters play in the kelp at its mouth. The Nature Conservancy retains ten acres as an educational center; special groups are allowed in by contacting the Conservancy at (415) 777-0541.

At **Gamboa Point,** almost a mile south of Big Creek Bridge, seals and sea lions converge on the slanted rocks offshore because they are easy to slide onto and off. A short distance farther south is a drinking fountain and mini-picnic grounds.

After Vicente Creek you come to an outpost of civilization along this essentially lonely South Coast. It's **Lucia,** perched 500 feet above the ocean, with a gas station (remember, gas is expensive along the Big Sur) and restrooms. The restaurant opens at 7 A.M.

and generations of visitors have stopped in to sample the homemade split pea soup, pie, or other viands. Weather permitting—usually it permits by noon—visitors can sit outside overlooking the ocean. The ten rustic motel cabins (408/667-2391) are perched on another even more spectacular spot a distance from the restaurant.

Lucia and some of the surrounding area is owned by the Harlans, descendants of Wilbur Harlan, who homesteaded here in 1895 after hiking down the coast from Santa Cruz. For many years mail for this lonely area was brought by mule over the mountains from Jolon; the Harlan homestead, near the end of the trail from Jolon, served as a post office. The Coast Trail from Monterey passed nearby also, so their home was a hub of activities, with extra guests often enjoying hearty meals, especially the buttermilk cornbread. At one time, in addition to the constant visitors, seventeen people sat down for meals each day. Each week the Harlans used up a fifty-pound bag of flour ground from their own wheat and corn. The family was almost self-sufficient, except for salt and cooking or sewing equipment. Twice a year, in order to buy these supplies, they would drive their hogs and cattle up over those steep mountains to Jolon. Once it took forty-eight trips back and forth before all the pigs were pushed across the Nacimiento River. Later, Walter Harlan bought supplies for his family and neighbors in San Francisco and chartered a ship to bring them down the coast. The coming of the ship was one of the festive highlights of the year for these isolated families; they would gather and sometimes party for days.

However spartan life might be, these pioneers managed to import teachers to educate their children. A saying went that they would train a mule to bring in a new schoolmaster, shoot the mule, and marry the schoolteacher. Others said the teachers were just too frightened to make the return trip. So they stayed, and usually ended up with a wedding ring. At the turn of the century, children of only four families attended the little redwood school on a tiny shelf above Lucia. As three of these families were of Mexican or Spanish descent and spoke Spanish at home, the American children learned to speak their neighbors' language. Later, when there were no more children to educate, the school was moved to its present location at Pacific Valley, eight miles south.

Shortly after leaving Lucia, on your left, you'll see the road leading to the **Immaculate Heart Hermitage of the Camaldolese Hermits,** an order of monks founded in similar mountains in Italy in 1012.

A sign by a white cross reads "We are here to live a life of prayer in silence and solitude and for this reason we regret we cannot invite you to camp, hunt, or enjoy a walk on our property . . . In view of the nature of our life, we are confident that you will cooperate." Before this sign was posted, trespassers were common; now they are rare. Visitors, however, are welcome to attend the daily masses or to buy crafts and homemade brandied fruitcake (which are also sold in the Hermitage Shop in Carmel). Men—not women—are also welcome to spend several days of retreat on this former Lucia Ranch, 1,300 feet above the ocean. For information, call (408) 667-2456. (When the Harlans sold this property, Lulu Harlan, a spirited woman who died in 1984 at the age of ninety-two, commented, "Our family sold to monks who are not on the right track of the Bible, don't want women around, and make money selling Immaculate Heart fruitcakes.")

You next cross over **Limekiln Creek.** Back when the highway was built, over 163,000 yards of rock had to be blasted out every 1,000 feet to get around Limekiln Point. The privately owned **Limekiln Beach Redwood Campground** (408/667-2403) occupies much of this steep canyon. One short hiking trail leads to four historic lime kilns that supported many people in the 1880s; another trail, where you must scramble over logs, goes to a lovely waterfall. Sixty sites are crowded inland among the redwoods or are right on the ocean beach close to otter country. There's no electricity, though.

The **Kirk Creek Campground** (408/385-5434) has thirty-three sites available on a first come, first served basis, with grills and picnic tables. This beautiful grassy area overlooks the ocean and a sweep of coastline. There are restrooms and also hit squads of aggressive raccoons who help themselves to your food unless it's locked in your car.

Next to the Kirk Creek Bridge, the **Nacimiento-Fergusson Road** twists up the Santa Lucias almost eight miles to the summit, then through thick trees, along the Nacimiento River, into an oak-dotted valley in the **Hunter Liggett Military Reservation,** and finally to the ghost town of **Jolon** and its nearby mission. The road is breathtakingly precipitous; many old-timers suggest it's better to drive down, where you have the inside lane and a view of the ocean to the horizon, with cars crawling along the highway like beetles and hawks riding the wind below you. Whichever way you go, it's an unforget-

The Nacimiento-Fergusson Road, twisting up the Santa Lucias almost eight miles to Jolon, is breathtakingly precipitous.

table experience, even more so in the spring when masses of lupine, poppies, and almost all the state's flowers make their appearance. At many switchbacks you can pause at cool folds, shadowed by redwoods and ferns.

The **Mission San Antonio de Padua** was founded in the Jolon valley in 1771. Now only a scattering of buildings and crumbled ruins of the old adobe Dutton Hotel remain to remind you of the time at the turn of the century when Jolon prospered because it was a natural stopping place for stage-coaches. Today the mission, which many say is the most evocative of any in California, slumbers peacefully before a backdrop of mountains. As you drive toward the long, graceful adobe building—if you ignore the khaki convoys that come and go or the Spanish-looking military headquarters on a nearby knoll—it is as if you turned back the clock over 200 years. It is cool under the arched outside passage where the few remaining Franciscan monks stroll with heads bent. It is cooler inside the church and museum. In the sunny garden courtyard where birds sing above the hum of insects, it is usually warm. Bats flit by at dusk in the passageway leading to the garden. "We are doubly blessed," one of the brothers remarked, "the bats not only keep the insect population down, they leave valuable fertilizer."

The Nacimiento-Fergusson Road is the only road over the mountain from the Big Sur that can be driven by the average car, and from Jolon it eventually connects with busy Highway 101 at King City or farther south. Occasionally it is temporarily closed by slides or while the Army is using it as a proving ground. (Soon after World War II broke out, thousands of acres here were purchased from William Randolph Hearst for this purpose.) There's not much activity going on for soldiers stationed in this isolated valley. There's only a service station, a dusty campground, a saloon that serves sandwiches, and a multipurpose store.

Back to Highway 1 after the spectacular Nacimiento Road, at **Mill Creek** you'll find picnic tables and a small rocky ocean beach where you can surf cast, rock fish, and skin dive, or just look.

The area south of Wild Cattle Creek Bridge to Prewitt Creek is known as **Pacific Valley.** There are four miles of relatively level road on this marine terrace, so you can get to the shore at many places. The **Pacific Valley Center** (805/927-8655) contains a gas station, grocery store, and restaurant where you can treat yourself to homecooked food and desserts (try the pies) to eat inside or outside on the deck. You are

The old adobe Dutton Hotel in the ghost town of Jolon used to welcome stagecoach travelers.

now arriving in jade country, and the gift shop here shows pieces that have been found by lucky local people.

At the **Pacific Valley Station** of the Los Padres National Forest you can obtain a permit to enter the Ventana Wilderness; you must also obtain a permit here or at another forest service station if you intend to build a fire.

At **Sand Dollar Beach,** there's a clean and pleasant picnic area with fire pits and a restroom. To reach the crescent-shaped and somewhat rocky beach, you cross a meadow pockmarked with gopher holes and descend the stairs. Perhaps because there is a short walk involved, the beach is often yours alone or shared only with hang-gliders. The **Plaskett Creek Campground,** half a mile farther south, has forty-four sites for self-contained RVs. This campground and Plaskett Creek were named for Ed Plaskett, who once ran mail over from Jolon.

You are now at the edge of **Jade Cove,** actually a series of coves stretching from here to Willow Creek, about two and a half miles farther south. Rock-hounds hunt for California jade at low tides here. The area is fairly picked over by now, although skin divers can bring in sizable pieces. The biggest prize, dug up in 1971, was a 9,000-pound boulder of

A resident of Gorda, a tiny settlement at the end of Big Sur, shows some of the jade he has collected and polished to sell.

nephrite jade, eight and a half feet long. You certainly can't equal that, but if you're persistent you're sure to find a few smaller pieces in dark, almost black green or the rarer blue-green color. It's easy to confuse this semiprecious prize with serpentine, but jade has a waxy, almost greasy feel and it's harder than steel, so you can test it with a knife. Before starting out, you might check out jade at a nearby store to see what you're looking for.

The most publicized place to hunt for jade is where the sign says **Jade Cove.** Park on the shoulder of the road three-tenths of a mile south of Plaskett Creek and take the stairs down the 150-foot cliffs to the rocky shore. An easier place to reach the also rocky edge of the ocean is at **Willow Creek.** Just south of the bridge a road twists down to the shore. Even if you're not hunting jade, and it can be found here, this is a beautiful place to watch the surf crashing in; white gulls posing; and dipper or water ouzels, those chunky brown birds, walking under the creek water. Also, there are restrooms. Rock fishing can be

sensational here, and sometimes you can buy fish from commercial fishermen in the early afternoon.

The next point, **Cape San Martin,** just south of Willow Creek, has one of the most spectacular views along the entire coast. The dirt road in is easy to miss; it's almost hidden behind a bluff. The road is also hard on cars, so park on the highway shoulder and walk the short distance in. If you're sure of foot, at the end of a narrow path on a saddle, you can reach a huge rock with a 360-degree panorama of the coast and of gray whales, if they are passing.

A dusty dirt road on the inland side of Highway 1 goes up into the remote **Los Burros Mining District.** Don't take it unless you have four-wheel drive or an armored truck—a few miners still work isolated claims and don't look kindly on trespassers. In 1887 W. D. Cruikshank discovered gold back in these mountains, and a minor gold rush was on. Near Cruikshank's Last Chance Mine, the town of Manchester flourished for a few years; then the gold became too unprofitable to mine. Near the turn of the century most of the ghost town burned to the ground, leaving only that necessity of necessities—a saloon.

The tiny settlement of **Gorda,** next south, is your last chance in Monterey County to gas up, buy groceries, and—if it's open—eat in the cafe. One of the residents collects and sells jade; walk up the steep path behind the buildings to his trailer to see his display. (At last reports Gorda was up for sale, so it may be entirely changed when you stop.) Since Gorda is the last stop on the Big Sur mailman's run, it is generally regarded as the end of Big Sur, although Nobel prize winner Linus Pauling, who lives south of here, considers himself still in the Big Sur.

At **Salmon Creek,** you're almost running out of Monterey County and you are running out of redwoods. It's their southernmost stand. Only a few stunted specimens survive near the creek. For a damp but exciting side trip, first park near the forest service station, where you must obtain permits if you intend to build fires or hike back on the mountain trails that start here. Then scramble up the creek, climb along a notch behind the waterfall, and peer out through the cascading water. If it's winter, perhaps you'll see steelhead trout on their spawning runs.

Two miles farther south you leave Monterey County and enter San Luis Obispo County.

The ornate twin towers of the Spanish-Moorish main castle, situated 1,600 feet above the ocean, were copied from a single-towered Spanish cathedral.

22

San Simeon, Hearst Castle, and Environs

After you cross the boundary into **San Luis Obispo County,** driving south on Highway 1, the first sign of commercial civilization is **Ragged Point** with its balconied inn overlooking miles of ragged coastline (805/927-4502). There are also restrooms, a service station, and a fast food stand with tables so you can enjoy your hamburger and fries outside. If you like to live dangerously take the path that plummets to the ocean from the grassy knoll behind the restaurant.

For several miles continuing south driving requires all your attention, as it has before you reached Ragged Point. Slowly you become aware that the hills roll instead of plunge. The ocean is still on your right, but now, with a few exceptions, it's closer and easier to get to.

Soon after passing Point Sierra Nevada, you see— jutting up on a point—the red brick **Piedras Blancas Lighthouse.** Cabrillo was supposed to have named this point in 1542 for its chalky white stone. (The whiteness is due to bird droppings.) Ever since

1874 the lighthouse has continued beaming its light twenty miles out to sea. Photogenic as it may be, the lighthouse is now automated and off-limits to the public. Even before the lighthouse was built, this point was popular as a lookout for whalers.

Further south, at a settlement called **Piedras Blancas,** you can gas up and eat anything from snacks to a sit-down meal. If it isn't foggy, the Piedras Blancas Motel (805/927-4202) has a view of Hearst Castle and may have space available when no vacancy signs are rife closer to the castle.

Some of the best abalone picking along the coast is in this area. Shore and rock fishing is popular, especially in the coves. Among other catches, lucky fishermen can land surf perch, greenlings, and cabezon. There are also tidepools that stretch for miles and cliff tops that are excellent vantage points to watch sea birds and whales.

Highway 1 hugs the shore for several miles, then turns inland slightly at the tiny coastal town of **San Simeon,** some 94 miles south of Carmel and over

200 miles south from San Francisco. Actually, San Simeon appears to be two towns. The gaudier, more commercial section known as San Simeon Acres and jammed with motels is mainly on the highway. Toward the ocean is a tiny, sleepy section, the true village of San Simeon. Its cluster of Spanish-style houses has, of course, red-tile roofs.

The old wooden **Sebastian store,** now an official state landmark, was built in 1852; mules pulled it on skids to its present location in 1878. Since then, the building has seen many changes. When Pete Sebastian, the present owner, was a child, he remembers three or four ships a week anchored at San Simeon Bay, each ship complete with wild-living stevedores. Boasting a Chinese seaweed operation and a whaling station, the area was slowly becoming Hearst country. During and after World War II, in order to practice amphibious landing maneuvers, 10,000 to 15,000 soldiers were stationed on the nearby Hearst ranch. Ten to fifteen employees of the store kept busy serving the men beer and catering to lesser needs. During this period, the tiny San Simeon post office handled thousands of pieces of mail. Now the Sebastian store, which is sublet to the Buddell family, caters mostly to tourists who want picnic supplies, souvenirs, guidebooks, and information.

William Randolph Hearst's father, George, had inexorably bought up all available acreage in the area from destitute rancheros and from the dairymen who replaced them. He paid 70 cents an acre for land. Then, by offering more than the going price of $1.25 an acre, he managed to accumulate 275,000 acres, which included fifty miles of ocean front. During his son's reign, building materials and art objects were unloaded at the San Simeon pier for the trip five miles up the hill to the castle. Some objects were stored in warehouses here until they could be used. Many of the Spanish-style homes were built to house working employees of the Hearsts; a few who have retired still live in them.

The original pier is no longer. Another pier probes ninety-two feet out into this delightful little cove, far enough for pier fishing. Virg's Fish'n (805/927-4676 or 927-4677) operates party boats here from March through October.

Hearst Castle on the Enchanted Hill is straight out of the Arabian Nights. You begin to see why it is the most popular state park attraction in California when you focus on the castle through telescopes near the Sebastian store. On a clear day, as you look up toward the Santa Lucias, you see—silhouetted against the sky 1,600 feet above the ocean—an ornate Spanish-Moorish castle fringed by palms,

with towers copied from a single-towered Spanish cathedral.

But the castle is only icing on the cake. If you're fortunate enough to have tour tickets and are bused five miles up the winding road to this state historic monument, here's just part of what's in store: Besides the miles of view and the 123 acres of gardens, terraces, and pools, you'll see what was once the world's largest private collection of historic artifacts: the former possessions of monasteries, cathedrals, and kings. In the 115 rooms of the castle itself (La Casa Grande) plus the 46 rooms of the three guest houses you may view hundreds of categories of art from priceless medieval paintings to 1920s-style white marble statues (akin to those sold to Forest Lawn Cemetery) to Cardinal Richelieu's bed, carved out of solid planks of walnut, to tapestries and carpets worth millions. The castle staff is still trying to track down the origins of many pieces. Eclectic it is! Hearst himself called it a giant art school. Megalomania may be the delusion of grandeur; this *is* grandeur.

William Randolph Hearst was born in San Francisco in 1863. Historians and others attempting to probe behind Hearst's façade conjecture that his complex personality developed during a childhood spent so much with his mother. His father, George Hearst, was frequently away caring for his interests: Although George Hearst had no formal education, he did have the golden touch. He studied geology on his own and his studies more than paid off; one of his lucky investments, for which he paid $450, was a one-sixth interest in the famous Comstock Lode in Virginia City, Nevada.

Phoebe Epperson Hearst, William's mother, was dedicated—with an iron will—to art, literature, and education. When he was ten, she whisked William off to Europe where he spent one and a half years developing his intense interest in art, antiques, and architecture. Hearst had tutors, attended private schools, and also did a stint in public school because his father felt he might learn about the "real" world there. His formal education ended at Harvard, where he was business editor of the *Lampoon*. He was asked to leave before he graduated. His prank of putting a donkey in the dean's office did not endear him to the authorities.

Hearst himself was a brilliant and complex man. In 1887, when young Hearst was twenty-four, his father—faced with a six-year term as senator—reluctantly gave him *The San Francisco Examiner*. William Randolph Hearst was on his way. Eight years later he bought the *New York Journal*; by 1923

Hearst owned twenty-two daily newspapers, fifteen Sunday papers, and nine magazines. According to Lincoln Steffens, Hearst was "tall, with thin lips and cold gray-blue eyes." His voice was high and soft, but his manner was firm. Some of his ranch and castle employees worshipped him. Others, especially union newspapermen, did not.

At the age of forty, the publisher from California met sixteen-year-old Millicent Murray doing a vaudeville act—or "turn," as it was known in those days—with her sister and her father, Willson Murray. Hearst and Millicent were married in Grace Episcopal Church in New York on April 28, 1903. They had five sons—the first was born in 1904—but by the 1920s they had separated permanently. Millicent raised the boys on the East Coast in a palatial home, complete with moat and drawbridge. (Of Hearst's five sons, three are still alive and active in Hearst affairs.) During the latter part of their marriage, Hearst spent most of his time at the castle. The couple never divorced; the reason often given is that she was Catholic. After his death, Millicent said, "William Randolph Hearst was a great man. Those who thought otherwise just didn't know him."

As almost anyone who attended movies in Hollywood's heyday knew, the woman at Hearst's side in his later years was movie star Marion Davies, an ebullient fun-loving blonde who made Hearst laugh or, at least, smile. One story, perhaps fanciful, has a teenager hired to canvass the castle grounds each morning during this period to erase the graffiti Marion and her comedian cohorts scrawled on the nude statues.

Hearst started the castle in 1919 shortly after his mother died. Then, as the only son, he came into the 240,000 acres here as well as other vast properties and the multimillions that his father had piled up. Hearst chose Julia Morgan, a distinguished Berkeley architect and protégée of his mother, to help design and build his castle. Julia, a remarkable woman for her day, was the first woman to obtain a degree in mechanical engineering from the University of California at Berkeley, as well as a degree in architecture from the Ecôle des Beaux Arts in Paris. She was a tiny ninety-five pounds of dynamite who wore horn-rimmed glasses and old-fashioned hats. During weekends on the enchanted hill, away from her flourishing Bay Area headquarters, she and Hearst pored over plans.

Julia was asked why the ornate castle was so different from the much simpler style she learned under the architect, Maybeck, when her credo had been, "buildings should be unobtrusive elements in the landscape." She replied, "My style is to please my client." All was not an architectural honeymoon, however. She and Hearst disagreed on occasion, especially when it came to lighting the castle. Hearst, the showman, wanted the castle spotlighted. Julia tried to hold out for more muted lighting. Hearst won, and guests who were driven up the coast from San Luis Obispo at night in limousines, could see the extravagant display from miles away.

Julia, whose office was destroyed in the 1906 San Francisco quake, believed in heavily reinforcing her buildings. The vast quantities of steel, iron, and cement needed to build the structures arrived by coastal steamer at San Simeon and had to be hauled five miles up to the site. Gradually the buildings were erected, and often reerected or changed as Hearst changed his mind. Many rooms were designed or built around a particular historic artifact.

Landscaping was also a challenge. Water was piped in from springs five miles away, and rich topsoil had to be brought up the hill. Hearst hired his head landscape architect, Nigel Keep, in much the same way he hired many editors and columnists for his newspaper empire: Keep, a partner in a San Jose nursery, noticed a tall man scrutinizing his trees, shrubs, and vines for an entire hour. The man then offered to purchase everything in the place. Keep assented, but talked the man out of buying the Bartlett pear trees because he was having trouble with them. Impressed by his honesty, the man—citizen Hearst himself—offered Keep a job at his "San Simeon hideaway." He said he would pay twice the gardener's current salary and added a free house and transportation up the hill. Keep accepted and stayed on until he retired in 1946.

Keep had twenty gardeners under him. Now, with help from nearby California Polytechnic State University, twelve gardeners keep up the acres of landscaping that include eighty-four varieties of roses, sixty-four kinds of shrubs, and nearly seven and a half miles of hedges. Because of the hilly terrain, hundreds of feet of retaining walls, balustrades, terraces, and ornate stairways were built, each profusely adorned with marble statues, well-heads, and sarcophagi, many from ancient Rome.

Hearst had a special affinity for trees, especially native oaks. When he wished to move one giant oak, girdles were designed and workmen planned for six months so that the forty-ton tree could be moved fifty feet. Hearst was also fond of wildlife. At one time he owned the largest private zoo in America, which included lions, a leopard, giraffes, and Barbary sheep—1,200 varieties in all. As guests drove

At one time, Hearst's private collection of priceless art, books, urns, and other artifacts was the largest in the world.

up the five-mile road, they saw signs: "Always Drive Slowly, Animals Have the Right of Way." To this day, zebras, tahr goats, Roosevelt elk, sandbar deer, and Barbary sheep roam the back slopes, along with native deer, foxes, wild boar, and an occasional mountain lion.

At one time, Hearst's acquisitions represented one quarter of the sales of art objects in the world. The results are staggering for quantity and, often, price-less quality: One artifact in the assembly room is an ebony jeweled cabinet in the shape of a temple, with hand-cut and polished quartz crystal windows deco-rated with lapis lazuli inlaid with gold. The silk Persian rug is valued at $8 million and has 600 knots to the square inch. The Etruscan vases are museum-quality. Much of the antique silver is twenty-four carat, so fine it needs to be polished only once a year.

When William Randolph Hearst began collecting, there was little market elsewhere for used castles and monasteries. One school of opinion contends that Hearst plundered countries of irreplaceable objects; another states that Hearst merely took advantage of a golden opportunity that eventually gave millions of Americans a chance to see these priceless objects.

Until 1958, however, only guests of the Hearsts could enjoy this artistic and scenic bounty. One of Hearst's famous guests, George Bernard Shaw, is said to have remarked—or perhaps it is just hoped that he did: "This is what God would have done if He had had the money." Other privileged guests in-cluded Churchill, President Coolidge, the Shah of Iran, the Empress of Romania, the King and Queen of Greece, and the Duke and Duchess of Windsor. Many movie luminaries commuted up from Holly-wood: Rudolph Valentino, Clark Gable, Buster Keaton, Greta Garbo, Cary Grant. The list goes on and on. Charlie Chaplin came so often he was called the court jester. Katherine Hepburn never made the trip. Recently, while interviewing her, Dick Cavett asked if she had any regrets in her long Hollywood career. "Yes," she replied, "I regret not accepting an invitation to San Simeon."

Mixed into this smorgasbord of famous guests might be Hearst editors or columnists and newsboys who had won subscription-selling contests. These visitors might share the ketchup and mustard with spur-of-the-moment invitees. One old Norwegian fisherman related how, when a storm drove his small boat into San Simeon harbor, a tall man invited him and other crew members to dry out and have dinner at "his little place up on the hill." Days later the Norwegian realized that he had been Hearst's guest.

William Randolph Hearst died in 1951. His sons and their families used the castle and ranch house occasionally, but upkeep was prohibitive. In 1958 the Hearst Corporation deeded the state 123 crucial acres of the enchanted hill and acreage near the highway for parking and other visitor facilities. There was a proviso, however. The Hearsts were skeptical: If this isolated monument failed to attract sufficient visitors, the deal was off. They need not have worried. From the beginning, Hearst Castle proved so popular that its profits have helped maintain other state parks.

Besides checking out the castle and grounds, the 900,000 or so visitors a year are also curious about Hearst and his lifestyle. "Why," they want to know, "did he build it?" One answer to that question might be found in a letter Hearst wrote to his architect: "We are tired of camping out on the campground on the hillside. I would like to build something a little more comfortable."

Whether Hearst Castle is a monument to one man's desire for acquisition, a giant toy, a memorial to his mother, or a glorified resort for collecting famous guests, or whether there is an element of truth to all of these suppositions, Hearst felt money was there to be spent, and spend it he did.

After the main castle, the 104-foot outdoor Neptune Pool now attracts the most attention. At one end a Greco-Roman temple façade reflects in the clear, blue water. At the other end is a grouping of white marble statuary, which includes mermaids and two mermen complete with two fish tails apiece and Venus being born from the foam of the sea. There's another pool inside, but the 345,000-gallon Neptune Pool was a favorite of Hearst and his guests. Today it is the envy of visitors who frequently inquire if it is still used. Although it is off-limits to visitors, it is open a few times a year for employees who can bring a spouse or friend.

The Hearst Castle guides are exceptionally pleasant and enthusiastic. Some are full-time state employees; others may be college students who work only during peak periods. They're all hand-picked. When the notice of openings was posted recently at a nearby university, 300 applied. Twenty were admitted; twelve completed the training period. After they have taken a 120-hour course and have soaked up additional lore from other guides and the castle librarian, most guides become zealots—some almost evangelical—about the castle and its contents. Their

enthusiasm is catching. Many vary their lectures slightly, tailoring them to the interests of visitors in their care. These can include American students, a busload of Japanese or Israeli tourists, or just plain families.

At present four tours are given every day except Thanksgiving, Christmas, and New Year's Day. Walking distance (with a lot of up and down) is about one-half mile for each tour, which takes about one and three-quarter hours. Children from six to twelve are admitted half price, and under six free if they ride on someone's lap on the bus. Because the tours are so popular, the state strongly recommends buying tickets in advance through nationwide Ticketron agencies (listed in the white pages of most phone books). If you plan your trip at least one month in advance, you can also reserve by mail from Ticketron, P. O. Box 26430, San Francisco, CA 94126; mark "Hearst" and dates requested on the outside of the envelope. (Ticketron requires cash or travelers checks.) A few tour tickets are sometimes available at the **Visitors Center** below the castle, but don't depend on it. Remember, it's a long way to drive to be disappointed. If the Visitors Center does have tickets, you may buy them only with cash or travelers checks. Sorry, no checks or credit cards.

Coastlines, which runs a bus service to the castle from the San Luis Obispo Amtrak and Greyhound or from the Monterey Airport and Greyhound, has some tour tickets available on southbound trips only. Bonusses are the friendly drivers, well versed about the routes. You can reach Coastlines at P. O. Box 587, Monterey, CA 93940 or phone (408) 649-4700.

The state recommends first taking Tour I, which can accommodate over fifty people. You navigate only 150 steps on this tour, which includes the gardens, pools, a guest house, and the main floor of the castle. Taking pictures on the tours is encouraged; guides often pause to suggest good shots. But flash; tripods; or large, bulky accessory bags are forbidden.

On the main floor of the castle you will be almost overwhelmed by the medieval-style Morning Room and the Refectory with its Sienese festival banners, Flemish gothic tapestries, and long Italian refectory tables glowing with priceless silver. Many visitors are most awed by the Assembly Room, where guests gathered before dinner to await their host and hostess, who descended from on high, appearing through concealed elevators in the burnished wood wall.

On the very popular Tour II, mainly of the Castle's upper floors, you walk up and down 356 steps. Highlights are the private rooms of Hearst and

A Greco-Roman temple façade reflects in the clear, blue water of the 104-foot outdoor Neptune Pool at Hearst Castle.

Marion Davies, plus the Celestial Tower Suite in the belfry. Yes, do look for bats near the belfry; there might be one hanging from the ceiling. Besides the ringing of the bells, a more frequent sound when the winds blow strong is the clapping of the huge, flat leaves of the palm trees. On Tour II you'll also see the second floor library, kitchen, and pantry. Space is so tight going up and down the many stairways and in the small bedrooms that the tour is limited to twelve. This is the perfect tour to take after Tour I, but—since it's so limited—reserve early!

Tour III concentrates on a guest house and the "new" Guest Wing in the castle, with its marble bathrooms (one is called the long john), and the gardens. It is limited to fourteen people and has 300 steps to wheeze up and down.

On Tour IV, geared for the visitors who want to take photographs, twenty people who can manage 283 steps can enjoy the formal gardens, including a hidden terrace, the unfinished bowling alley, and the wine cellar with its vault. Rumor has it that Hearst tried to keep Marion's partaking of liquor at a minimum and, therefore, the alcoholic beverages under lock and key. Some of the vintages stored here would bring tears of envy to the eyes of wine connoisseurs. (One of the wine-producing Rothschilds from France stayed at the castle for many months during World War II.)

How about taking all the tours in one day? Even if you have the stamina of a goat and can run blithely up and down all 1,089 steps on all four tours, it's just too much to take in. Each tour must leave from the Visitors Center down below and return. Then, there are details to be taken care of during the day, like eating; you can't take food or drink along on any tour. If you can get your tickets timed right, two tours a day are plenty. If you're there over lunch time, you can grab snacks at the Visitors Center. There are other necessities here, also, like restrooms and a souvenir shop.

Where to stay? Getting to the castle from Los Angeles or San Francisco takes time, especially if your route is south along twisting Highway 1. Unless you start at 3 A.M., you'll have to stay overnight somewhere nearby. Awaiting your money is an array of motels along Highway 1 at the south end of San Simeon and on into Cambria. The closer to the castle, the more apt they are to be filled with members of special tours. To reiterate once again, reserve early, particularly during holiday weekends and vacation periods. Travelers who need to be economical might find less expensive housing at Cayucos, on the ocean farther south, or in Paso Robles, inland on Highway 46 from Cambria.

Big motels, many with restaurants and pools, stretch along within view of Highway 1 in the more commercial area of San Simeon: the Green Tree Inn, San Simeon Lodge, San Simeon Sands Motel, Silver Surf Motel, El Rey Inn, and Cavalier Inn to name a few. Travel agents and motor clubs will be glad to help.

You can also write to the various Chambers of Commerce for information. Perhaps the most knowledgeable about the entire area is the Chamber of Commerce in San Luis Obispo (805/543-1323), forty-two miles south of San Simeon, at 1039 Chorro Street, 93401. Or you can contact the smaller Chambers of Commerce: P. O. Box 1, San Simeon, CA 93452 (805/927-3500); 767 Main Street, Cambria, CA 93428 (805/927-3624); 151 Cayucos Drive, Cayucos, CA 93430 (805/995-2206; and 1113 Spring Street, Paso Robles, CA 93446 (805/238-0506. The Morro Bay Chamber of Commerce, 385 Morro Bay Boulevard, 93442, has a toll-free number which you can call for motel information: (800)231-0592.

Two agencies operate along the coast where, for a membership fee plus, of course, overnight fees, you can bed down and breakfast in a private home. Perhaps the most well known is Megan's Friends (805/528-6645). Homestay (805/927-4613), P. O. Box 326, Cambria, CA 93428 offers private suites in homes. The large Bed and Breakfast International (415/525-4569), 151 Ardmore Road, Kensington CA 94707, has listings in the area. The J. Patrick House (805/927-3812), 2990 Burton Drive, Cambria, CA 93428 advertises a fireplace and bath with every room. The Pickford House (805/927-8619) is a new bed and breakfast inn in Cambria.

Those traveling in RVs or with skinny wallets will find several campgrounds within easy driving distance of the castle. A good investment might be the guide and map to California State Parks available at most state parks. Or send $2, which includes tax and mailing, to Distribution Center, Department of Parks and Recreation, P. O. Box 2390, Sacramento, CA 95811. The guide lists San Simeon State Beach (805/927-4509), five miles south of San Simeon and right on the beach, with 115 primitive sites. There are two state park campgrounds at Morro Bay, thirty miles south of San Simeon. **Atascadero State Beach** (805/543-2161), on the ocean just north of the first turnoff to Morro Bay, is open during the summer and has 104 family campsites. Trailers are allowed, but there are no hookups. **Morro Bay State Park** (805/772-2560) has 115 sites, plus a restaurant, rental boats, and more. It's beautiful and protected. No wonder it has a seven-day limit in summer, fifteen days other periods.

If you're staying in the more commercial part of San Simeon or have time, look in at the **Plaza del Cavalier Shopping Center.** Besides a fancy general store and restaurant, you'll find shops specializing in leather, jade, and seashells. Headquarters for the California Wood Carvers Guild is in a big, friendly room with fireplace overlooking the ocean. The Guild has 1,700 members, and some of their carvings are shown in the museum and gallery here.

If you need a stop to picnic and rest, the **William Randolph Hearst State Beach** more than fits the bill. It's on the ocean, with trees, picnic tables, and restrooms. You'll see the entrance across from where you turn in to the castle parking area. The Hearst Corporation hopes to develop resort facilities, including a golf course, in this area. That's still in the future, so it's fortunate you can enjoy this pleasant, easy-to-get-to coastline now.

The easy-to-get-to arc of beach south of San Simeon is popular with wind surfers.

The Soldier Factory at 789 Main is probably the most famous establishment in Cambria.

23

Cambria, Harmony, and Cayucos

Although its population is a mere 3,750, **Cambria,** "where the pines meet the sea," is the first sizable coastal town south of the Monterey Peninsula; San Simeon, its northern neighbor, admits to a permanent population of around 127. Very little of Cambria is visible as you're driving on Highway 1. Blink your eyes and you may miss the turnoff inland to the business section. Going south, San Simeon blends almost imperceptibly into Cambria. You can walk along the beautiful shoreline here for miles. (See page 86.) When you reach the area across Santa Rosa Creek near the county park your easy hike stops, interrupted by cliffs and no trespassing signs.

Once you get away from the coastal trail along **Moonstone Beach** Drive, finding your way may take longer than you anticipate. If you look at a map of Cambria you'll see that the town is divided roughly into four pockets. Most residents live to the west of Highway 1, one segment near Moonstone Beach and another in the pine-clad hills further

south. The downtown or business area is split into **West Village,** also known as Cambria Pines-by-the-Sea, and the old or **East Village** a half-mile away on Main Street. Both business areas contain galleries, restaurants, and shops, but more of this later.

This somewhat arty town boasts that it has no industry (except tourists?) and describes its climate as mild—no smog—with clear blue skies, light seasonal fog, and ocean breezes. Temperatures average 50 to 70 degrees year round. Besides the artistically inclined, a large portion of its population—many retired—occupy vacation homes or cabins. The present assortment of these is a far cry from the adobe home of an even earlier settler, Don Julian Estrada, who was granted Rancho Santa Rosa several years after California's missions were secularized in 1834. The adobe, set among fruit trees by a shallow lake or lagoon, presided over the rancho, which was small for its time and contained only three Spanish leagues (a league is more than 4,400 acres). Much of the area that remains undigested by Cambria's grid of streets was once a portion of this early rancho and is now owned by descendants of the first settlers.

Don Julian liked pomp and ceremony and dressed the part in velvet and brocade encrusted with silver and gold. Hospitable to a fault, he believed in lavish entertaining of in-laws, relatives, visiting priests, neighboring settlers, and strangers. Walter Colton, a prominent Monterey citizen, commented, "If I must be cast in sickness or destitution on the care of the stranger, let it be in California; but let it be before American avarice has hardened the heart and made a God of gold." At the frequent fiestas which might continue for days, there was much dancing, eating, and showing off of horseback prowess. The fiesta highlight was often a fight to the death between a snarling bear and several bulls.

Previously, the rancho had been an outpost of the Mission San Miguel, founded in 1797. However, centuries of Indians, probably Salinians, camped here previous to that to hunt the abundant game. (Salinians are said to have had such patience while hunting with bows and arrows that they could infiltrate a herd of deer.) An Indian horse trail connecting San Simeon with San Luis Obispo ran through the rancho property. Occasional Indian artifacts are still found along this former trail and by Santa Rosa Creek.

After the white man's diseases had taken their toll, and after the trauma of secularization, only seventy-five Indians lived or worked on Estrada's rancho. They helped grow corn, barley, and wheat and raised wild cattle and horses, with exciting twice-a-year roundups. This romantic and extravagant way of life faded away in a few decades. In 1862 Estrada was forced to sell all but 1,500 acres of his Rancho Santa Rosa. In his delightful book, *Up and Down California: 1860–1864,* William H. Brewer, a surveyor, tells of staying with another don further south on the remnants of what had been a 70,000-acre rancho. Brewer blamed that loss on dissipation and "spending thousands of dollars on a single spree [fiesta]."

True, living in such high style on credit did prove Estrada's undoing when he needed to come up with cash for the expenses of proving his title to the rancho. Domingo Pujol, a rich Spaniard, lent him money. Then came a knockout blow, the drought of 1863–1864, when almost all the livestock in the entire area was wiped out. By then most of the rancho Indians had been killed by an epidemic; only three remained to help rebuild Estrada's herds. Don Julian sold all but 1,500 acres to Pujol. A few years later he sold everything but a few acres surrounding his home to George Hearst.

Don Julian died in 1871, proud but nearly penniless. Five years later his last small acreage was swallowed up by Hearst. When the adobe home started to crumble, William Randolph Hearst bulldozed it flat. (Hearst later ran into financial troubles himself and had to sell much acreage.) Thus, an era of openhanded hospitality—of romance—had passed. Even the site of Estrada's adobe is buried near the asphalt of Highway 1.

Some of Estrada's more prudent neighbors barely survived, and their much diminished lifestyles left something to be desired. Brewer comments, while visiting an American who owned an 80,000-acre ranch, "he lives quite stylishly for this country—that is, about half as well as a man would at home who owned a 100-acre farm paid for."

Why was the town named Cambria? This may have come from the Latin word for Wales. Before settling on the name Cambria, the town went through many changes, starting with Santa Rosa; then Rosaville; San Simeon; and Slabtown, a nickname developed because of nearby lumbering ventures.

Several historic buildings more than 100 years old are still standing, mostly in east or Old Town Cambria. The Squibb-Darke home, built circa 1877, is on Burton Drive; you can spot it by the windmill in back. The home is delightful, with roses growing over old, unpainted fences. The jungle of bushes, trees, and plants that shade the house have been left to grow mostly unhampered, unclipped, and unpruned because, according to the late Paul Squibb, "vegetables and plants have rights, too."

The nearby Brambles restaurant is in a cottage that is more than 100 years old. So is the restored Santa Rosa Catholic church, erected around 1870 and worth a look. To reach it, stroll by the post office, library, bank, grocery, and other businesses; cross Main; and continue on Bridge Street.

Across from the old Squibb home at 4070 Burton Drive is a two-story collection of tourist-oriented shops called the Old Village Mercantile. The **Seeker's Gallery** is around the corner on Center Street. If you have time to visit only one gallery in Cambria, pick this one, for you'll see museum-caliber fine art. Seeker's specializes in contemporary American handblown art glass, but they also carry porcelain, clay, metal, wood, and other media, even handmade masks. The owners, who escaped from high-pressure jobs, now travel widely to visit artists in their studios before selecting one-of-a-kind pieces that bridge the gap between craft and art. Prices can run into the thousands, but some items like marbles and paperweights are in the modest range. It's hard to talk to the owners without catching some of their enthusiasm; you're welcome at the Seeker's Gallery even if you just look. Also in this same complex is the Greenroom, a gift and apparel shop that has an old-time jazz band playing free every Saturday.

The Schoolhouse Gallery, in the old Santa Rosa one-room schoolhouse built in 1881, shows works of local artists from noon to 3:30 P.M. every day except Tuesday. This nostalgic little building, complete with belfry and front porch, is on Main Street halfway between the east and west Cambrias. The transplanted and rebuilt one-room jail, originally built in the 1880s, is nearby.

Before you visit west Cambria attractions, pop into the Chamber of Commerce (805/927-3624) at 767 Main, Cambria, CA 93428. The friendly and helpful volunteers will give you maps and pamphlets, some on offbeat excursions.

The **Soldier Factory** (805/927-3804) at 789 Main is probably the most famous establishment in west Cambria. This thriving industry which ships all over the world was started in the garage of Jack Scruby in 1957. Scruby first concentrated on tin soldiers; now he also turns out thousands of pewter figurines, painted and unpainted. Walk inside the factory past the replica of a British guard and you're in a fantasyland of unicorns, dragons, clowns, medieval jesters, and pixies. There's a centaur and a carousel horse, and figures from Alice in Wonderland and the Wizard of Oz. The metal chess sets include an Arabian Nights Fantasy set and a Good-versus-Evil set. The Soldier Factory is open 10 A.M. to 5 P.M. seven days a week, but the real factory that turns all this out is closed weekends.

Nearby Townes Emporium, which sells antiques and gifts, is easy to find because of the seven-foot-high, turreted Cambriona dollhouse on its roof. This miniature house was created by Victoriana, around the corner at 1 Arlington. There Weldon ("Bud") and Betty Boothe conduct a shop dealing in miniatures and dream of the time they can start a whole miniature village in Cambria, complete with scaled-down Hearst Castle. Other shops in the neighborhood are worth a visit. Across Main Street is the Thistle Book Store, popular with locals and a good center to gather information about the area.

Almost every article and pamphlet on Cambria mentions **Nitwit Ridge** on Hillcrest Drive; go up

the hill from Main Street and turn onto Cornwall Street, which turns into Hillcrest. If you're into funque and junque, you'll find it here, although you can glimpse only the outside of this potpourri from the postage stamp–size parking turnoff. Art Beal, now in his eighties, is the self-described eccentric who started building in 1920 and continued on, adding rocks encrusted with abalone shells, driftwood, bits of glass, and whatever else came to hand. A concrete deer or elk stares down at you; there are also bridges, objects dangling from gates, and more.

If you prefer pretty pebbles and shells in their natural setting, take a shoreline walk that includes many of Cambria's natural highlights. Do this preferably when you have an extra few hours and the tide is out. Start at the southern end of San Simeon State Beach where Highway 1 connects with Moonstone Beach Drive and continue south for about two miles. If the occasional clambering up and down rocks is too much, you can cheat by strolling onward on Moonstone Beach Drive. About half a mile south, look back for a view of the Piedras Blancas Lighthouse blinking away seven miles north. Unless you become sidetracked picking up moonstones, you soon arrive at Leffingwell Landing, a rocky promontory clad in dark green Monterey cypresses and pines.

William Leffingwell, a rancher who arrived in 1858, established a sawmill and delved into the ship unloading business. Lumber and barrels were dumped into the ocean to float ashore or be towed in. Smaller cargo was loaded onto rowboats. This included passengers, who had to wade to and from the shore. At today's **Leffingwell's Landing** you'll find picnic tables, restrooms, and ample parking. Offshore, or at the next promontory south, you may glimpse sea lions and seals hauled out on rocks or otters playing, dining, and sleeping in kelp beds. Farther out, in late November through March, you may see gray whales migrating.

To get to the second bluff, scramble down to the beach by the old highway bridge and cross the usually dry creek. Once again you'll be walking on tiny, colorful pebbles (usually varieties of quartz) as you will in another tiny cove or after you cross Santa Rosa Creek. Who knows? You might even find a silky, translucent moonstone. That happens once in a blue moon. To get to Shemal, the county park off Windsor Boulevard, you may have to return to Moonstone Beach Drive. By now, you've gone almost two miles. This is a pleasant walk, even on overcast days. It's often spectacular at sunset; for this event you'll probably be joined by Cambria citizens out to walk dogs or just to enjoy the ocean-washed air and views.

Perhaps because they're at the bottom of steep, rocky bluffs and hard to get to, the shoreline south of the county park has interesting tidepools. Take Ardath Drive off Highway 1 toward the ocean and continue on through tree-oriented homes to the end. Drive a short distance to a turnaround where you'll find a bench hewn out of a log. If the tide is low, you can scramble down to the beach here.

If you like exploring back roads, take the bucolic Santa Rosa Creek Road five miles toward Paso Robles to Linn's Fruit Bin (805/927-8134), open every day except Tuesday and Wednesday and every day during the pick-your-own-berry season. At this small family farm you'll not only find freshly picked produce but delectable preserves and pies.

Where to stay? Since Cambria is so close to Hearst Castle, you'll find a plethora of motels. However, thousands of the people who arrive daily to tour this monument also need a place to sleep, so reserve early through your automobile association or travel agency. If you are caught without a roof over your head, as a rule of thumb motels on Moonstone Beach Drive (with views) are more expensive. The Cambria Pines Lodge and Health Spas (805/927-4200), as its name indicates, is in the pines. This twenty-two-acre resort has a pool, saunas, and a pleasant garden room restaurant. Occasionally small motels at the very eastern end of Main Street may have inexpensive and vacant rooms without frills. The nearby campgrounds are mentioned in the chapter on the Hearst Castle area.

Where to eat? You have a wide choice in the 4000 block of Burton Drive. The Flying Frog Restaurant (805/927-5656), besides the obligatory frog legs, features seafood and Mexican food at surprisingly modest prices. You can eat outside on the deck, too. The nearby Brambles Dinner House (805/927-4716) and the Grey Fox Inn (805/927-3305) both strongly advise reservations. So does the equally fancy Moonraker (805/927-3859), 6550 Moonstone Beach Drive. Visitors with large families or large appetites might try the Chuck Wagon Restaurant (805/927-4644) at Highway 1 and Moonstone Beach Drive. Here it's all-you-can-eat seven days a week. But if it's daytime and the weather has cooperated, instead of looking at the ocean through a window, why not enjoy a picnic at one of the many parks and beaches within sight and sound of the spray? Cambria has just the place to stock up. It's Picnique in the Pines (805/927-8727), a tearoom at 727 Main where you can take out a basket of picnic fare. Another place to pick up a picnic lunch or join the locals munching fish and chips or hamburgers is Bob and Jan's Deli (805/927-4909), 2292 Main.

Going south from Cambria on Highway 1, after you pass Highway 46, the road to Paso Robles, keep your eyes peeled to the left or you may miss the turnoff to the dollhouse village of **Harmony.** Coming north, it's easier to spot the shops, both miniature replicas and real, in or near the old dairy buildings.

The town was founded around 1910 by a Swiss dairyman. The colorful plaque on the wall of the main building says the name Harmony came because the feuding among the dairy farmers, which occurred from 1869 until the early 1900s, finally ended. For

Harmony, population eighteen, has a store and its own post office, where musicians and artists rent boxes for the cachet of the postmark.

a few decades, when Highway 1 ran right through town, Harmony flourished; as a hospitable gesture, motorists were treated to ladles of fresh milk.

On his way to or from his castle at San Simeon, William Randolph Hearst frequently stopped to buy the top-quality butter and cheese. One legend has Rudolph Valentino also stopping by, although briefly. To commemorate this event, for many years Harmony boasted a memorial porcelain toilet with a plaque that read: "In the early 1920s, while in the company of William R. Hearst and Pola Negri, Rudolph Valentino had a call of nature. Guilda Williams, who lived here, was kind enough to let him use her bathroom facilities. When the little house was remodeled, the pottie was placed here in memory of Rudolph." Guilda later revised the story, saying it was not Valentino but Marion Davies who stopped with Pola Negri. In any case, the pottie, which had been turned into a planter, disappeared. The story, however, lives on.

In the late thirties, although the main dairy operation was moved to San Luis Obispo, Harmony still carried on a few dairying activities. After changing hands several times, the tiny town was sold in 1977 for around $400,000 and the tasteful restoration began that still continues. Now, besides restrooms and a pleasant garden with benches, there is a restaurant and a pottery works where you can watch potters in action (and swallows that nest under the eaves coming and going). Metalsmith Randy Stronsoe shows many of his nationally famous works in the **Harmony Valley Gallery.** You can also watch a woodcarver and see samples of Martin Donald's handmade paper.

Donald, who is an ordained minister, conducts weddings in the chapel, which was previously a wine-and-cheese-tasting-room; his wife runs the town antique shop.

Although the Donalds are the only permanent inhabitants and the rural population totals a mere eighteen, Harmony has its own post office: Musicians and others rent post office boxes here to get that Harmony postmark on their mail. At last report a few boxes were still available. If you're in the market, write the Town of Harmony, P. O. Box 9, CA 93435. For information on Harmony, on weddings here, or on the special events, like chamber music performances, phone (805) 927-8288.

Back to Highway 1, the seaside cliffs that hug much of the ocean provide great views at almost every turn. If you're in the mood for a wide, sandy beach, complete with free fishing pier, continue on to

Cayucos about six miles north of Morro Bay.

Cayucos, population just over 2,000, sprawls along quiet Estero Bay. The name Cayucos is perhaps a bastardization of the words *kayak* and *canoe,* after the Aleuts who paddled kayaks to hunt sea otters. The Cass Home, built by town founder "Captain" James Cass between 1867 and 1875, is on Ocean Avenue just back from the pier. Cass, a New Englander, sailed around the Horn and settled on 320 acres soon after the breakup of the original Rancho Moro y Cayucos 8,845-acre land grant. His once splendid house, now unpainted and with broken windows, sags in a weed field. It is definitely for sale. Whether time and weather will win out or whether a group or private party will restore this historic gem was still a question when this book went to press.

In order to serve this prime dairy and farming country, Cass and a partner erected a store, a warehouse, and, in 1874 built the 940-foot fishing pier. The **Cayucos pier** serves fishermen especially during spring and summer runs of bocaccio and jacksmelt. The best pier catches during August through October are white croaker, young rockfish, and walleye surf perch. To make your fishing more enjoyable you'll find restrooms, bait and tackle shops, and fish-cleaning facilities at or near the pier. From May into October, when the water is calm, you might want to rent a skiff to go after bottomfish. Or how about climbing on a party boat and going after the big ones?

Not interested in fishing? Walk out on the pier anyway for a front-row-center view of many sea birds: perhaps brown pelicans, cormorants, murres, and shearwaters. You could also be lucky enough to watch the antics of sea otters.

Grunion sometimes run on Cayucos beach during night high tides in spring and early summer, but you can take them only by hand. These fish spawn in the upper reaches of waves soon after the tide begins to recede. The female grunion digs a small pocket in the sand with her tail and deposits her eggs, which are immediately fertilized by the male. The next wave covers the eggs and carries the spawners back to sea. In about two weeks, when the next series of high-tide waves exposes the eggs, the larvae hatch. Early Indians who witnessed grunion runs described them as "little fish who come in and dance on their tails by the light of the moon."

Skin diving is popular in Cayucos; so is surfing. As for swimming, Estero Bay is relatively placid and there's a lifeguard on duty during the summer. Some swimmers describe the water as invigorating, others as downright chilly. In any case, you'll find sufficient white sand for sunbathing if the sun is visible. If you prefer tamer swimming, try the pool at Hardie Park, across Highway 1 inland from the pier. You'll also find picnic tables, barbeque pits, and tennis courts here.

A short drive south at Whale Rock Dam (watch for the sign) there's freshwater fishing for trout, bass, catfish, and bluegill. Some optimists still try for clams at minus tides along Cayucos beaches, but clams are no longer plentiful. The same goes for marine life in the tidepools below the cliffs to the north of town. Too many visitors have taken away shells, rocks, and tiny crabs.

If you're an antique buff, you'll find a number of shops along Ocean Avenue, or you can visit the Cayucos Meat Market Antiques (805/995-2206) on 151 Cayucos Drive—inland from the pier and Cass house—which also doubles as the town's Chamber of Commerce.

One of the interesting spots in Cayucos is the **cemetery,** just inland to your left going south on Highway 1. The oldest gravestone, moved here after the cemetery opened, is dated 1841. Cass, the town founder, is buried here as is Elisha H. Packwood, who died in 1865 after an encounter with a grizzly bear. According to the "cemetarian" who works here, Packard—although unarmed—managed to deal the bear a death blow before expiring himself. Other deaths recorded on gravestones were from being gored by a bull, run over by a hay rack, and thrown from a horse. Some headstones show round porcelain replicas of the deceased. Virginia Pierce is pictured with her father, who holds a can of beer. One flat tombstone features a champagne glass and the inscription: "This one is on me. Ed Upham

1902–1976," followed by, "I kept telling them I was sick."

Where to stay? Considering its size, Cayucos bulges with motels, including the AAA-approved Cypress Tree Motel (805/995-3917) and the Unique-View Motel (805/995-3225). The Shoreline Motel and Restaurant (805/995-3681) is right on the beach. Many motels have kitchen facilities. Get a complete list from the Cayucos Chamber of Commerce. Better reserve early for holidays, especially over the July Fourth weekend when Cayucos explodes with festivities, most of them at or near the pier.

Many locals eat at the Sea Shanty on Ocean at the south end of town—save room for their pies. Perhaps the most postcard-photogenic of local restaurants is The Way Station (805/995-1227), in a restored nineteenth-century travelers' rest stop at 78 Ocean Avenue. Friendly Carlin and Margaret Soule, who run the restaurant, double as chefs and gardeners. Whether or not you intend to eat here, look at the lush garden in back. You can lunch, dine, or enjoy Sunday brunch inside or overlooking this garden; sometimes guitar music plays in the background. There's also a wine cellar and antique shop on the property. The equally ancient-appearing Cayucos Tavern in the next block north, actually built circa 1974, features two large oil paintings of topless cowgirls.

From **Morro Strand Beach State Park,** just south of Cayucos (take the Twenty-fourth Street turnoff from Highway 1), you can stroll over nine miles of sandy beach right on into Morro Bay. You'll be interrupted by the Standard Oil pier at midpoint and you'll share long stretches only with occasional surf fishermen.

24

Morro Bay

If you like beaches, birds, and other wildlife, consider **Morro Bay,** "where the sun spends the winter." Continue barreling along Highway 1 and you may notice only huge, cone-shaped **Morro Rock** and the three 450-foot-high smokestacks and grid of pipes of the Pacific Gas and Electric (PG&E) plant. But if you pause and really savor Morro Bay, you are in for many happy surprises.

The town—population 8,400—is gift-wrapped on three sides by parklands: **Atascadero State Beach** on the ocean to the north, **Morro Bay State Park** adjoining to the south, and protected sand dunes to the west resting between placid Estero Bay and the ocean. All this plus grasslands, hilly overlooks, and more!

Since flowers seem to grow thicker and larger here (yes, fog does help) and the estuary and nearby marsh teem with marine life, Morro Bay is among the ten top areas in the United States where land and sea birds gather. In fact, in 1971 the whole town was designated a bird sanctuary. The Audubon Society, Box 160, Morro Bay, CA 93448, puts out a free bird-watching pamphlet and map. As many as 250 varieties have been spotted on a specific day, especially in the fall and winter.

Added to Morro Bay's natural bounty, fishing is good and there's a lively marina as well as facilities for golf and other sports, including outdoor chess. No wonder there are so many motels—more than thirty. Write for a list from the Chamber of Commerce, 385 Morro Bay Boulevard, Morro Bay, CA 93442 or call toll-free for motel information (800) 231-0592. Although there are hundreds of campsites, many commercial RV parks and camps are filled to the brim with permanent guests. The saying goes that people come as tourists and return as retirees.

Monarch butterflies winter here, also. From October to March they hang in great golden clusters from eucalyptus trees. The ancestors of these trees which make the air pungent and attract nesting great

A close-up of Morro Rock shows the sand dunes at the foot of this ancient volcanic monolith.

blue herons were planted by Franklin Riley, who homesteaded here in 1870 and built the town's first house.

Don Gaspar de Portola and his men camped here on their march up the coast in 1769 to rediscover Monterey Bay. Their journal describes the area as pleasant and notes a big rock "a little less than a gunshot from shore." Three years after the Portola jaunt hunters were sent down from Monterey, then on the verge of starvation. At what is now nearby Montaña de Oro Park enough grizzly bears were shot to feed Monterey for three months.

The grizzlies were finally wiped out, but food (clams, that is) are still available along the mudflats during minus tides in fall and winter—with a fishing license, of course. Geoducks that may tip the scales at many pounds like the muddy area three feet down,

gaper clams prefer two feet down, and Washington clams are happy a foot down. Ignore the small bent-nose clams half a foot below the surface; they're chock full of sand.

Getting across the channel to the mudflats and digging the clams out of all that black ooze is not for everyone. First you search for the clam's hole or the tip of its siphon. Then you ready your shovel and dig around the telltale signs of occupancy, leaving the clam in a muddy island in the center. Then comes the hard part. You lie on your stomach in that ooze and grope around until you grab the unhappy clam, then pull, pull, pull. Watch for those stray waves or the turn of the tide. But, at least that chilly saltwater will wash off part of the mud on your clothes.

For centuries before the whites arrived, Chumash Indians lived in this area, clamming, hunting, and fishing. Some archaeologists contend that the Indians or their predecessors arrived forty-seven centuries before Christ. On the huge sand spit facing the town you can find shell mounds: ancient garbage dumps where the Indians deposited clam, cockle and mussel shells, and deer and rabbit bones.

A trip out to the spit is worthwhile but difficult. You have to hike in a healthy distance from the southwest near the Los Osos Valley–Pecho Road or somehow manage a boat ride across the bay. Once there you can spot the tracks of many animals and may startle a great blue heron enjoying a siesta.

These big birds nest from January to August in rookeries among the eucalyptus trees on Fairbanks Point between the state park museum and the Golden Tee Motel (an excellent place to eat for nongolfers, too). You'll see the great blue herons silhouetted high in the trees or flying off for food. It's an impressive sight. These lords of the shallows are four feet high with a wing spread of six feet. Few fish, small crabs, or other unfortunate prey that they spot escape their stilettolike bill. Back at the rookery—even with your eyes closed you're aware of their presence because of the incredible racket—the huge nestlings squawk loudly at any parental arrival or departure. You may see some of the youngsters tottering on the tips of high branches, debating whether to try their wings.

Besides the great blues you'll see many varieties of birds in this sanctuary: busy sandpipers; curlews; willets; and godwits, whose bills curve up toward heaven. Inland are the hawks, red-winged blackbirds, meadowlarks, and other song birds. Along the cliffs you may see oyster-catchers after mussels; the clownlike pigeon guillemots and swallows; or you may startle turnstones and plovers, who fly off flashing their black and white wing patterns. Beyond the surf line are other birds, but to really enjoy, get a good bird book, adjust your binoculars, and watch the flying extravaganza with more know-how.

Visiting Morro Bay's jewel of a museum is a must; continue south on Main Street and watch for the signs soon after you enter **Morro Bay State Park** (805/772-2560), where you'll also find a beautiful campground with 135 sites including twenty hookups for trailers. At the State Park Museum of Natural History (805/772-2694), you'll find displays on Indians, great blue herons, and pertinent natural life in the area. On weekends movies on natural history are shown at 10:30 A.M., noon, 2 P.M., and 4 P.M. The museum possesses restrooms and a path on the bayside leads to a small snack bar. There's an excellent

view of Morro Bay from the museum's balcony, although there's a wider, really spectacular overlook on Black Hill to the east.

To reach this lookout with its sweeping panorama of sea, marsh, and mountains, turn inland at the north edge of the golf course. Take the first road off to the left (it may be unmarked) and continue on to the parking lot. Then, after a steep but pleasant ten-minute hike, you're standing on the top of the 665-foot-high hill tucked into the string of volcanic peaks leading inland.

Morro Rock, which guards the harbor to the north, is the end of a spine of seven (or nine—controversy rages) extinct volcanic cones perhaps 50 million years old. Juan Rodríguez Cabrillo, a Portuguese navigator, first saw this monolith in 1542 on his voyage of discovery for Spain. This rock, somewhat optimistically called "The Gibraltar of the Pacific," has shrunk considerably over the years. In the 1880s, although it was of inferior quality for this purpose, rock was quarried off its side to provide breakwater for coastal towns. "Gibraltar" was attacked again in the early 1930s to help build a jetty to connect it to the mainland and to add a breakwater.

Not until 1968 was the much hacked-at monolith declared State Historical Landmark No. 821. Now it is administered by the California state parks. In order to protect a pair of endangered peregrine falcons nesting at the top, carrying firearms or climbing the rock are strictly prohibited. So do your climbing armed only with binoculars.

Standing on the strand or parking lot by the rock you may thrill to the rapid wing beats and incredibly swift dives of the nesting pair of **peregrine falcons.** You might even be lucky enough to see their graceful loop-the-loop air ballet during courtship. You are more likely, however, to see flocks of cormorants who nest on the rock or to watch sea gulls, brown pelicans, and other sea birds riding the updrafts. Some land birds seem to like the rock, too.

The main turnoff from Highway 1 into town is Main Street. Turn on to Morro Bay Boulevard, which deposits you on the Embarcadero at the water's edge in ten short blocks. En route, the Chamber of Commerce (805/772-4467) is on your right at 385 Morro Bay Boulevard.

Main Street runs slightly inland at an angle from the Embarcadero. It doesn't have bobbing boats, but some of the town's more interesting restaurants, galleries, and bookstores are on this street. The Book Peddler at 842 Main specializes in out-of-print books and memorabilia. Across the street at 845 Main is the

Some Birds You'll See on or near the Coast

Here are a few of the birds you may glimpse along the ocean's shore. Those tiny shore birds that run back and forth with great self-importance, constantly probing for food and twittering, are **sandpipers.** When they're running along the shore they sometimes look as if they were on wheels. You'll see them all year except summer, when they're off breeding in the Arctic (yes, these tiny birds fly all the way to the Arctic for this). **Sanderlings** are the most abundant sandpipers. They feed at the very edge of the surf, barely rushing back in time. When startled, they emit a short, sharp "twit." Other sandpipers are hard to identify. Many birders call them all "peeps."

Dowitchers are stolid-looking birds with long straight bills. They eat with a sewing-machine motion. **Kildeers** are robin-sized, with a white band on the forehead and two black convict bands across a white chest. Their cry is more nearly "ki-dee." They're great actors. If you get close to a kildeer's eggs (in a shallow scoop—no nest) it will hop ahead of you, dragging a wing pitifully as if it were broken. When it decides it's lured you away far enough, the bird bolts for home. **Plovers** are the size of kildeers but have a different coloration.

Curlews are large, brown birds with long bills that curve downward. **Godwits** are a mottled brown; their bills curve upward (toward God?). **Willets** are smaller cronies of godwits and curlews, and much more numerous. Identify them in flight by the dramatic white stripes on their black wings. They emit a shrill "whee-wee-wee." **Avocets** have blue bills that turn upward, white undersides, and wide black stripes on back and side to the tail.

The most common sea birds are **gulls,** the noisy, scolding scavengers that help keep beaches clean. **Western gulls** are the most noticeable. They are large and dark; look for the heavy yellow beak. **Heermann's gulls** have white heads that contrast with their gray bodies and scarlet bills. They're the gulls that emit that mad laughing. They sometimes follow a pelican's thrilling dive to snatch his catch. **California gulls** are white; you'll see them here only in winter, for they nest inland. These gulls were credited with saving the crops of Utah pioneers from plagues of grasshoppers.

Cormorants look grotesque as they perch on offshore rocks, with their long snaky necks and long, slightly hooked beaks. These large black birds are superb at fishing. Some Japanese use them as slave fishers, placing a ring around the neck of each bird so that it can't swallow any large fish it catches. **Brown pelicans** look even more bizarre than cormorants with their big, pouched bills, but wait until you see their thrilling dives.

Grebes, or **hell divers,** hang out on the surf line or in lagoons. They are Olympic-caliber divers. **California murres** fly in lines close to

Sea gulls, the most common bird along the coast, do a valuable job of scavenging the ocean's edge.

the water with rapid wing-strokes. **Scoters** are diving ducks, often seen this side of the breakers. **Coots** (mud hens) are numerous in freshwater ponds. On shore they waddle like old men.

To complete this brief look at birds, go inland just a short distance, get your binoculars ready, and you might see some of these: **Steller's jays** start scolding the minute you step into their conifer-forest headquarters. They're dark blue, with a large near-black crest and are impudent thieves. **Allen's hummingbirds** flit and hover wherever there are bright flowers. They have green backs and brilliant throats, sides, and tails. **Goldfinches** look like canaries, but they're not.

California quail are those gray-and-brown birds with black-and-white faces plus black,

curving head plumes; you'll see them scuttling across your road or path into the bushes. Their cry sounds like "Chicago." If you see tiny brown birds with black and white streaks, they probably belong to one of the many species of **sparrows.** The female **house finch** looks like other sparrows, but the male boasts a bright crimson head and breast. You'll probably see house finches lined up on a telephone wire.

If you want to learn more about coastal birds, see the *Field Guide to Western Birds* by Roger Tory Peterson, published by Houghton-Mifflin; or *Birds of North America,* by Chandler S. Robbins, Bertel Brunn, Herbert S. Zim, and Arthur Singer, published by Golden Press.

Fishing and pleasure boats are berthed in the busy harbor at Morro Bay.

Coalesce Bookstore (805/772-2880)—"people coming together"—which moved up from Harbor Drive. There's no hustle-bustle here. You can browse at length along with local sandal-clad intelligentsia or chat with the friendly owner, Linna Thomas. Ask about the wedding chapel in the back, which is occasionally used for autograph parties and poetry readings.

Most first-time visitors head immediately for the **Embarcadero** to stroll past the small sea-oriented shops and galleries or visit the mournful-sounding sea lions at the small aquarium. The majority of the numerous eateries feature fish and chips. At some the

lemon juice arrives in a tiny plastic bag. While you eat you can enjoy the sight of sea gulls circling, boats coming and going, and pelicans skimming the water. The Galley (805/772-2806) is popular with the senior set. If you arrive early enough to be seated, you can enjoy a hearty but modestly priced bowl of clam chowder as you look at the bobbing boats.

What makes this Embarcadero different from others at small touristy seaports? It's the Centennial Stairway of recycled redwood that leads down from a stone pelican at the end of Morro Bay Boulevard at Market to a giant outdoor chess board. Playing chess here you get your exercise, also. Chess pieces weigh from eighteen to thirty pounds each, and you may end up lifting 1,000 pounds before a game is over. On Saturday at noon, local chess buffs often demonstrate. The public is allowed to play, but first call the Recreation Department at (805) 772-7329. During the Harbor Days Celebration in mid-October, live chess players in full costume — alias local thespians — replace the usual chess pieces.

Going south along the Embarcadero you have a close-up look at the local fishing industry. There's also a boat launching ramp and The Cannery at 235 Main where you can buy freshly caught fish. Eventually you reach the Morro Bay State Park and museum mentioned earlier.

Going north you arrive at a complex of city T-piers where you can fish for halibut, perch, and crab without a license. Many party boats operate from here and along the Embarcadero. One of the best known is Virg's Fish'N (805/772-1222), near the rock, which lets you try your luck from 7 A.M. to 3 P.M. From December into February they also have whale-watching trips.

With its somewhat Polynesian ambience, the Harbor Hut (805/772-2255) presides over this bustling area and offers drinking, dining, and live entertainment. Nearby you can buy tickets for a relaxed hour's cruise on the Tiger's Folly, which paddlewheels around the bay.

On the excursion you may wonder at an unor-thodox houseboat that vaguely resembles a galleon usually "parked" near the sand spit. Sandal and his son, Prince Paka Diogenes, are probably in residence living their secluded life fishing and meditating. The handmade houseboat can be occasionally moved with the help of sails and an anchor, which is thrown out ahead of the boat and then the line pulled taut. Wherever Sandal anchors he takes on the responsibility of protecting something, whether it is the great blue herons or erasing graffiti from the rock.

North of the rock, **Atascadero State Beach** stretches for more miles than you may care to walk. It's usually air-conditioned, read *breezy,* and lures surfers. If you want to avoid the wind and the sand in your lunch, you can escape to Lila Kelsey Park in the concrete embrace of the PG&E plant. Here, behind a windbreak, you can munch your lunch at a picnic table; you can barbeque, too.

If you're early, and lucky, you may be able to reserve a campsite right at the edge of this surf-washed beach. Atascadero Beach State Park (805/543-2161) has more than 100 sites. But, even if you don't intend to stay, check out this stretch of sandy beach with its view of the rock. It's long enough (three miles) and big enough (seventy-five acres) for you to find a private spot to put down your ice chest. Then you can beachcomb, stroll, surf fish, or do anything else that's legal while you listen to the waves and the cries of birds.

San Luis Obispo

25

San Luis Obispo

San Luis Obispo, population 35,740, rests at the foot of San Luis Mountain in a broad and still relatively uncrowded valley. It's inland from the coast an easy nine miles or so. This often means sunshine when chill fog hovers at the ocean's edge.

Since San Luis Obispo is approximately halfway between San Francisco and Los Angeles and reached by both Highways 1 and 101 (in fact, it's difficult to get to and from some parts of town without being swept onto Highway 101), this is a logical point to pause on your trip. You have a choice of dozens of motels and inns. The Chamber of Commerce lists twenty-nine in town plus a dozen nearby. This includes the world's first motel, the twenties-style Motel Inn (805/543-4000) at 2223 Monterey Street.

The San Luis Obispo Chamber of Commerce (805/543-1323), located at 1039 Chorro Street and open seven days a week, is one of the most enthusiastic along the coast. Stop by early for maps and

folders to preview the attractions that appeal to you. It's near the plaza before you get to the mission, which you will want to see anyway.

In addition to sunshine and easy access, other attractions include a well-groomed creek that is especially picturesque as it wanders by the mission and plaza. History buffs can have a field day visiting the dozens of well-preserved, old-time buildings that include adobes, Victorians, and brick turn-of-the-century structures. Most of these historic buildings are on the San Luis Obispo Heritage Home Tour, which lists almost forty Queen Anne and other vintage homes that you can cover in an eight-block area south of downtown. Get the free map and guidebook at the Chamber of Commerce.

Several downtown buildings retain their old-fashioned ambience. The one-time Sinsheimer's Bros. Store, built in 1884 at 849 Monterey Street, still has an iron-front façade. Muzio's Grocery, across the street, was built over 100 years ago and still has wooden floors and an enticing selection of gourmet foods. Using bricks from his personal brickyard, the Ah Louis Store on nearby Palm was started in 1874 by Ah Louis, a leader of the 2,000 Chinese railroad workers then in the area. Presently it's an Asian gift shop operated by descendants of Ah Louis.

Eating in downtown San Luis Obispo should pose no problem; over sixty establishments within the town's border serve everything from fast food burgers on up. For midday munching, try the 700 to 1000 block on Higuera. Several delis and restaurants here back up to the creek, so you can eat outside overlooking the greenery of the **Mission Plaza.** You can investigate the Spindle, Country Culture (yogurt), the Bakery Cafe, and, further west, the Creamery. Or enjoy your own sandwich on one of the benches right by the creek; here you can watch swallows darting after insects.

For evening dining, locals may head for restaurants along the ocean, perhaps in Shell Beach, Cambria, and Cayucos. In town you might try Chocolate Soup (805/543-7229) at 980 Morro Street, where you can sample homemade soups and desserts plus sandwiches and other fare, including that caloric chocolate soup. At the Apple Farm (805/544-6100), 2015 Monterey, also well publicized, you can dine on American food: chicken and dumplings, turkey and dressing, or prime rib. For Mexican fare, many locals visit Pepe Delgado's (805/544-6660), 1601 Monterey. The Farm Boy Restaurant (805/543-1214), 1114 Marsh, serves down-to-earth food around the clock.

As for shopping, so many stores are jammed together the compact downtown area has sometimes been called one large department store. Book stores like Gabby's (805/543-9035), 894 Monterey, or Phoenix Books (805/543-3509), 1127A Broad, which features old but revivable volumes, are run by local enthusiasts who take the time to chat.

Rather than wander around town, if you prefer your shops in tourist-oriented complexes, investigate the Network from Higuera through to the creek. Two blocks west, the Creamery, another complex of boutiques and shops, also backs up to the creek. As its name implies, it was once a working creamery. Another historic note: The nearby Harmony Valley Creamery, now extinct, has been transformed into a mortuary. If you can't find what you want downtown, try the **Madonna Road Plaza** or the **University Square Center** near Cal Poly, the latter geared more for student-age shoppers.

As in days of yore, the mission and its manicured plaza are the hub of much of the downtown activities, informal or scheduled. The mission, founded in 1772 by Junipero Serra, is the fifth in a series that stretches up California from San Diego. Three years before the mission was founded, Gaspar de Portola and Father Juan Crespi passed through the area on their way to rediscover Monterey. After they made note of the many bears that could provide food and the friendly Indians, they recommended building the mission.

Local Chumash Indians helped make the adobe bricks for the five-foot-deep walls—the mission also doubled as a fortress. After the thatched roofs were set afire three times by unhappy Indians, the mission fathers reroofed with red clay tiles. Some historians say these tiles were formed by workmen shaping the clay over their upper legs to give the tiles the right taper to mesh together; the tiles also provided drainage.

The mission grew prosperous until it was secularized in 1834 and its property was parceled out as huge Mexican land grants. The last Franciscan missionary of this period lived on in the aging mission in abject poverty until not one Indian remained. Later, whiskey sellers who plied their wares nearby were the prosperous ones and bandits were rife. One notorious bandit and his men took over the town for a short time in 1853, sleeping in the mission garden.

William H. Brewer, who surveyed up and down California during the Civil War period, liked the beautiful, green grassy valley but dismissed San Luis Obispo as a "small and miserable town."

As the years passed the mission continued to disintegrate. Then in 1880 the church and priests' quarters were enclosed, incongruously, in clapboard, a belfry was added, and the roof shingled. This saved the adobe walls from further crumbling. Recently the two crucial buildings were restored to pristine glory. Since the mission hospital, Indians' living quarters, and storehouses did not receive the clapboard treatment, they disappeared, making the present mission complex seem small compared to missions like San Antonio de Padua at Jolon.

A tiny museum of religious and Indian relics is tucked away inside the present mission, which now serves as a parish church. The grassy plaza stretching to the creek is pleasantly landscaped and moderately quiet, as no cars are allowed in. It's quiet, that is, unless the Fiesta or other celebration is in full cry. Even during these periods, the garden—half hidden in back of the church—gives you a feeling of serenity, of what it must have been like during the short period of tranquility in the few decades after the mission was established and expectations were high.

In 1894, when the railroad arrived, San Luis Obispo could no longer be referred to as a sleepy Mexican village. Today you would never mistake it for a suburb of New York City, but most townspeople and visitors feel this is one of the town's charms.

Just west of the mission plaza area on Monterey in the small County Museum, open 10 A.M. to 4 P.M. Wednesday through Sunday, you can view a potpourri of historic items from baskets and relics of the Chumash Indians to costumes and tools of the pioneer white settlers. It's much like poking through an attic jammed with centuries of nostalgia. The town art center is across the street.

Some irreverent people have dubbed the **Madonna Inn** (805/543-3000) a "dinosaur's playpen." It is an eye-stopper (no, it's not a religious shrine). You reach it by taking Higuera Street south to Madonna Road. Long before you cross Highway 101, you'll glimpse its shocking pink turrets, gables, and much, much rock work. Alex Madonna started it in 1960 when outside work for his construction company languished; he put the men to work here adding more rocks, waterfalls, more rooms, a restaurant, more shops, a wine cellar, a rodeo area, and yet more rooms. A must is a visit to the men's room to view the seashell urinal, complete with waterfall.

Each room in the Madonna Inn has its own personality. You decide which room fits your lifestyle by perusing colored postcards of each room in the small reception lobby. Not everyone is a devotee of Madonna's brand of architecture. Nevertheless, perhaps as a commentary on the sterility of many motels, the Madonna Inn parking lot is frequently full, and there's often a waiting list for the rooms.

The **Madonna Plaza,** referred to earlier, is a short distance away on Madonna Road. Here the mix contains a supermarket, hardware store, and other purveyors of staples.

For a quiet interlude away from shopping centers and shocking pink inns, take the turnoff on Madonna Road to **Laguna Park** and **Lake,** a tiny dot of water with vistas of rolling hills and a full contingent of panhandling ducks. Recreation facilities also feature picnic tables, and wind surfing rentals and instructions; you don't need a license to fish. There's a jogging and fitness run and a nearby golf course (805/549-7309) at 1175 Los Osos Valley Road.

Outside the northeast boundary of San Luis Obispo on the opposite edge of town is **California Polytechnic State University (Cal Poly),** with its 375-acre central campus, plus 4,800 additional acres earmarked for farming and field studies.

Go Mustangs! This popular institution insists that its 15,000 students, now about 40 percent women, learn by doing. Agricultural majors may be responsible for sheep, swine, poultry, or a cow. A student may adopt and train a horse—rodeos are big on this campus. Crop science or ornamental horticulture majors often plant and reap the results of their labor. These students frequently live in a dormitory next to their projects.

You can visit the pampered livestock; especially endearing in the spring are the lambs, piglets, colts, and calves. You can buy student-grown produce and dairy products—don't miss the sinfully rich ice cream—at the Campus Store on weekday afternoons. A small florist shop in the Ornamental Horticultural Unit is open to the public for sales Monday through Saturday. Also of interest, particularly in late summer and late fall, is the nearby All-American Garden where experimental ornamental plants are grown.

Before heading for any of these points of interest, first pick up a campus map at the information desk (805/546-1154) in the Administration building, which is within the horseshoe-shaped Perimeter Drive surrounding the older inner campus. Also, be sure to get a parking permit here. Many students drive cars and parking is closely monitored. You can enter the campus off Grand Avenue or on Highland Drive off Highway 101.

Cal Poly boasts that there are more T-squares per capita on its campus than anywhere else. Possibly this is because 14,000 students have attended its architectural school, the largest in the country. In line with its motto of learning by doing, architecture students have erected many experimental structures back in Poly Canyon off Mountain Drive, which is off Perimeter Road. The canyon, stream, and surrounding hills are bucolic and beautiful. As with the agricultural units, a caretaker is usually on hand to answer questions. However, the gate to Poly Canyon is open weekdays only, from 7:30 A.M. to 5:30 P.M.

Cal Poly also has collections of antique printing and newspaper equipment plus antique airplane engines, which can be seen by appointment. Before you leave the campus, treat yourself to lunch or dinner at the university's pleasant and moderately priced Vista Grande Restaurant—if you are lucky enough to find a spot in the huge parking lot off Grand Avenue.

The Cal Poly campus may be huge, but it doesn't seem large enough when 100,000 students, relatives, and friends crowd in for the annual Poly Royal Celebration and open house the last full weekend in April. If you don't have a student attending Cal Poly, avoid San Luis Obispo during this hectic weekend. Off campus, as well as on, streets are packed and so, of course, are motels.

Cal Poly isn't the only college near San Luis Obispo. The two-year **Cuesta College** is six miles west of town off Highway 1. The buildings are newer, parking is easier, and there's the historic **Hollister Adobe** with Chumash Indian artifacts; open only 1 P.M. to 4 P.M. on Sunday. But it's Cal Poly that rouses almost evangelical fervor.

Go Mustangs!

Just outside of San Luis Obispo on Highway 1, this mossy barn with a fading Mail Pouch ad on its roof begs to be photographed.

26

San Luis Obispo Back Country and Beaches

As you comb the coast from Carmel through the Big Sur and south, you are aware at every turn that this is one of the world's most beautiful and spectacular shorelines, but the steep Santa Lucia Mountains virtually cut you off from the back country east of the Big Sur. In San Luis Obispo County, it's easier to reach the back country and you'll find that it, too, is beautiful in its own way.

This is rural California at its best, with oak trees, orchards, singing birds, and vineyards. In the spring the green fields and gently rolling hills are thick with wildflowers, but the countryside is as attractive in its golden phase during fall and winter when the vineyards put on their scarlet and yellow show and the orchards are pregnant with nuts and fruit. At intervals, as if to add interest, volcanic rocks jut up on the placid landscape. And this countryside has barns that beg to be photographed; two of the more famous are just outside the town of San Luis Obispo: the mossy barn on Highway 1 with the fading Mail Pouch ad on its sagging roof and the octagonal barn at the very southern end of Higuera Street.

If you've arrived on twisting two-lane Highway 1, chances are you'll opt for four-lane Highway 101 going home. This means you'll go through **Paso Robles,** about thirty miles north of San Luis Obispo. The town, strung out along Highway 101, was started in the early 1800s because of its thermal sulfur hot springs, which were advertised as curing everything from debauchery to cutaneous disorders. However, because it was too near a railroad crossing, the hot springs were closed.

Paso Robles now is the center for a healthy agricultural industry in livestock, almonds, grain, and wine. The county fair in August is really big! The town is also a good place to buy fishing and sporting equipment. Since Paso Robles is only about half-an-hour from the coast and its many motels often have moderate prices, you might consider staying here in this sunny town. (It can be too sunny in the summer.)

Contact the **Chamber of Commerce** (805/238-0506), 1113 Spring, Paso Robles, CA 93446 for a list of inns, motels, and RV parks.

Even if you don't stay, check out the Paso Robles Inn (805/238-2660) and its gardens, a cool restaurant popular with locals, and a cocktail lounge with cowboy ambience. The rear portion, originally built in 1891, still stands. The Inn, which has been modernized, is a nostalgic reminder of opulent resort days and the price is right. Also worth a look are the turn-of-the-century houses and the old Catholic church—now Joshua's restaurant—on Vine Street, parallel to the main street. Other oldies are near Chestnut and Eighteenth streets.

Take the Highway 46 turnoff just south of Paso Robles if you're bound for Cambria and Hearst Castle or if you just like beautiful back roads. En route you'll enjoy canyons and hills undulating all the way to the ocean; at one point you'll see 100 hills. The small and friendly family-run York Winery (805/238-3925) is on York Mountain Road, which loops off Highway 46. The winery, reached through an arcade of oaks, is open from 10 A.M. to 5 P.M. daily.

Going east about seven miles inland on Highway 46, you'll arrive at one of the most charming wineries in the area, the Estrella River Winery (805/238-6300). The grounds are immaculate, with rose bushes at the end of each row of vines; a viewing tower has a 360-degree panorama of the countryside. Tasting and tours are from 10 A.M. to 4 P.M. daily. Do try the white Zinfandel; it's ambrosia.

Templeton, the next small town south of Paso Robles off Highway 101, was founded in 1887 by Swedes from Minnesota who immediately erected a great, gray Lutheran church. To attract tourists, many buildings have been restored and repainted in the style of the old Western days. Antique shops have moved in and there's also a bed and breakfast place, the Country House Inn (805/434-1598), at 91 Main. The most imposing edifice in Templeton is the grain elevator.

Succor is near, however: Several interesting wineries are nearby. The oldest, Pesenti (805/434-1030), 2900 Vineyard Drive, Templeton, lets you taste their premium and jug wines from 8 A.M. to 6 P.M. Monday through Saturday, Sunday 9 A.M. to 6 P.M. At another old-timer, Las Tablas (805/434-1389), on Winery Road off Vineyard Drive, you can sample Zinfandel and generic wine from 9 A.M. to 5 P.M. daily.

Atascadero, next south, was dreamed up in 1913 as a model community. Soon after putting in sunken gardens and erecting the big Italianate dome-shaped administration building that you see from Highway 101, the promoter bogged down with financial difficulties and was jailed for mail fraud. For years after, the town took after its name, which translated roughly means "stuck in the mud." The inhabitants make light of their mud-soaked situation by putting on a Mudhole Follies every year.

If your destination is the coast, take Highway 41 west out of Atascadero, which ends up practically at the foot of Morro Rock in Morro Bay. If you're headed for San Luis Obispo going south on Highway 101, continue on and enjoy the tree-clad mountains and overlooks before you arrive.

Back to Highway 1 going north of Paso Robles you'll see signs directing you to the **Mission San Miguel Arcangel,** founded in 1797. Even if you're not a devotee of missions, stop to see the thirty-four varieties of cactus on the grounds. Another highlight is the museum with a wishing chair. According to Indian legend, women who sit in it get their wish for the husband of their choice. There are also picnic tables and restrooms.

The mission's padres had the honor of producing the first wine in California, this in stone vats. After secularization, the mission deteriorated. In 1929 it was returned to the Franciscan friars, who restored it to its former ambience. The church interior is stunning, with original paintings and decorations done by early Indian neophytes.

Across the street, appropriately named Mission Street, is another vignette of the past sandwiched in between the railroad tracks and busy Highway 101. It's the well-preserved **Rios-Caledonia Adobe,** which was once a stagecoach stop.

You can save time by *not* stopping at the town of **San Miguel.** This hamlet has had two heydays, one when the railroad arrived in 1886 and another during World War II when the now almost-deserted Camp Roberts was host to 45,000 troops. San Miguel's population then was over 4,000. At present it's less than 1,000, and dogs doze on the main street in front of boarded-up hamburger stands and defunct service stations.

According to its Chamber of Commerce, when it comes to scenery and recreation, San Luis Obispo county has almost everything going for it. In addition to back country roads and ambling through gently rolling hills dotted with peaceful farmlands and vintage barns and vineyards (as a bonus, there's often a small, friendly winery at the end of that back road), the ocean's edge is only ten minutes away.

Rows of vines stretching to the mountains are evident as you drive along Highway 101 through California's big inland valley.

Even here you have choices: rugged, untouched Montaña de Oro; sunny, funky Avila Beach; or Shell Beach with its string of restaurants.

Montaña de Oro State Park, just south of the Morro Bay sand spit (take the Los Osos Valley Road, which turns into Pecho Valley Road), has often been called wild. The shock of surf against fifty-foot bluffs is dramatic; this almost 10,000-acre mix of hiking trails, streams, peaks, coves, canyons, and tidepools is also unspoiled.

Park headquarters (805/772-2560) at **Spooner's Cove** is in one of the old wooden buildings that were part of the A. B. Spooner ranch at the turn of the century. Before that, it was a portion of the Pecho y Islay land grant. An ancient campsite used by Chumash Indians is on the bluff south of the cove. The present state park campground nearby on Islay Creek has fifty primitive and somewhat windy sites with pit toilets. A short distance away is a twenty-five-unit horse trailer camp. Campsites are on a first come, first served basis until Memorial Day. Then reserve through your local Ticketron.

These facilities plus asphalt roads and picnic tables overlooking the sandy beach at Spooner's Cove are the only signs of civilization. This, according to many visitors, is all to the good.

For some of the best tidepool searching on the Central Coast, take the trail along the bluffs just south of the picnic area for half a mile, then scramble down to Corallina Cove. If the tide is low you should see a bountiful supply of marine life hiding out in the cracks, crevices, and pools here. Quarry Cove, a short distance farther south, also has fascinating tidepools as does Hazard Canyon, a mile and a half north of Spooner's Cove. Once again, a reminder: After you've enjoyed looking and learning, leave all the marine plants and animals where you found them!

One of the easiest and most rewarding of the park's forty miles of hiking trails is the three and a half miles along the sea bluffs south of Spooner's Cove. Inland during spring and early summer the fields are blanketed with miles of the wildflowers that gave the park its name, especially fiddleneck, goldfields, wild yellow mustard, and California poppy. Seaward, the constant pounding of the surf has sculpted the bluffs into a gallery of shapes and sea caverns that reach far into the cliff under your feet; you can feel the earth reverberate as the surf pounds in. Offshore, you may see otters playing in the surf at their southern limit, seals or sea lions, and perhaps great gray whales on their annual migration.

If you want a more energetic hike, try the steep trail to **Valencia Peak,** 1,342 feet high. Besides viewing up to 100 miles of coastline you can often find sea fossils high on the peak; many millions of years ago this area was part of the ocean floor and

At Montaña de Oro, as at other beaches, sea birds join you in combing the edge of the coast.

was turned on end after a giant geological event. An easier but often dusty trail (actually a road) follows the north bank of Islay Creek. If you get too dusty or hot, two chilly but invigorating waterfalls await you just over a mile up the road.

Many devotees of Montaña de Oro State Park prefer **Hazard Canyon.** The trail in starts one and a half miles into the park boundary; watch for cars parked along the road. Walk through a grove of eucalyptus trees to the rocky beach; en route early or at dusk you might glimpse black-tailed deer. At the ocean you'll often meet surfers and see children sliding on the tilted slabs or on the sand dunes. If you have the stamina and the yen to stumble over sharp rocks, you could walk all the way to Morro Rock. But there's enough to enjoy for a full day right here in this huge untamed park.

Avila Beach, also ten miles from San Luis Obispo, is about as different from untouched Montaña de Oro State Beach as possible. This tiny town, with a population of only a few hundred, is tucked into a cove just south of Point San Luis, which protects it from most (not all) offshore winds. As a result it's often sunny, and you can swim without turning blue with cold. The average annual temperature is a pleasant 70 degrees. Inevitably during summer and holiday weekends the beach is jammed with sunseekers enjoying the miniature boardwalk and sandy beach.

Sprinkled among the hotdog stands are restaurants that have a more varied menu, especially good fresh fish and seafood, like the Old Custom House and the Jetty Restaurant, which serves hot clam chowder with actual clams in it.

Aloof from all this, high on a spit of land to the south of **San Luis Obispo Creek,** is the elegant red-tile roofed San Luis Bay Inn (805/595-2333). With its balconied rooms with views, pool, restaurants, hot tubs, and tennis court, a guest need only descend from the heights to enjoy the golf course, which meanders over the creek and behind the town.

With so much recreation going on, this isn't the prime area to study nature, although you might see black-crowned night herons roosting along the creek. You will see and hear gulls, however, on and off the pier at Port San Luis, just north of Avila. The gulls are there because there's plenty of fishing going on: from commercial fishing boats, sport fishing boats, pleasure craft, and from people dangling lines off the pier, which doesn't require a license. Port San Luis Sportfishing (805/595-7200) is one of the outfits that ventures out after rock cod, salmon, and albacore in season.

You can enjoy all this activity and also have an excellent view of Avila from the Olde Port Inn (805/595-2515) at the end of the pier. You can also quaff a beer or taste the reasonably priced sea fare here. The Inn advertises a seafood buffet Monday night, gourmet dining Tuesday through Sunday, and lunches daily from 12 P.M. to 3 P.M. The Olde Port Fish Company next door offers fresh fish daily.

What else is there to do in Port San Luis if you're not interested in fish? You can take a quick look at the bumpy volcanic formation just north of the parking lot. Perhaps by the time you read this, the 1983 storm damage will have been repaired and the lighthouse will be open to the public.

Port San Luis has almost no permanent residents. Then why is there all that traffic coming and going? The answer is the nearby **Diablo Canyon** PG&E nuclear generating plant. You'll see the guards blocking the road in and you may even get caught in the center of one of the many demonstrations by dedicated and patient locals and visitors opposed to the plant. If you haven't made up your mind yet on Diablo Canyon you might visit the Information Center, off Highway 101 near the Avila Beach turnoff.

Also on or near the turnoff are two hot spring spas. Sycamore Mineral Springs Resort (805/595-7302) has small private tubs and a huge twelve-footer for groups. Guests can soak in the hot tubs for half price. There's also a small cafe in the main building. The Avila Hot Springs Spa and RV Park (805/595-2359), also on Avila Road, has two pools, one at 88 degrees and another at 105 degrees. But hot spring spas are now very popular, so if you want to indulge, reserve ahead.

A mile south of Avila Beach—take the Cove Landing Road off Avila Road—is another popular beach, **Pirate's Cove.** The view of San Luis Bay is not the only reason for its popularity. Clothing is optional; dispense with your bikini and tan every round inch.

Shell Beach, south of Pirate's Cove, is an easy ten-minute drive from San Luis Obispo. Perhaps this is why it has several antique dealers and a string of restaurants, many with ocean views. Spyglass Inn (805/773-1222) is one. Trader Nicks (805/773-4711), actually in adjoining Pismo Beach, is another. If you're on a tight budget, try the early-bird specials; the sunset may be more spectacular earlier, anyway. Another well-known restaurant, this with a Western air, is F. McLintock's Saloon and Dining House (805/773-1892).

The residential part of Shell Beach cascades primly down a marine terrace to the ocean. There are two staircases—one is at Morro Avenue, the other at Palisade Avenue—that let you reach the rocky shore and tidepools. Both are off Ocean Boulevard, which hugs the seacliff. Even if you don't descend to the tidepools, you can enjoy the many sea birds that perch on rocks offshore, and you might spot seals, sea lions, and otters.

Pismo Beach, next south, is popular with dune buggy enthusiasts, so it is noisy and often crowded. P.S.: Those delicious Pismo clams that made it all worthwhile have virtually disappeared from the beach. So you may not want to visit just to see the two sand dunes now protected from vehicles. However, swimming is good, you can fish off the pier, and 500 campers are permitted on the sand with no designated sites. If the noise bothers you, head north. San Luis Obispo County, like all of California's Central Coast, has a bountiful choice of beaches and back country havens to suit every taste.

27

A Year Full
of Events

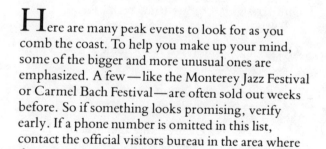

Here are many peak events to look for as you comb the coast. To help you make up your mind, some of the bigger and more unusual ones are emphasized. A few—like the Monterey Jazz Festival or Carmel Bach Festival—are often sold out weeks before. So if something looks promising, verify early. If a phone number is omitted in this list, contact the official visitors bureau in the area where the event takes place.

Chamber of Commerce
  80 Eureka Square
  Pacifica, CA 94044
  (415) 355-4122

Santa Cruz County Convention and Visitors Bureau
  Church and Center
  Santa Cruz, CA 95060
  (408) 423-6927 or 423-1111

Monterey County Convention and Visitors Bureau
  380 Alvarado
  P. O. Box 1770
  Monterey, CA 93940
  (408) 649-3200

Monterey County Fairgrounds
  (408) 372-5863

Chamber of Commerce
  Forest and Central
  Box 167
  Pacific Grove, CA 93950
  (408) 373-3304

Big Sur—sorry, folks, visitors are on their own.

Chamber of Commerce
  767 Main
  Cambria, CA 93428
  (805) 927-3624

Chamber of Commerce
    151 Cayucos Drive
    Cayucos, CA 93430
    (805) 995-1200

Chamber of Commerce
    1275 Embarcadero
    Box 876
    Morro Bay, CA 93442
    (805) 772-4467

Chamber of Commerce
    1039 Chorro Street
    San Luis Obispo, CA 93401
    (805) 543-1323

Chamber of Commerce
    1113 Spring Street
    Box 457
    Paso Robles, CA 93446
    (805) 238-0506

JANUARY

Whale-watching also in December and February; from
    overlooks all along the coast, watch the migration
    south of the gentle gray giants.

Twelfth Night Burning of Christmas Trees, Carmel
    Beach.

Bing Crosby Pro-Am Golf Tourney sometimes in early
    February. This is the big one, with celebrities.
    Bring rain gear and hip flask.

FEBRUARY

Beachcombing is at its best now into March, if winter
    storms have cooperated. Try near mouths of
    creeks and rivers.

Fungus Fair, features hundreds of wild native
    mushrooms, Santa Cruz Museum, 1305 East Cliff
    Drive (408/429-3773).

Mardi Gras, San Luis Obispo.

Heritage Home Tour, San Luis Obispo.

Almond orchards around Paso Robles are decked out
    in their pink and white blossoms in late February
    and early March.

MARCH

Gray whales are back on their return trip from Baja
    California; many are mothers with babies.

Steinbeck Birthday Celebration, Salinas (408/758-7311).

Kite Festival, Capitola (408/462-2026).

Good Old Days Celebration and Victorian Home
    Tour in Pacific Grove; or in early April.

Hunt Meet and Steeplechase, sometimes in early
    April; Pebble Beach (408/649-3200).

APRIL

Wildflowers are at their best, especially on backroads
    inland from the coast. The Jolon Valley is
    spectacular; so is Point Lobos, and the apple
    blossoms may be out around Watsonville.

Wildflower Show, over 500 species, Pacific Grove
    Museum (408/372-4212).

Butterfly Criterium Bike Race, Pacific Grove.

Polo Matches, Monterey Fairgrounds or Pebble
    Beach.
Adobe Tour, Monterey.

Quilt Show, P. O. Box 1025, Pacific Grove, CA
    93950.

Kite Flying Contest, Carmel Middle School, Carmel
    Valley Road.

Poly Royal (Cal Poly); join 100,000 visitors, San Luis
    Obispo (805/546-2576).

Marine Lab Open House, sometimes in early May,
    Moss Landing (408/633-3304).

MAY

Last chance to enjoy the coast before the summer
    crowds descend, especially at Santa Cruz, the
    Monterey Peninsula, and Big Sur.

Mussel quarantine begins on May 1, if not before.

Portuguese Chamarita parade and free barbecue in Pescadero, usually six weeks after Easter; in Half Moon Bay usually seven weeks after Easter.

Santa Cruz Spring Fair, arts, crafts, food booths, exhibits, and entertainment, Pacific Garden Mall (408/475-7115 or 423-6927).

House and Garden Tour, Monterey.

West Coast Antique Fly-In, Watsonville Airport (408/724-3849).

Shark Derby, Moss Landing (408/633-5202).

Bonsai Show, Buddhist Temple, Seaside (408/394-0119).

La Fiesta; San Luis Obispo celebrates its Spanish heritage with parades and dances.

Wine Tasting in the Park, Paso Robles.

Art in the Park, Morro Bay.

JUNE

Miss California Pageant, state finals for Miss America; Santa Cruz.

Harbor Festival and Boat Show, Santa Cruz Yacht Harbor.

Merienda, Monterey's birthday celebration.

Antique Classic and Vintage Car Show, Pacific Grove.

Surfabout, surfing contests, including wind surfing; Carmel beach.

Fiesta, San Antonio de Padua Mission; Jolon.

Steinbeck Festival, Salinas (408/758-7311).

Winston Grand National Races, sometimes in July; Laguna Seca (408/373-1811).

JULY

Bass Derby to celebrate the striped bass runs continues through August in Pacifica.

July Fourth Celebrations explode all along the coast: Coastside County Fair and Rodeo, Half Moon Bay; La Honda Days Celebration and Barbeque;

July Fourth Parade, Seaside; Fireworks, Coast Guard Pier, Monterey; Fireworks, Salinas Fairgrounds; Fireworks, Cayucos pier; July Fourth in the Plaza, San Luis Obispo.

Rodeo; the big one for roping and riding, Salinas (408/757-2951).

Obon Festival, Monterey Fairgrounds (408/394-0119).

Clint Eastwood Invitational Celebrity Tennis Tourney, Carmel Valley.

Bach Festival; a two-week music fest, reserve early! Carmel.

Flea Market; a big one! Moss Landing (408/633-5202).

Feast of Lanterns, Pacific Grove.

AUGUST

Mozart Festival; eighteen or so concerts scattered from the plaza to Cal Poly, sometimes held in late July, San Luis Obispo (805/543-4580).

Flying Disc (Frisbee) Championships, Cabrillo College, Aptos (408/475-7565).

Arts and Crafts Festival, Custom House Plaza, Monterey.

San Luis Obispo County Fair; "The biggest little fair anywhere," Paso Robles.

Monterey County Fair, Monterey Fairgrounds (408/372-5863).

Concours d'Elegance, classic cars, Lodge at Pebble Beach.

Historic Auto Races, Laguna Seca (408/373-1811).

Scottish Highland Games, Pebble Beach.

National Horse Show, Monterey Fairgrounds (408/372-5863).

Fiesta, Monterey History and Art Association, Monterey.

Flea Market; the granddaddy of them all, San Juan Bautista (408/623-2454).

Sandcastle Contest, Capitola (408/423-6927).

Pacifica Frontier Days, last week in August.

SEPTEMBER

Artichoke Festival, Castroville (408/633-3402).

Quilt Show, Pacific Grove.

Watercolor Show, Pacific Grove Museum.

National Begonia Festival, Soquel Creek, Capitola (408/423-6927).

Monterey Jazz Festival, Monterey Fairgrounds; reserve early at their office, 444 Pearl Street or call (408) 373-3366 or 775-2021.

Festival of the Saws (musical saws), Louden Nelson Community Center, Santa Cruz (408/429-3504).

Carmel Mission Fiesta, Carmel.

Santa Cruz Mission Days Fiesta and Parade, Santa Cruz.

Gem and Mineral Show, Monterey Fairgrounds (408/372-5863).

Central Coast Wine Festival, Paso Robles.

Wild Game Barbeque, San Luis Obispo.

OCTOBER

Pumpkin season is in full glory, well worth a roll of color film, near Half Moon Bay.

Monarch Butterflies return! Welcome Back Monarch Day, Natural Bridges State Park, second or third week; Butterfly Parade and Bazaar, Pacific Grove.

Harbor Festival, Morro Bay.

Sandcastle Contest, Carmel Beach (Good luck discovering the date.)

Mussel quarantine usually ends October 31st, but check.

NOVEMBER

Ye Olde English Market, Monterey Fairgrounds (408/372-5863).

Community Thanksgiving Potluck Dinner, Monterey Fairgrounds (408/372-5863).

Christmas Crafts Fair, Cocoanut Grove, Santa Cruz (408/423-2469).

California Wine Festival (or in early December), Monterey Conference Center and big hotels (408/64-WINES).

DECEMBER

Christmas in the Plaza, San Luis Obispo.

Christmas Parade of lighted boats, Morro Bay.

Festival of Trees, Monterey Fairgrounds.

Christmas Crafts, La Playa Hotel, Carmel (408/624-6476).

Renaissance Fair, Sunset Center, Carmel (408/624-3996).

Singing Christmas Tree, Pacific Grove (408/373-0431).

Mexican Christmas Procession and Party, Monterey Conference Center.

Residential Christmas Tour, Pacific Grove.

Candlelight Concert, Carmelite Monastery, Carmel.

Music for Christmas Series, Carmel Mission.

Christmas Eve Midnight Mass, Carmelite Monastery, Carmel.

Grand Prix Formula 5000 Races, Laguna Seca (408/373-1811).

Index